Trials & Truffles

EXPATS IN BRUSSELS

T.D. ARKENBERG

For Jim, my husband, best friend, and adventurous companion
&
Brussels, our beloved city of chocolate

Also by T.D. Arkenberg

Final Descent
Jell-O and Jackie O
None Shall Sleep
Two Towers
A Belgian Assortment

All of life is a foreign country.
(Jack Kerouac)

*The world is a book, and those who
do not travel read only a page.*
(Saint Augustine)

Table of Contents

Preface

Love stories are complex. Seldom, as Shakespeare suggests, does the course of true love run smooth. Most romances travel bumpy and twisted paths that careen between tender affection and intense dislike. Detours, distractions, and diversions vex the novice and veteran lover alike. Where an amorous journey ends is anyone's guess.

Our love story happens to involve a city. Despite repatriating to Chicago a few years ago, my husband and I recall our Belgian adventure with great affection. But Brussels, our home for two years, required a patient lover. The city of truffles, creams, and pralines was a place we had to endure before we fell under its spell, a healthy dose of bitter along with the sweet.

I

Uprooted

Deracinate (16th cent. French, déraciner*):*
  To uproot; to take something out of its native environment
                                          (The Free Dictionary)

Chapter 1

"Paris or Brussels."

"Huh?" I pressed the phone closer to my ear to block out the music and chatter inside Starbucks. Talkative mothers enjoying regained freedom at the start of a new school term filled the small shop. Conversations focused on recent summer vacations, kids' new teachers and coursework, and vows to return to exercise regimes.

The voice on the other end of the phone belonged to my partner Jim. The surging excitement in his tone suggested good news. We'd been together for fifteen years. I was accustomed to his heavily rationed exuberance. "It's all right," delivered in deadpan monotone, was Jim's customary reply to a spectrum of things: a fine meal, a killer cocktail, a cute puppy, and practically any number of compliments for which I fished.

"They're recommending Paris or Brussels," he replied louder. His words came at a quickened tempo. "Well actually, the Paris office is in Cergy, a suburb. HR's simply not sure yet. They're still analyzing both options. Financial considerations, you know. But be thinking, Paris or Brussels."

I understood Jim's shorthand; the news wasn't unexpected. We'd spoken about the high probability that his employer, a global provider of consumer data and analytics, was considering him for an overseas assignment. But until that moment and his mention of two concrete alternatives, a move hadn't felt real. I'd given relocation only high-level consideration. With five decades of life under my belt, I wasn't naive. Plans often fell through—the loftier an initiative, the higher the likelihood of failure and disappointment. A transfer to Europe was about as lofty as things got.

The wheels in my head creaked into motion. Soon enough, they'd be spinning as fast as jet engine turbines. With relocation inching closer to reality, the process of reviewing the consequences to our little household would begin. At that moment, however, my initial thoughts of being uprooted from friends, family, and our home were overwhelmed by Jim's unbridled enthusiasm.

For a partnership to last, you don't stifle your mate's happiness, and you certainly don't stand in the way of his or her dream. We'd built our relationship on a foundation of sacrifice and compromise. Jim had made plenty of both for me. It was my turn to return the consideration. And Europe was no consolation prize. The idea of an international move was intoxicating, an opportunity for new experiences and personal growth. Turning an idea into reality was always the hard part.

"What's your preference?" he asked.

"Well, Paris certainly is appealing."

I'd adored Paris since first setting eyes on the magical French capital as a teenager, thirty-five years earlier. For me, Paris meant blue skies, stunning architecture, great food and art, and grand style. After that initial trip, I returned half a dozen more times including two visits with Jim that involved plenty of romance. Sex in Paris should be on everyone's bucket list. If it's with someone you love, all the better.

"Simply because the office is in the suburbs," Jim added, "doesn't mean we have to live there. We could get a place in the heart of Paris. Imagine that."

Ooh la la!

As he spoke, my fingers flew to the keyboard of my laptop. Google search results for Cergy were sparse. On paper, the city of fifty thousand residents twenty miles northwest of Paris resembled our suburban

Chicago hometown of Arlington Heights. But similarity and familiarity didn't appeal to me. If we were moving to Europe, I wanted a unique experience, something quite different from our American life. When dining out, I seldom ordered hamburger or pork chops, reliable staples of a home-cooked meal. Where is the fun or adventure in that?

"Not too thrilled with living in the suburbs," I said into the phone. "But central Paris is very expensive. Granted, Belgium's not as exciting as France, but your new boss is based in Brussels. That's a positive, at least from a professional angle." My arguments were as much for my benefit as for Jim's.

I was less familiar with Brussels, having visited the Belgian capital only once before, exactly twenty years earlier, on a holiday with my parents.

I remembered the city of one million people as unremarkable, smaller than other grand European cities. Courtesy of my former employer, United Airlines, I also had the good fortune to visit Amsterdam, Madrid, London, Berlin, Rome, Athens, and Istanbul. All were flashier and more exotic.

In sharp contrast to Paris, Brussels I recalled as drab, damp, and gray with only a smattering of architectural gems. Critics often cited the city's lack of sophistication, calling it provincial and boring—the Cleveland or Pittsburgh of Europe. Even Hercule Poirot, Agatha Christie's French-speaking Belgian hero famous for employing his "little gray cells" to solve murders, suffered the chronic humiliation of having to clarify his nationality: "No, no, monsieur, I am *not* French...I am Belgian!"

Brussels does have a sweet side. Famous for rich, creamy delicacies made from cocoa beans, it's a veritable city of chocolate. Well-known brands include Godiva, Leonidas, Neuhaus, Mary, Côte d'Or, and Pierre Marcolini. One might think the country's taps ooze with rich chocolate. But humankind doesn't live on chocolate alone.

"Well, something to think about," Jim said, his enthusiasm still strong. "The final decision may be out of our hands. Let's wait to see what HR says. In the meantime, I'll research housing options."

I laughed gently into the phone, knowing he'd launch into overdrive researching apartments in Paris and Brussels. He loved real estate and devoured HGTV. *House Hunters International,* a popular show featuring foreign-bound expatriates, was one of his favorite programs.

"We'll talk more when you get home tonight," I said. "And by the way, sweetie, congratulations. You've wanted this for so long."

I yearned for Jim to find happiness and fulfillment in his professional life. Although his job gave him purpose and a modicum of satisfaction, his employer's corporate culture frustrated him—a scarcity of teamwork and camaraderie, as well as uninspired and insensitive leadership. He fought hard to fit in, suppressing frustrations while eking out small victories by injecting, wherever he could, his brand of nurturing and strategic leadership.

His shoulders bore the weight of tremendous pressure. Since I'd let go of my executive role at United Airlines five years earlier, Jim's paycheck was our primary source of income. Despite his firm support of my writing efforts, I was nonetheless wracked with guilt. Was it fair for me to pursue my passion while duty and an unrelenting stream of living expenses obliged Jim to suit up every day to battle corporate dragons? I sometimes wondered whether my quest to become a writer was a self-indulgent dream, maybe even a quixotic one at that.

"Babe?" The enthusiasm in Jim's voice tempered.

"Yes?"

"Just realized I've been talking a mile a minute."

"No worries. I completely understand."

"This move will have a huge impact on you. You need to know that I understand that. Are you really sure about this? Sure you want to move?"

"Of course."

Even if I'd had doubts and major misgivings, my answer would have been a resounding yes. Jim urgently needed a fresh perspective, an energy boost from a new challenge. A European assignment would breathe life into his flagging spirit. Such a career-enhancing shoulder tap wasn't likely to come again. The job in Europe was a doozy—responsibility for replacing a fragmented network of analytical platforms with a new, more powerful and consolidated system. The role would provide professional growth for which he longed.

Personal benefits of an overseas posting were equally immense. We loved to travel. Both of us had studied abroad. In addition, Jim had once interned for a U.S. conglomerate at its European headquarters outside Milan. As a result of these experiences, living overseas didn't scare us. We had many friends and acquaintances—expats and locals—scattered across the globe.

The opportunity also represented redemption of sorts, a second chance for Jim to realize a dream. Two years before, this same employer had sought to export Jim's leadership skills to its Eastern European branches. Units in the former communist bloc struggled under a legacy of centralized economies and a hierarchy entrenched in the outdated command-and-control leadership dynamic. Jim was the right guy to steer the desired transformation.

That plan, however, had come to a crashing halt. None of the countries where the company wanted to transfer Jim recognized our relationship. As a same-sex partner, I had no legal standing to qualify for a resident's visa. The experience left us both crushed, hurt by dashed hopes as well as the sting of discrimination. Jim overcame that earlier disappointment by diving into his work. But the experience left him wounded. Drawing comparisons with advancing careers of colleagues at his former employer, he worried that his career had stalled. He'd given up his job at Daimler Financial, a company and culture that brought him great satisfaction, to stay in Chicago where I was then a vice president for United.

After we ended our call, my head swirled with Jim's big news. Pushing my writing aside, I sat cupping the Starbucks coffee. My eyes glazed over as I contemplated the future. Sure, the transfer might fall through, but I shook that idea from my head. In all likelihood we were on the verge of moving. Living in Europe excited me, but the reality of making such a move was daunting.

Relocation meant big changes. Could I handle more upheaval in my life? When I left United, I abandoned a great career, a hefty paycheck, and a positive trajectory toward a comfortable retirement for the biggest gamble of my life—to reinvent myself as a writer. I gave up financial independence, a firm sense of purpose, and regular validation of my worth.

Money and power aren't everything. But in our culture, they represent more than most people admit. My role as a successful executive defined me. My job heading large organizations and leading big groups of people filled me with great satisfaction. Strings of accomplishments stroked my confidence. I enjoyed respect and a broad professional network. Employees sought my counsel. Colleagues answered my calls and emails. I felt valued.

Five years later, I was struggling professionally. Reinventing myself proved difficult and frustrating. Agents, publishers, bookstores, and others in the publishing industry rarely answered phone calls or replied to my emails. I went from respected executive to unknown and unproven author. My confidence sagged, my ego bruised. Yet, I persevered. Wasn't this what it meant to "pay one's dues?"

But my hard work was about to bear fruit. My debut novel was on the verge of publication. What would happen after that milestone, I didn't know. Recurring feelings of vulnerability, insecurity, and fear popped up along my journey of reinvention. At times, the depth of these emotions surprised me. *Had I blundered? Did I choose the wrong path? And if I did, what's next?* The corporate world had forgotten me.

My choice, therefore, seemed singularly obvious—continue to forge ahead as a writer and hope for success. Insecurity still dogged me. Would I find myself, one day, farther along a narrowing path, lost inside a forest of self-doubt with no escape? Maybe relocation and a fresh perspective were things I, even more than Jim, needed. Europe represented a new path, an exciting adventure that might provide an alternate way forward.

Sitting in Starbucks on the cusp of big change, my emotions teetered from excitement to apprehension and all points in between. After taking a deep breath and sipping the tepid coffee, my eyes dropped to the computer screen. In a flurry, my fingers tapped out searches of Paris and Brussels.

Chapter 2

"Belgium it is, babe. January 1." Jim's voice carried the exuberance of an ear-to-ear grin. His reaction wasn't unexpected. An expat assignment was one of his longstanding professional goals. Additionally, the new opportunity sweetened the bitter aftertaste of the aborted posting of two years earlier. Financial considerations and proximity to his Brussels-based boss drove the company's decision. I didn't mind. I preferred living in the center of a small European capital rather than on the pricey periphery of a larger one, even if that city was Paris.

Moving to a country with advanced civil rights laws held great appeal. Although gay rights in the United States were on the cusp of great change after a June 2013 Supreme Court ruling, large swaths of the country still had contempt for couples like us. Politicians and preachers spewed nasty rhetoric to denounce the court's ruling. Our struggle persisted. Western Europe was far down the path in righting injustice. In 2001, the Netherlands became the first nation to legalize same-sex marriage followed two years later by Belgium. In early 2013, France became the tenth Western European nation to grant equal status to same-sex couples.

For two gay men, therefore, the transfer meant more than a mere change of venue. We were heading to a society that respected, dignified, and granted legal status to our fifteen-year commitment—not simply tolerance but genuine acceptance. We'd join a long line of American expats who left behind a culture often hostile and intolerant of those outside the mainstream. Perhaps writer James Baldwin and entertainer Josephine Baker had said goodbye to their homeland hoping, as we did, that America might one day evolve.

With our destination set, reality hit. We had three months to move our household from Chicago to Brussels. Transplanting ourselves wasn't going to be easy. People to tell, tasks to complete, and a long list of questions—a veritable maelstrom of activity. We didn't know what we didn't know. Perhaps all life-altering journeys begin with a mix of excitement, apprehension, and fear. Our emotions jumbled. But whereas Jim focused on the uncharted path ahead of us, well-worn ruts of the past consumed me.

"I'd prefer not to sell." That pronouncement marked my first line in the sand.

My parents had built the original house forty-six years earlier. Acquiring the property after their deaths, Jim and I updated and expanded the 1960s colonial. We poured our love and lives into the place. Built on the original foundation, our new home filled us with pride and gave us great joy. I wasn't ready to let go of that rich history and emotional investment. My roots burrowed deep, literally. I'd planted, from seed, the fifty-foot maples that graced the yard.

"Probably won't have to sell. Depends on the economics," Jim said.

He understood my attachment to the house. After fifteen years together, he also knew that my tolerance for upheaval was reaching its limit. He'd already expended a great deal of relationship capital to nudge me overseas.

"Speaking of which, when will you see the expat package?"

Jim's assignment was open-ended but not permanent. Based on experiences of expat friends, we planned on an absence of two to five years. After that we'd likely return to Chicago.

"Any day now," he replied. "But will you be okay with renters?"

"Don't have any choice. It'll be fine, really." A mortgage and high property taxes didn't give us the luxury of leaving the house vacant.

"We'll have to clean it of course… when we get back. Spruce things up too."

Jim nodded. "We can use some of the rent to refurbish. What do you think we'll have to do when we get back?"

Clever boy! I recognized his tactic of diffusing a stressful discussion by engaging in collaborative problem solving. In one short conversation, he'd transported me to Europe and back again into a new and improved version of our beloved house. I played along.

My eyes scanned the sunny kitchen before looking to the yard. "To start, painting. Inside and out."

"Floors too," he said, eying a section of wood stained by a prior pet. "Love to refinish all of them."

"Depends on wear and tear."

He studied my face. "So, you understand there'll be wear and tear?"

"Of course. I'm fine with that. Great opportunity to refresh and update."

Jim grinned. My positive attitude pleased and, I suspected, surprised him. "We'll see what they offer in my package."

"As well as what we can get in rent."

Regardless of what we did with the house, downsizing was a must. To what extent, we wouldn't know until we found a Brussels home. European dwellings were notoriously small. Additionally, our three-car garage and basement were loaded with items we wouldn't need. Storage was a ridiculous waste of money. A good third of our possessions, therefore, would have to go.

One afternoon with Jim at work, I walked through the house. Dressers, desks, closets, and boxes brimmed with old stuff—Jim's, mine, and remnants of my parents' past. "A hazard of moving into the family home."

I spoke the words on a sigh to our golden retriever. Now nine years old, Sadie was two when we rescued her. After I left the corporate world, during most days she was my sole companion. A terrific listener too. When I practiced reading my manuscript drafts aloud, her big brown eyes focused on me, her snout resting on the floor. Every writer should have such a captive and earnest audience.

"Ah, but where to start, Sadie girl, that's the problem." She batted her long golden eyelashes in sympathy. "Basement, closets, spare bedrooms. Guess it doesn't matter where I dig in first."

Things could have been worse. After our parents' near-simultaneous deaths a decade earlier, my siblings and I had sorted through furniture, artwork, and clothing. Before our major rehab project, a second sweep reduced a layer of clutter. But old letters, bills, photos, cards, and other keepsakes from my parents' fifty-year marriage remained scattered throughout the house. Stuff stashed away in drawers and closets seems subject to laws of inertia.

Weeding had fallen to me because Jim had neither the context nor emotional attachment to the family archive. He could have reviewed his files blindfolded. In fact, he had filled a contractor bag with his old papers and plopped back onto the couch before I tackled my first closet, or so it seemed.

Medical bills and insurance statements from my parents' final illnesses filled several drawers. The files transported me back to those dark days. Kneeling down, I rubbed my hand along Sadie's silky fur. "Perhaps it'd be better to let Papa Jim discard everything. Would be easier, that's for sure." Her golden head nodded in agreement.

A tall cherrywood dresser contained my father's personal history—decades-old pay stubs, utility bills, postcards, letters from his mother during World War II, and even his dog tags and white sailor's cap. There were reminders of his deep faith: rosaries, a prayer book, even the Saint Joseph icon buried in the yard to help sell my parents' first house, and the round silver medal affixed to the dashboard of the family Ford before St. Christopher fell out of favor. Other mementos served as testimonials to a father's pride: report cards, swimming medals, school photos, Valentines, and art projects crafted by kindergartener hands nearly half a century earlier. The dresser stood as a veritable time capsule. *Time to let go.*

Among my mother's keepsakes: a hospital wrist band and condolence cards for a baby that never made it home, black and white photos of high school days, antique costume jewelry, a christening gown. A packet of letters fastened with red ribbon drew my keenest interest. Postmarks dated the correspondence to the months before my parents' May 1952 wedding. Patuxent River Naval Air Station was typed as the return address. The Navy recalled my father during the Korean conflict. Sitting on the floor, I pulled one letter after another from their brittle yellowing envelopes. My father's letters spoke of wedding preparations, love for his fiancée, and the adventure before them. With words of assurance, he detailed the arrangements for moving his bride to Maryland. Dad was 25, Mom only 20. *Sixty years,* I thought. *A lifetime has come and gone.*

Reading my parents' correspondence and handling old family treasures triggered smiles, laughter, and tears. Memories served as stark reminders of time's inevitable passage. *All over in the blink of an eye.* All the more reason, therefore, to embrace our adventure.

As black bags filled with leftovers of my parents' lives and painful deaths, I became numb, depressed, even irritable. I didn't understand my reaction, not completely. On one hand, I grieved again for the loss of my parents. But that wasn't all. Our impending move from a place where I felt rooted and secure triggered an invisible spark that would smolder unseen, flaring only after we relocated.

One evening, Jim pulled me into a hug. "You okay, sweetie?"

His cashmere sweater caressed my cheek. "Fine…I'm fine. Just so much…stuff."

In the weeks before the move, chronic bouts of sadness and despair continued to grip me. A simmering stew of emotions surfaced as anger. I retreated into myself, finding solace in music and long walks. As was my habit, I didn't share my innermost feelings with Jim or anyone else. How could I articulate what I myself didn't understand? For me, this represented more than a physical move. In addition to a profound goodbye, the undertaking was about to upend my highly-prized equilibrium and launch me on a sometimes harrowing journey of self-reflection and discovery.

Jim wanted to hold off announcing our move until he received the final transfer package. "Otherwise," he explained, "people will ask too many questions for which we have too few answers. Sketchy details only distract and confuse."

Negotiations on the package, a mix of financial and quality-of-life terms, took about two weeks. Jim paired our short list of "asks" with logical rationale. For example, because of differences in electric current, we wanted an allowance to buy new appliances. Transporting Sadie safely to Europe was another concern. Having worked for an airline, I was all too familiar with pets lost or killed in transit. Most mishaps happened during connections. At substantial cost, we retained a highly recommended pet transport service and a guarantee that Sadie would travel on the same nonstop flight with me.

Jim handed me a copy of the agreement. "Didn't get all we wanted, but I'm okay."

So was I. Perspective drove our satisfaction. We considered the posting an adventure. Like travel, this was an investment in personal and cultural enrichment.

Time had come to share our news. Close friends and family would learn in person. The grapevine, though swift, was sloppy. "No, we're not joining the Peace Corps to raise yaks and live in a yurt in Outer Mongolia." I offered up a contemporary solution. "We could simply post it on Facebook. Then everyone hears at the same time."

Jim rolled his eyes. "My mother would have a fit."

The prospect of that conversation gave him concern. We weren't sure how Barbara would feel about her baby boy, the favorite son, moving to Europe. Although we saw her and Jim's stepfather infrequently, the proximity of our respective homes comforted her. How would she respond to news that a seven-mile separation was growing to four thousand miles, and a fifteen-minute drive becoming an eight-hour flight?

We delivered the news over breakfast in early October. As with most difficult announcements, anticipation was worse than reality. "I know it's what you wanted," she said. "And it's not forever." Neither upset nor weepy, she reserved her tears for later.

"That's right, two years max," Jim replied, trying to soften the blow.

Jim's stepdad Michael offered a comforting smile. "We'll visit, of course."

"We can Skype too," Jim added with enthusiasm.

"*Every* week, promise." Barbara stared at Jim until he nodded in agreement.

"We'll see you more than we do now," I said.

As for me, my closest relatives consisted of two older siblings. Unlike parents, brothers and sisters fall into the "advise and move on" camp. They had their own lives and interests. The house and its contents topped my brother's list of concerns. He treasured family mementos. "No worries," I said to calm him. "You'll get first dibs on anything we decide to toss. As for the house, we're renting, not selling." More resigned than happy at the news, he promised to visit Brussels. Jim and I had our doubts.

With respect to my sister, an ocean wasn't significantly different from the five-hour drive that currently separated us. In many ways, Brussels was less foreign and a great deal less scary than the city of Terre Haute, Indiana, where she lived. When I phoned with the news, she replied with earnest joy, "How thrilling."

Our social circle responded with surprise and support. For friends with whom I worked at United, a European move was cause for celebration. Brussels was a friendly destination for standby travel. Our workout buddies began planning a group vacation. And although my writer friends would miss my presence at our weekly sessions, they understood that an expat adventure was fodder for creativity and literary inspiration. Reaction is *always* a matter of perspective.

As preparations for our big move shifted into high gear, life didn't stop. In between the many relocation tasks, we squeezed in other commitments. In late September, we flew to New York City for a friend's fortieth birthday. In October, we attended a Christening at which I was godfather to a friend's daughter. An unexpected and unwelcome disruption came in the form of jury duty. I was impaneled for a week-long criminal case. Coincidentally, my first book launched during the trial, tempering much of the excitement. Jim and I made time to celebrate our October birthdays and host our annual Halloween gathering. And yet, the clock kept ticking.

"How do we even begin finding a place to live?"

Jim replied with a glint in his eye, embracing the challenge as a lover of real estate, open houses, and HGTV. I had every confidence he'd find a place we'd both like. We had similar tastes and understood that compromise kept harmony in a relationship. As proof, we had survived the multiphase renovation of our home without argument or discord.

The relocation package gave us a budget and access to a local housing specialist. Jim sprang into action. Our answers to a battery of e-mailed questions helped the expert, a knowledgeable Belgian named Guy, to focus his search.

"This is your opportunity to live in the kind of place you want," I said to Jim as he launched into house-hunting mode. "Your best chance to live in the city. Get it out of your system," I added with a wink. Early in our relationship, Jim had agreed to move to the suburbs though a city condo was more his style.

"A loft?"

"If that's what you want."

The allure of an historic capital was strong for both of us. Living in the city center would allow us to dive into our adopted culture. Like tourists for whom O'Hare Airport and suburban malls are their only taste of Chicago, we didn't want a bland, sanitized version of Brussels. Practicality drove our preference as well. I wouldn't have a car.

After taking a first cut at Guy's recommendations, Jim gave me digital tours of his top picks. Huddling together on our sofa over a laptop, we culled the prospects.

I scanned the photos. "Looks like I could live in any one of them."

Suspicions lingered, however. Flattering angles and photoshopped glam shots were as deceptive in peddling real estate as profile pictures were in luring matches on Internet dating sites. Friends considered our search too limited. We took a view that too many choices thwarted decision-making. If twelve properties didn't yield a winner, one hundred wouldn't be any better. Exhaustion was another consideration.

Jim and I flew to Brussels after Thanksgiving for our "Look See" trip and a chance to confer with Guy in person. Our flight arrived Sunday morning. Both of us had been to Brussels, Jim for business and I for a holiday twenty years earlier. But this visit was different. Unlike a soured vacation, this trip didn't include an early-checkout option. We were sizing up the place to put down roots.

We made our way to the hotel using the airport train and Metro. I shrugged off Jim's suggestion of a taxi. "If we're going to live here, may as well get used to public transport. Let's approach this as natives." After only a minor glitch with a ticket dispenser that didn't read our U.S. credit card, we were on our way.

The Sofitel, brightly decorated for Christmas, was located in the heart of the city's premier shopping district. Dior, Vuitton, Versace, and Tiffany were among the luxury brands whose stores lined the avenue. After short naps and showers, Jim and I went for a walk to, as I said, "get a feel for our new home."

"And some food," added a grinning Jim.

Though gloomy and damp, the weather offered up mild temperatures for the last day of November, at least by Chicago standards. Best of all, there was no snow. We'd learn soon enough that gray skies, drizzle, and mild temperatures were the norm in Brussels…year-round.

Despite the daunting task of finding a new home in a city foreign to us in many ways—language, culture, customs, logistics—our adrenaline surged. This was one more great adventure to share, our personal episode of *House Hunters International*. But instead of choosing from three homes, we had twelve to judge.

Guy picked us up Monday morning. Like many locals we observed, the thin, taciturn, and middle-aged man chain smoked and assumed a sphinxlike expression. "Hope you're rested up for a long day." He spoke in French-accented English. "We have ten properties to see, a good mix of old and new."

I grabbed the back seat, leaving the front for wide-eyed Jim. Outside the car window, Brussels whirled by in a blur—a quick left, a right turn, a sprint along the ring road, a crawl down a narrow side street. The pattern repeated throughout the day. I gave up trying to piece together landmarks and memories from my earlier visit. The city of twenty years before didn't matter anyway. Like my parents' mementos, details of the past were mere clutter. Only current-day Brussels mattered. Words like *diverse, shabby, crowded, trams, old, traffic,* and *gray* popcorned in my head—my first impressions of our soon-to-be home from a fast-moving car. Parts of the city were quite grand and, above all, interesting, exotically foreign, and authentically European.

Turning to me from the front seat, Jim's expression assumed the look of a kid at Christmas. "What do you think, babe?"

"Good, all good. It'll be great living here." I didn't lie. I'd begun to mentally insert myself into the cityscapes that flowed past the window. Reminiscent of my quest to reinvent myself as a writer, this was a "no regrets, no turning back" moment.

Our whirlwind tour took us to properties in the town center as well as into neighboring communes primarily to the east. Suburbs were off our list. Unfortunately for Jim, so were lofts. They simply didn't exist in Brussels, or none was on the market. Guy didn't say much. During viewings, I tried to read his body language. Was that a raised eyebrow or a scowl, a nod of approval, perhaps? I grasped for any help in making a decision. As the day progressed, we became familiar with the unique personalities of each commune. Each successive viewing helped crystallize our priorities with respect to the layout, location, and character of our ideal home. Nearly twelve hours later, my head hurt. Property photos snapped with my phone blurred together as did the images in my mind.

Over dinner, Jim and I discussed our options. We tried to distinguish one property from another. Several, unforgettable for the wrong reasons, were easy to dismiss. One had a wooden "outhouse" complete with half-moon cutout inside the master bedroom. Another repelled us with a Pepto-Bismol pink kitchen. An apartment in the diplomatic quarter looked as if its occupants had taken flight in haste. A filthy bathroom, unmade beds, and a half-eaten meal on a grimy kitchen table didn't exactly scream, "Rent me."

"My hunch was right," I said to Jim. "The Internet could make a shack look like Buckingham Palace."

With a last-minute addition, three viewings were set for Tuesday on top of second looks at two places from day one. When our hunt ended, the two units from day one remained our top picks. In character and lifestyle options, they were stark contrasts. One property consisted of the ground floor and lower level of a handsome townhouse in a residential neighborhood. It included access to a large walled garden. The other was brand new, a modern apartment in a busy square lined with restaurants. That three-bedroom unit was on the top floor of an attractive midrise building. Vintage opulence versus fresh contemporary.

"Tough choice, babe. What do you think?" Jim asked.

I'd have guessed that Jim preferred the newer unit. His tastes ran more modern than mine and he often spoke of liking "high-rise" living. However, his tone and expression suggested that he also struggled with the decision.

"How about we walk around each place?" I suggested. "We can compare the neighborhoods. See which is better for Sadie."

Sadie was accustomed to a large, fenced yard where she spent hours lounging on lush grass. Despite Jim's assurances that he'd walk her, I remained skeptical. Our walkabout made the decision easier. Although she hadn't accompanied us to Brussels, Sadie broke our deadlock. As her loyal subjects, we understood that our little princess would not be amused to discover that she had no grass. The vintage apartment with a garden, therefore, was the winner.

With an offer extended, we headed to the airport. Having found a place, we checked that major to-do off our list. Many tasks, however, still lay ahead. The biggest of these was the physical move itself. While we awaited our flight, satisfaction turned to agitation. Jim's face tensed when he listened to his voice mail, a message from our realtor in Chicago.

I waited for him to disconnect. "What's wrong?"

"Miriam wants to see us ASAP. Issues with rental prospects."

Chapter 3

Saying goodbye to Chicago is easy in winter. The harsh season blemishes the pretty face the city presents to the world the rest of the year. Days meld together in monotonous gray. Bloated clouds bring sleet, snow, freezing rain, and graupel, the menacing name for ice pellets that coat a snowflake. Such weather, awesome to a child, cozy to a romantic, and inspiring to a poet, is a damn nuisance to any clear-headed adult.

Returning from our house-hunting mission, Jim and I faced bitter cold and a succession of winter storms. Stalactite-sized icicles dangled from the eaves of our snow-piled roof. Clearing the driveway, we suffered chapped faces, sore limbs, and achy backs as mountains of white rose along its edges. The constant drudgery weighed us down. In prior years, lighted wreaths, evergreen boughs, and holiday cocktails pulled us through those dark days. But with our focus directed elsewhere, we didn't have time for a Christmas tree, let alone the three that usually adorned our home over the holidays. Carols of joy and good cheer served as background to our chorus of swear words. *Screw your white Christmas!*

Even if we had time to celebrate, we weren't in the right mindsets to do so. If only Santa fulfilled the Christmas wish lists of expats: reliable renters, swift and painless moves out of one home and into another, safe transit of our beloved pet, an end to damn snowstorms.

Jim voiced a constant refrain during those busy weeks of December.

"Wish we were already there."

I sympathized with his lament. Besides the fatigue of moving chores, a weariness I shared, Jim straddled two jobs, with a foot on each continent. His anxiety was palpable—a jockey on a promising new mount eager for the starting gate to open. And we still didn't have a renter. Our realtor's voice mail suggesting difficulties compounded our stress. Bracing for bad news, we set up a meeting.

Miriam swept into our kitchen on a whoosh of cold air, her expression and energy signaling urgency. Tossing me her coat, she swooped onto a chair at our kitchen table and dropped a bulging canvas bag to the floor at her feet. Petting Sadie's head, she nodded her acceptance to my offer of water.

"Successful trip to Brussels? Found a place? Happy with it?" Although phrased as questions, her staccato delivery informed us that casual banter wasn't on her agenda.

Jim and I exchanged perplexed looks. Although he'd taken the lead in renting out our house, I'd known Miriam longer. The friendship between our families spanned decades. I considered her smart, tenacious, and always professional. Friends I referred to Miriam expressed satisfaction with her services in selling their homes. With our abbreviated timetable, we considered ourselves lucky to secure her services. Besides, commissions that agents earned for renting a property were nothing compared with a full-fledged sale.

Handing Miriam a bottle of water, I joined Jim and her at the table. "From your message, it sounds as if you've hit a snag with potential renters."

Heaving a sigh, Miriam sat back. Her pained expression continued to signal bad news but still she didn't speak. Again, Jim and I looked at each other before I adopted a more direct approach. "What's the issue with renting the house?"

Taking a deep breath, she seemed to formulate a reply while she extracted a thick folder from her bag. Opening it on the table, she pushed a clipped stack of papers toward Jim and me. After a glance at the top sheet, we stared at her, our expressions seeking clarification.

"It's the comps." A firm nod of her head suggested that she'd offered the definitive answer. "Take a look for yourself." She undid the clip fastening her papers, a stack identical to the one she handed us.

Jim and I scanned several listings. Although they shared our postal code, the homes were nowhere near the caliber of our house. Our place had more square footage, a larger yard, and a state-of-the-art kitchen. The confusion on Jim's face mirrored mine.

"Look there," she said, pointing to a listing. "$1,000 less per month than what you're asking. Same number of bathrooms."

This was a far different assessment than our initial conversation. When we first contracted with Miriam, she had enthusiastically supported our proposed rent figure. In addition to reeling from the insinuation that our prized castle was a shack, we'd already spent our projected rental stream—at least in our heads.

Jim waved a few pages in the air. "Bathrooms are only one feature. These homes are nothing like ours."

As Jim's usually solid patience thinned, I jumped in, skipping to the financial hit. Since the expat opportunity first surfaced, every decision seemed to have a negative impact on our bottom line. "Just what are you suggesting?"

"W...well, it's, um, um, entirely up to you of course, but, um, um, maybe five or six hundred less than your current ask. A place to start anyway."

My exasperation revealed itself with a furrowed brow, cocked head, and wide-eyed glare. My frazzled nerves couldn't absorb much more stress. Anger, borne of frustration and fatigue, was on a constant, unpredictable simmer. I understood the cautionary counsel in Jim's eyes. Most couples become skilled at code and mental telepathy. *She's a friend,* he was thinking. *She's doing us a favor. Above all, there's no time to find another agent.*

Miriam looked from me to Jim and back at me again. Sitting farther back in her chair, she gently tapped the table with her fingers.

"Perhaps you'd like to talk it over?"

"No," I said, practically barking my reply. "I think Jim will agree. Let's try to find a renter at the rate we agreed…with *you*…at this very table…just *two* short weeks ago."

Jim turned to Miriam. "We haven't even had one person across the threshold."

Jim and I were convinced that our house showed well. After the re-hab, strangers stopped to tell us how much they loved the place. House and party guests alike praised the design and décor. Family in the con-struction trade marveled at the craftsmanship. It even featured in our town's annual house walk. We were convinced that we needed only to lure prospective renters inside. As simple as that sounded, getting anyone through the door wouldn't be an easy task in the two weeks before Christmas.

"Okay, let's see what happens." Miriam's tone of resignation paired with a look of disbelief.

Jim shrugged. "We'll know soon enough."

I nodded. "We've got every confidence in you *and* the house."

After fetching a basket of booties for use by prospective renters and an envelope with glossy brochures promoting our home, Miriam went on her way.

Closing the door, I turned to Jim. "How about some wine?"

He sighed. "How about something harder?"

They weren't fancy cocktails, but our rum and vodkas created some much-needed holiday magic.

With our departure fast approaching, not a day passed without some urgent task, decision or impediment. Practicing bilingual sar-casm, I called it the *angst du jour*. Among major loose ends was the fact that we couldn't book our flights because we didn't have our residency visas. And we didn't have our visas because of a process as Byzantine as one might expect. In addition to filling out online applications and sending our passports to the office of Belgian Consular Affairs in New

York, we were required to see a physician. Having received no explanation, we reasoned that the Belgians wanted to ensure we weren't seeking residency to infect their nation or, worse, bankrupt their national health service with chronic diseases.

"You really think they'd deny us residency because of a health issue?"

Jim shook his head. "Don't know. Would be pretty embarrassing though."

"Yeah, imagine. Visas denied due to athlete's foot and chronic jock itch."

The laugh we shared did us both good. Humor, though often hard to muster, was the best stress reliever. We could visit our own doctor. However, we didn't want to take a chance that the paperwork with lengthy instructions in French, Flemish, and English wasn't completed to a bureaucrat's exact specifications. Fortunately, their list of approved doctors included one based in Chicago.

"What's wrong?" Although Jim had trained himself to ignore my chronic grumblings, he paid attention to gripes that rose above a droning mumble.

"This is ridiculous. You know how much I hate doctors and physicals." We'd already been over the medical requirement several times. Our health was good. Neither of us took any regular medication. I resigned myself to enduring the most invasive physical exam that my wild imagination could conjure. But phobias, by definition, aren't rational and certainly never well-behaved.

"Sorry, babe. I know how much you hate this. If we didn't have to see a doctor, we wouldn't."

Logic may have told me that the situation wasn't Jim's fault, but he was a lightning rod for my vexations. After all, he had instigated our overseas move. Besides, if you can't vent your petty annoyances at a dearly loved spouse, at whom can you? I allayed fears of the discovery of an array of terminal diseases with fantasies about a tall, sexy doctor who looked and spoke like suave actor Gilles Marini.

But cynicism threatened even that salve. The stranger examining my prostate might end up resembling chubby-fingered Hercule Poirot.

I fretted about our late-afternoon appointment all morning, my ears ringing with my late mother's counsel about clean underwear. As for our visit, we received a single instruction: bring $150 in cash—*each*.

"All set?" Jim asked, rushing into the kitchen from his home office. I mumbled my reply as I put on my coat and scarf. "After the exams," he added, "how about drinks? We'll be close to Marty's."

Clever boy! Dangle a martini as reward for my turning my head and coughing. Cozy, quaint, and unpretentious, Marty's had become one of our favorite annual Christmas traditions. Serving up healthy doses of chilled vodka and vermouth, the festively decorated bar would cap off an unnerving experience.

Although we were familiar with the North Side, we didn't know the hospital. As Jim pulled into the parking lot, my stomach knotted. I feared a blood pressure surge that might disqualify me for a visa. We agreed that my exam would be first, to get it out of the way.

I stepped out of the car and into the crisp air. Across the street stood a dingy hospital, its unremarkable facade lit by amber streetlights. The building didn't inspire health or wellness. The drab exterior consorted with an equally dreary interior. *Haven't I seen this place in "American Horror Story"?* As we made our way down an empty L-shaped hallway, the air wafted odors more stale than medicinal.

Jim pushed open the door to a small waiting room. "Here goes."

An older woman looked up from her desk. "Mr. and Mr. Arkenberg, I presume."

I anticipated being directed to chairs. Instead, she told us to follow her. Walking through a short corridor, Jim and I exchanged confused looks. Was this to be a joint exam, similar to a couple's massage? After a light knock, the woman ushered us into a cluttered office.

"Poirot, *not* Marini." My soft mutter drew a quizzical look from

Jim. The doctor, an older man of medium build with glasses and graying hair, shook our hands and directed us to chairs across his desk. *Odd,* I thought, seeing no examining table. Identifying himself as a Belgian native, he made small talk about our upcoming move.

"Before we begin," he said, his tone, manner, and expression turning serious. He glanced from Jim to me, undecided where to direct his words. "There's the matter of…the fee."

"Oh, yes, yes, of course. Got it right here." Jim withdrew cash from his wallet. "$150 each, right?"

"Correct." The doctor grabbed the three $100 bills, discreetly verifying the amount tendered before placing the cash in a desk drawer. "I'll write out a receipt when we're done. Let's get started, shall we?"

Here goes. But instead of a physical, the doctor simply asked us questions about our lines of work.

"An author?" His jaw dropped; his eyes widened. "Tell me about your writing."

For several minutes, we discussed my book and our favorite authors. The good doctor showed more interest in my writing than my family did. Every minute spent discussing my book, I reasoned, meant one less minute poking around my privates.

His excitement ebbed only after a glance to his desk clock. "Time, time, time. It's getting late. Formalities and all."

Although less jittery than when I first arrived, my nerves kicked in. But instead of grabbing a stethoscope and thermometer, the doctor pulled two documents from a file folder. "Simple health questionnaire," he said, nodding at us with a smile. "I can see your general health is good." He rattled off a series of questions, first with me, then Jim. Our answers seemed mere formalities as his pen moved swiftly down the page. After handing us a receipt, he wished us good luck in Brussels and bade us good night.

I practically skipped to the car. "Waste of good clean underwear, but best damn physical I ever had."

"Oh, do tell me about your book, Mr. Author," Jim said, mimicking the doctor. "Sheesh," he added. "I could have had a heart attack and died at his feet while he chatted away with you."

A snort accompanied my laugh. "Look at the bright side; we've both been given clean bills of health and we're one step closer to Brussels."

"But $300 poorer. Let's get a drink."

Chapter 4

Our work was like the multiheaded Hydra of Greek mythology; when we crossed one task off our list, two more popped up. Once we secured our housing, we identified the furniture, accessories, and artwork we'd ship to Brussels. Our Chicago house had a small crawl space in which we planned to store a few things that we didn't want to transport to Brussels and I didn't have the heart to discard. Enough leftovers still remained, however, to furnish a small dwelling.

As we inventoried our belongings, Jim shook his head. "If it were up to me—"

"I know, I know. You'd get rid of everything."

He flashed a sly grin. "It's liberating." A decade earlier, he had sold almost all his possessions when he moved in with me.

"So you've told me. But there's something to be said for history and emotional attachment."

He shrugged. "I'm just saying..."

I glared my reply. "My brother will take a lot of the leftovers. For the rest, we need an estate sale."

Jim's ears perked at the suggestion, but his expression signaled doubt. "Great idea, but how can we pull something like that off in three weeks?"

"Leave it to me."

After making calls to realtors for recommendations, I found a woman both eager and available to conduct our estate sale. She was a bit aggressive for our liking, sizing up our stuff with the rabid-eyed glare of a dog in a butcher shop. But at that late date we were beggars, not choosers. Tenacity, we understood, sells.

A few days before the appointed sale, the woman's voracious team descended upon the house like a school of piranhas. Jim and I stood aside as they priced anything that wasn't locked away, and some that was. With a third of the sale proceeds fueling their exuberance, we were surprised they didn't tag Sadie.

Less than two weeks before Christmas, over a Friday and Saturday, more than two hundred and fifty bargain hunters traipsed through our home in search of treasure. They snatched up several pieces of furniture including a sectional sofa, dining room chairs, guest beds and dressers, and our kitchen table. The estate sale team suggested we leave the house during the event. Distance was healthy; my mind flickered with flashes of family history attached to each item. Letting go, however, was the price of moving forward.

Some things not intended for sale such as a fine linen tablecloth disappeared whereas others such as a Bose CD player were sold for a proverbial song. We neither fussed nor complained. The sale brought us one step closer to our goal.

One could rightfully expect us to catch our breath after the great purge that netted us, even after the piranhas' share, several thousands of dollars. But no! *Always time to rest in the grave* was my motto. The day after the estate sale, we hosted an open house, a gathering intended to function as both holiday party and farewell. In retrospect, the plan probably was too ambitious. In only a few days, a legion of movers would invade. But at the time and for several weeks afterward, we were flying so high on adrenaline that we didn't realize that our minds and bodies needed a break.

The last of the estate sale treasure seekers were barely out the door when Jim and I turned our attention to party preparations. First order of business, restore the house to some semblance of order, then clean, and finally stage with whatever furniture remained. Thank heavens for potted poinsettias—they make anyone look like Martha Stewart. The red flowers masked the Spartan décor and lent the house an air of holiday cheer. That night, we practically fell into bed, satisfied and exhausted.

Dawn arrived too soon. We raced to Costco for food trays and party supplies, prepping for a crowd of unknown size. For expediency, Jim had used Facebook to broadcast the party to more than one thousand of our closest friends. How many would actually come ten days before Christmas, we didn't know.

We were also celebrating the launch of my debut novel, *Final Descent*. The book, which had hit Amazon six weeks earlier, represented a milestone in my journey of reinvention. Five years earlier, I had planned on taking a short break before throwing myself back into the corporate world. Jim told me to take my time. He saw the toll that United's chaotic culture had taken on my health. Executive coaches, however, discouraged me. "Get back in the game while your skills are fresh," they said. "Employers don't like lengthy lapses in employment history." A good severance package and Jim's encouragement propelled me forward in my dream of a writing career. Finishing the book wasn't easy, and the road to publication wasn't the traditional path I'd envisioned. But writing gave me purpose.

Attendance at the open house overwhelmed us. Despite a dense snow pack and frigid temperatures, parked cars lined our block, spilling into side streets. Guests consisted of friends and family as well as people we hadn't seen in years, including a large contingent from United. I spent the party at my writing desk, signing copies of my book. I felt like a famous author. The line of "autograph seekers" snaked out the office and into the dining room. The wonderful mix of guests, more than four hundred in all, reminded us of the many great people in our lives. We couldn't have asked for a more affirming sendoff.

Two days later, movers arrived. You never realize the extent of your stuff until you move. Watching our worldly possessions disappear into scores of cardboard boxes and crates overwhelmed me. Over three days, the shipping container intended to transport our things, first by rail to Baltimore and then by freighter to Antwerp, filled to capacity.

Although relieved to have that part of the move behind us, watching the truck pull away made me wistful. We'd reached the point of no return. Shouting "*Stop!*" was no longer an option. Not that I would have. Like a tethered boat buffeted by high winds and surf, my emotional self tossed and turned. Thrill of adventure drew me to Brussels, but emotional bonds anchored me to home. I repeatedly assured Jim that I embraced our move. "No matter what happens or how hard this may be for me," I said more than once, "I believe with all my heart that when we're old and sitting in rockers side by side, we'll consider Brussels the highlight of our lives. I'm sure of it." That was my long-term vision anyway. Only time would reveal the prophecy's accuracy.

Miriam phoned as we were neck-high in packing boxes. "Great news," she said. "Two parties want your house."

"Told you so" was in our minds if not on our lips when she informed us that neither balked at the rent. Competitive offers had come from the first two parties who viewed our house. In finding not one, but two qualified renters, Miriam was our hero.

Both offers were acceptable, but we chose the expat from London. His request for a three-year lease mirrored our lease in Brussels. He and his partner had no children, a plus for wear-and-tear considerations. But their offer was contingent upon something on our list of undesirable items—a cat. We loved animals. But not being cat people, we feared permanent odors and scratches.

"They say he's well behaved," Miriam assured. "You can meet him if you want."

Good grief, an interview with a cat. After more persuasion by both Miriam and Jim, I relented. "Very well, a cat named Bach can't be all that bad."

"One more thing, sweetie." Jim's tone suggested unwelcome news. "They want the house on January 1."

"What? Impossible. That's less than two weeks away. How will we ever be ready?"

"Let me see what I can do." Prodded by a desire for domestic harmony, Jim negotiated. He got us an extra week, but still the pressure was on.

With a firm date, we tackled the remaining tasks. We felt so confident, we agreed to host our annual Christmas dinner for immediate family and close friends. Improvisation would again be key. Using only disposable cookware, I prepared a lavish dinner, serving our ten guests on folding tables and chairs later packed away in the crawl space. China and silverware were from my late mother's collection, which I was giving to my brother. Again, potted poinsettias made the house look festive and warm.

Although we still lacked visas and flights, we sailed toward departure. But a storm always follows fair weather. With the best of intentions, Jim decided to freshen the walls for the tenants. He bought small cans of paint, applying it liberally throughout the house.

"Oh my God," I blurted, viewing his handiwork. Haphazard brush-strokes of fresh paint streaked the walls. "We can't turn the house over to tenants in this condition."

With the smirk of a precocious toddler, he asked, "Why not?"

"The walls look like Pollock paintings, *bad* Pollock paintings."

Hiring professional painters would be costly, not to mention unlikely, during the week between Christmas and New Year's. We had one choice: tackle the Herculean task ourselves. Jim's parents came to the rescue. Over many long, tiring days, the four of us repainted a four-bedroom house. It looked magnificent, but regrettably we wouldn't be around to enjoy the fresh paint job.

I surveyed the house. "Makes for a damn good story." Was I laughing or simply hysterical? It didn't matter. Jim, my Pollock prodigy, was merely relieved by my clemency.

Less than a week before year end, Jim made daily calls to the Belgian consulate until, at last, he announced that the visas were approved. "They waited until the end of December, citing my January 1 start date as rationale."

I shook my head. "And they couldn't have told you that weeks ago?"

The twisted logic should have been a clue to the way things worked in Belgium. Jim immediately booked our flights. He'd fly out first, on January 2, to prepare for work and start getting our new house ready. Sadie and I would fly out one week later.

Despite offers to stay with family and friends, Jim and I remained in the house, sleeping on a borrowed air mattress. It was my wish, a chance to exert a bit of control over a situation that was spinning rapidly forward. "It's our house," I explained to Jim. "Why wouldn't we want to stay here as long as possible?" It may not have been very comfortable, but at least for me, our home radiated love.

New Year's had a more profound meaning that year. Out with the old—house, friends, lives. In with the new, however, was shrouded in mystery. We rang in the new year in our customary fashion with our workout buddies and dined with Jim's folks on New Year's Day—both bittersweet goodbyes, farewells of indeterminate length.

As Jim packed for his evening flight, my mood soured. One more piece of the goodbye puzzle in place. After loading suitcases into the car with Sadie, I drove him to O'Hare.

Jim squeezed my leg. "Wish you were coming along."

"I'll be there in a week."

"Love you."

"Love you more."

I snapped photos before he disappeared into the terminal. Once again, my stomach knotted with a feeling of wistful loneliness.

Sadie and I returned to a house empty except for the air mattress. The silence was deafening. I buried my face in Sadie's soft golden fur. "It's just you and me now, girl." I was too exhausted, feverish, and achy to make room for depression. With my forehead hot to the touch and my entire head throbbing, I collapsed onto the mattress and slept. Sadie cuddled at my side. Our conditions may have been Spartan, but for three days and nights I was comforted by the familiar. This was still our home.

Jim called every day from Brussels. He was living in a hotel until he could arrange for rental furniture. "You'll love it here," he said, describing walks around our neighborhood. "Several restaurants on our block. Found a great café where you'll want to write and a pet store for Sadie." He was doing his best to warm me up for adventure.

High stress marked my last day in the house. Alone and still feverish, I felt compelled to tidy. Where the energy came from, I didn't know. Perhaps the work was a ritualistic cleansing necessary for me to move on, or simply the product of a Polish-American mother who taught me never to welcome visitors into a dirty house. For twelve hours I cleaned linen closets, bathrooms, pantry, and kitchen, filling several bags with trash. After dropping off the air mattress at Jim's parents, I bought a bottle of champagne, cat treats, and a card, leaving these items on the kitchen counter as a welcome for our tenants.

At nine o'clock that night with the house clean and empty, I called to Sadie, "Come here, girl. One final photo." With wagging tail and toothy smile, she sidled up to me and we posed for a selfie. "Poor girl. If you only knew what's coming."

After a teary-eyed walk-through, I loaded three suitcases and Sadie into my car. On a dark, bitter-cold night, we pulled away from the house. Sadness swept over me.

Friends invited Sadie and me to stay with them for the final four nights before our departure. I'd sold them my car, which allowed me use of the vehicle until the end of my stay. I could simply leave the car in their driveway.

My departure date arrived. I was a basket of nerves: excitement, apprehension, fear. Concern for Sadie topped it all. Because of her size, she had to fly as cargo. The service collected her several hours before my flight. Worries rattled me when the pickup guy wasn't the same person with whom we'd been dealing. "Last-minute substitution," he said. When he asked for our transport kennel, my stomach sank. We had repeatedly informed the service that we didn't have one. After some calls, he assured me that a shipping crate would be provided at the airport. Reluctantly, I lifted Sadie into his car and kissed her good-bye. *Will I ever see her again?*

In a kind gesture, my brother met me at O'Hare for a final coffee and goodbye, assuring me again that he'd visit. After the last hug, I passed through security. Concern for Sadie remained my focus. After boarding, I informed the flight attendant about her. "I'll speak with the captain," she said. "I'll keep you updated." Most airline personnel are sympathetic to passengers traveling with animals. Several minutes before departure the flight attendant returned. "Captain's well aware of Sadie. We won't leave without her."

My Brother Scott

Departure time passed. I gestured to the flight attendant. A flash of concern swept across her face. After making a call, she walked over. "Your dog's safe. She's—" The pilot's voice crackled over the speaker, interrupting her. "Ladies and gentlemen, I'm sure you've noticed that our departure time has passed. We're just waiting for some guy's dog to board." The flight attendant and I exchanged grins.

As the plane pushed from the gate, I sat back and closed my eyes. Our big adventure had begun.

II

Fresh Transplants:
Our First Year

Trees, plants, and shrubs were never intended to be transplanted. That's part of our modern-day culture. Even in the best of circumstances, new plants will show some signs of stress. (mrtreeservices.com)

The Grand Place, Brussels

Chapter 5

Pushing my loaded luggage cart past idle customs agents, I waited for the opaque double doors to glide open. My stomach fluttered with nerves as if I were stepping onto a stage. Perhaps I was, in my new and unrehearsed role as an expat spouse.

Entering an airport's international arrivals hall always fills me with anticipation. Like Carroll's, Baum's, and Homer's heroes, I've had frequent journeys deliver me into foreign worlds where nothing is as it was at home. Guidebooks and travel tips go only so far. Strange lands must be explored, their uncharted paths navigated firsthand. After flirting with familiarity and easing into routines, however, it's usually time for the trip home. My current tumble through the looking glass was different. Neither vacation, business trip, nor student exchange, this plunge dropped me into a new world where I'd steep without time frame or return ticket. How much time and effort were needed to shed the unsettling mantle of outsider?

A mix of eager faces greeted me, their anxious eyes scanning each arriving passenger. My gaze moved swiftly past these expectant strangers until I spotted Jim. The sight of his handsome face, kind eyes, and broad grin calmed me. Here, more than four thousand miles from Chicago, Jim represented home, a safe haven of unconditional love. After exchanging a welcome kiss, we pulled each other into a warm embrace.

"It's legal here," I said, stealing a second kiss. Jim chuckled. Even if our simple display of ordinary affection elicited glares and judgmental sneers, I didn't care. Those who've never had reason to be guarded about their love wouldn't understand the power that comes from asserting one's truth.

Jim squeezed my hand. "I'm so happy you're finally here."

"Me too."

"I missed you. Seems longer than just a week."

"You can say that again."

Our reunion elated me. But my euphoria was shallow. My mind remained unsettled, teeter-tottering between our exciting new adventure and the rich, established life left behind. And although I didn't recognize it, I was exhausted—physically as well as mentally—from three months of constant upheaval. Still, that welcome embrace from the man I loved brought a momentary flicker of normalcy and joy to my life.

Our homecoming wouldn't be complete until we reunited with Sadie. It pained us to leave the airport without her, but a government veterinarian needed to review her papers and inspect her general health. With pre- and post-travel exams and a battery of vaccinations, Sadie's health underwent much more scrutiny than our own. After she cleared, the pet transport service would deliver her to our door.

"With what that service charges," I said to Jim more than once, "Sadie should have flown first class and been chauffeured home in a stretch limo."

As we walked to the airport parking garage, Jim relayed an incident in the arrivals hall. He'd wanted to take my photo after I cleared customs. Although he opened with a chuckle, his tone and expression turned serious, suggesting something other than a humorous anecdote.

"I took a few practice shots," he explained. "As I'm reviewing the photos, I sense my personal space invaded. You know the feeling?" I nodded, recalling an incident on the Paris Metro several years earlier when two guys tried to pick my pocket. "I look up," he continued. "Two big, bearded guys are glaring at me. One says something in French."

I laughed. Jim didn't understand a word of French. "What'd he want?"

"Hell if I knew. They nodded to an old guy in a white tunic. Had one of those religious white caps on his head. When I asked if they spoke English, the bigger one got angrier. Barking in French, he pointed to my phone. His buddy made a grab for it."

"Wow! Were they trying to steal it?"

Jim shook his head. "Don't think so. I heard, 'delete' and 'police.' Guessing they wanted me to get rid of the pictures. Think it's against the law?"

"To take a stranger's photo?" I shrugged. "Don't think so. How could that be illegal...in Belgium?" I'd heard of cultures that objected to photos—something about capturing the soul—but never anything illegal. "What'd you do?"

"Didn't want any trouble, especially with you arriving. I deleted the photos as they kept saying 'police.' I held up my phone and said, 'I delete, I delete.' After final sneers, they walked back to the old guy."

"We're not in Chicago anymore, Toto."

That was my welcome to Brussels—a surreal incident worthy of Dorothy in Oz, Alice and the Red Queen, and Odysseus and the Cyclops. What odd customs and strange people would we encounter on our odyssey in the coming days, weeks, months, years?

As Jim drove out of the airport, he detailed his week's accomplishments as well as the tasks remaining. Both lists were daunting. Despite all he'd done, only half our mission was complete. We'd only just begun to settle in. Our current car, furniture, and visas were only temporary. We had no bank account, credit card, or Wi-Fi, not to mention friends or social circle of any kind. We were transplants without roots.

Jim tried to be excited for both of us—an advance scout eager to retrace his cleared path and share exotic new marvels with those trailing behind. "You'll really love the neighborhood, I'm sure of it. Can't wait to show you the café where you'll want to write. It's really cool, and close to the house. Very bohemian. You'll see."

As adorable as I found his attempt to enthrall me, his pep talk fizzled. My mind lingered on something important left behind, my writing. More than two months had passed since I'd written anything. Of course, I had good reasons. The move simultaneous to the launching of my debut novel drained my time and energy. My efforts stalled as I neared completion of an initial draft of my third novel. I wanted to finish that first draft, get the story down as they say, before polishing up my second book, which I hoped to submit for publication later that year. All those lofty plans now hung suspended in the air. Time was one thing, but rekindling the writing bug was the bigger issue.

The production gap marked my longest since embarking upon my new career five years earlier. Taking my first sips of Brussels air, I worried that the energy, mindset, and conviction needed to return to pen and paper would elude me. An inability to regain my focus compounded my anxiety like an insomniac who lies awake fretting about sleep. Concern somersaulted on itself. Without writing, I was purposeless, wandering a strange sea with no rudder or wind for the sails—adrift.

Adrift. The word scared me. My ears rang with the harsh warning delivered with a clipped and authoritative accent. I recalled a conversation overheard a few years earlier at my local Starbucks. A tour guide, German by her Teutonic looks and accent, shepherded several couples who were transferring from South Korea to Chicago. The expats were on their "Look See" trip to choose a place to live. The German's voice sounded loud and distinctive. Though her words were different, her message was this: "Finding the right community is important. It's not the husbands I worry about; they have their job and coworkers. Not the children either; they have schools and classmates. No, it's *always* the spouse who has the issue. And why? Because they have *nobody*, no support network. They're *adrift*. If an expat goes home early, it's because of the spouse." Her dire warning drew my gaze to the wives. I wasn't sure they fully understood the cautionary words delivered in heavily accented English, but I certainly did. Studying the women's faces, could I detect the doe-eyed spouses who might remain adrift?

That Starbucks encounter, I guessed, was neither chance nor co-incidence. I now faced the same predicament as those Korean spouses. But were the tour guide's words a warning of what might be or a dire prophecy of my certain fate? In a way, my situation was even more precarious than those spouses. They had each other, companions on their foreign adventure. Even among our expat friends, while husbands worked their wives usually networked and socialized with other expat women. Most had children. No, as a male spouse without children I was alone. Writing could be my life preserver. But adrift and floundering, I worried that it might remain beyond my reach.

As we neared Brussels city center, skies grew darker. Drizzle hit the windshield. I nodded over the dashboard. "Better than snow."

I had left Chicago buried under several feet of snow. Clear skies brought severe arctic blasts, a climatic phenomenon the weather people called the polar vortex. That Midwest winter was on track to be among the coldest and snowiest on record. Brussels, by pleasant contrast, didn't have a trace of white. Despite a latitude north of Winnipeg and Quebec City, Brussels enjoys moderate temperatures courtesy of the North Sea and Atlantic Ocean. On average, winters never get too cold nor summers too hot. Yet the maritime climate had cons—a chronic cloud cover with long rainy spells. The northern latitude also meant dark winters. Early January had barely eight and a half hours of daylight, nearly an hour less than Chicago.

Passing under Place Louise with its quaint trams and glittering luxury boutiques, Jim maneuvered the car off the inner ring road and into the narrow lanes of Saint-Gilles. Tall, narrow houses of brick, stone, and wood lined the streets of our new commune. Most looked shabby, neglected. Public greenery consisted of only a few scattered trees planted in small beds that jutted into parking lanes.

Gray, gray, gray, I thought. *Everything's so damn gray!*

"Almost there." Anticipation mounted in Jim's voice.

The street sign read *Rue d'Ecosse*, and below that, *Schotlandstraat*— the French and Flemish for "Scotland Street." Brussels was bilingual. Our house at number 4 was near the top of the block.

Jim gave a gentle squeeze to my thigh. "Here we are."

Our New Home

The four-story townhome was the nicest building on the eclectic block. Built in 1881, the stately edifice had the charm of residences lining Paris boulevards. The ground floor was constructed of gray stone while cream-colored stucco trimmed in gray decorated the floors above. Security shutters, also gray, covered three sets of windows of our ground-floor apartment. One half-story below street level, bars protected the windows of our guest bedroom and bath. Above, wrought iron adorned Juliet balconies of the second and third floor apartments.

Tall, gray entry doors led into a cobblestone foyer that originally functioned as a covered carriageway. Murals lit by bronze coach lamps depicted Flemish land and seascapes. A second set of double doors of beveled glass accessed an enormous walled garden where, in the past, a carriage house and stables might have stood. Two marble steps led up from the cobblestones to a landing. There, columns of red-veined granite flanked the doors to our apartment. To the right of our entry doors, a wide staircase of warm alderwood ascended to six more residences.

Our apartment was immense by European standards. More than two thousand square feet spread over two levels. The main floor was grand—eighteen-foot ceilings trimmed with plaster that looked like whipped-cream piping of a fancy wedding cake. Cream-colored walls outlined in gray framing seemed worthy of exhibiting large canvases of Rubens or Rembrandt. Wood panels adorned with lion head carvings covered the lower third of the dining room walls.

A modern stairwell led down to a former basement that had been converted into bedrooms and bathrooms. The lower level was contemporary—unadorned white walls, walk-in closets, bleached wood floors, and a mix of track and can lighting. In the master suite, a wall of sliding glass doors opened onto a private patio.

A large terraced garden stood at the rear of the building. Glass partitions between the dining room and kitchen and a wall of windows at the back of the house showcased the natural beauty. A turn of the head took one's view from a grimy Brussels street scene visible out the front windows to a lush, green oasis out back. We'd snared a splendid apartment in which to build a comfortable life.

Jim unlocked our front door and pushed it open. "Welcome to our new home, my love. Shall I carry you across the threshold?"

"Only if you want to end up in the emergency room," I replied with a laugh. I had four inches and forty pounds on him. "I'll settle for a kiss."

As he showed me the rented furniture, I tried hard to be upbeat. The overnight flight and concerns for Sadie exhausted me. Two more hours passed with no word of our dearly loved pooch. Growing more anxious, Jim left an urgent message with his contact at the pet transport company. Because of the early hour in the United States, he got voice mail.

"Unacceptable," I bellowed.

"I agree, sweetie. But there's not much we can do."

Seething with frustration, I grew more agitated. Two hours later, sometime after noon, Jim's phone rang. Jim put his contact on speakerphone.

"I was able to track Sadie down," the woman in New York said. "She's waiting to see the inspector. Bit of a backlog. Should be anytime."

"This wasn't supposed to happen," Jim said. "That's why we hired you. It's maddening." He recounted the earlier mix-ups involving the substitute driver and missing transport kennel in Chicago.

"I'm sorry," she replied. "There's really nothing we can do. I'll keep you advised."

We felt helpless, stressed, and tethered to house and phone.

"You must be famished," Jim said.

"No!" I snapped.

Jim put on his coat. "Well, I am. I'll run next door and grab a sandwich. Sure I can't get you one?"

"No!"

Ten minutes later he returned with two sandwiches that we ate in silence. I was hungry after all.

Our Wi-Fi and Internet access was limited to Jim's phone. Besides feeling disconnected, I didn't have any way to divert my worry. Unpacking provided distraction.

"Want some help?" Jim asked.

"No!" I snapped again. Sometimes space is good for a relationship.

After emptying my suitcases, I tried to nap. Concern kept me awake. Around two o'clock in the afternoon, I wandered upstairs. Jim was seated on the couch, scanning his phone. He looked up, his half-hearted smile informing me that he had no news...no good news anyway. "Sadie's still at the airport, they say."

Additional calls to the woman in New York grew increasingly tense. She tried to calm us, but we lost all confidence that anyone knew Sadie's whereabouts. Wild imaginings hijacked reason. Sitting in silence, we feared the worst as dusk darkened the room.

A little after four o'clock, Jim's phone rang. He repeated our address to the caller, nodding at me with a smile. Hanging up, he practically squealed with joy. "He's got our girl."

Minutes later at the sound of the front door buzzer, Jim and I jumped to our feet. "She's here!" Darting outside, we huddled behind the van as the driver opened the back doors. Sadie's head was visible through the wires of a wooden crate. Glaring at us, her coal-black eyes looked tired and very unhappy.

She remained aloof for the rest of the night.

"She's pissed," Jim said.

"She won't stay mad long. She'll bounce back to her old, lovable self after a good night's sleep. I think we all will." We fell asleep, our little family reunited under our new roof.

Saturday promised a full day of exploration, errands, and recovery. But reprieve from the prior day's stress was short-lived. We awoke to a text from the property management company overseeing our home in Chicago. "Call ASAP."

I groaned. "That can't be good."

Jim shook his head. "Nope."

But it was too early to call the States. Jim ran out for coffee and croissants, which we ate speculating what had happened in Chicago.

Jim got off the phone, his expression a mix of frustration and despair. "It's the house."

"Yes?" I braced for bad news.

He took a deep breath. "Our tenants are dealing with a massive leak."

My jaw fell. "What?"

"Melting snow. It's seeping into the house." With frozen gutters and a thick snow pack, the melting snow closest to the warmer roof had nowhere to go. A waterfall descended two stories into the kitchen, damaging drywall and window blinds. "Our tenants tried to clear the roof," he added. "They need permission to involve our insurance agent."

I sighed. "He won't be happy."

The policy was less than ten days old. In order to rent out our home, we had to convert from a homeowner's policy to rental dwelling coverage. Doing so required a switch in insurance companies and agents.

My blood pressure spiked. "We've never had this problem." Images of our home pained me. Mold and structural damage were concerns. I felt as if we and our house had failed our new tenants. They'd resided in the house for less than one week.

"Damn, damn, damn! I haven't been here for twenty-four hours. That damn house doesn't want to let us go." I felt trapped, our stubborn roots refusing to let go. "Why is this happening?" Was it karma, the universe, or merely a cloud of bad luck?

Jim looked at me, concern in his eyes. My tears and rant were an overreaction. But I didn't understand that at the time. My emotions muddled, swirling together at high speed. Exhaustion, anger, fear, excitement, depression, and grief churned to the surface before plunging back into the maelstrom only to bubble up again. With only one day into our grand adventure, a toxic mess of emotions consumed me.

Chapter 6

Problems with our Chicago house haunted us for months. Deep snow made the roof too dangerous to inspect, but clues suggested ice damming. Blocked by frozen gutters, melting snow trickled down the roof and into seams in the house's soffit. A relentless cycle of snow and bitter cold made repair impossible until spring.

Timing couldn't have been worse. Jim struggled to get his arms around a global role while also learning the complex choreography of working with a demanding and combative boss. And despite exhaustion and frazzled nerves, I mustered every ounce of strength to put down new roots in Brussels. Calamitous events in Chicago threatened to paralyze my progress or, worse, send me over an emotional cliff. Sensing my fragile state, Jim told the property management company to delete me from all communication. Jim had one advantage. Because this was not his family home, he could be more objective and emotionally detached. Although I was selfish to let him shoulder the burden, I needed the "Ignorance is bliss" reprieve.

Jim doled out updates in filtered sound bites. Most of the time he waited for me to ask. One of my rare inquiries informed me of a dispute. A contractor brought in by our property manager pointed at the roof's design. "Too many peaks and valleys." Our architect and builder, unsurprisingly, rejected the notion. They offered their own opinion: "Simply a bad winter. Ice damming's a problem everywhere."

Nonetheless, we hoped they'd offer a solution. They did not. In addition, our insurance agent sought to limit the liability of the new policy. Poor Jim tried to coordinate the mess from four thousand miles and seven time zones away.

"The house is acting like a jilted lover. Exacting revenge because we abandoned it." My words, which sounded like a tag line for a Stephen King novel, reflected my harried mind.

Costs of the debacle made us shudder. We'd received only one month's rent and were already in the red. Cash outflows included a sizeable insurance deductible, reimbursement to our tenants for out-of-pocket expenses related to cleanup, and charges for clearing snow from the roof. None of this included the broken hot-water heater replaced days before our departure.

Unexpected damages were only part of the equation. We accepted the posting aware of financial risks, considering the European adventure an investment that offered many intangible benefits, both personal and professional. We were expats in name only as Jim's employer had transferred him onto the local Belgian payroll. A housing allowance, access to tax accountants, and property management services for our Chicago home cushioned the financial blow. But Jim was no longer covered by an employer-sponsored retirement plan. Missing years of contributions and company matches would leave a permanent hole in our golden years. Unlike many expat contracts, Jim's had no allowances for annual flights home, language lessons, enculturation courses, or other assimilation perks that benefited employees and their families. My transition benefit was limited to a magazine subscription, a monthly periodical containing features for expat spouses.

Despite distractions with our Chicago home, Jim dove into his new job. He felt pressured to show a return on his employer's investment for moving us to Europe. Regularly leaving the house before six o'clock in the morning, he didn't return until eight o'clock at night or later. From my own corporate experience, I understood his commitment and challenges as a new manager. Success depended on pulling his widely scattered team members together quickly. Many weren't thrilled with their new boss. The stereotypical American parodied on television and in film is loud, brash, pushy, and uncultured. Jim's new team didn't yet know that he's none of those things. He embraced the philosophy that good leaders focus on *results* and *relationships* with equal and uncompromising fervor. Individuals, he knew, might follow a manager who stokes intimidation and fear, but not for the long term, and not with any true, game-changing passion. Trust and respect were key ingredients for high-performing teams. Earning them required sizeable investments of his time and personal effort.

Jim teetered on a quivering tightrope. Integrity demanded adherence to his values while survival meant conforming to a corporate culture reflective of most contemporary companies: quick wins on short horizons, action valued above leadership, and tactics prized over strategy. His new boss, a long-tenured Belgian, was heavily steeped in the corporate culture—a recipe for personal success and survival I'd seen before.

Nurturing his fledgling team while balancing the expectations of his demanding boss consumed Jim's time and energy. A lesser person might sacrifice the team in order to manage up. Not my Jim. Although often frustrated that commitments to his people left little time for me, I recognized his deep satisfaction. Coaching and mentoring brought him joy, giving him purpose, satisfaction, and camaraderie.

As Jim poured himself into work, my isolation deepened. Sadie was a fine and comforting companion, but without a social or professional network, my world felt very small. Strings of dark, gloomy days accompanied by incessant drizzle wore me down. A need for human connection coupled with a love of adventure pushed me from the comfortable cocoon of our house. With a red Chicago Blackhawks sports cap and black raincoat holding the chilly dampness at bay, I spent my days exploring Brussels. Winding streets and narrow lanes were a far cry from the easy-to-follow grid layout of Chicago and its suburbs. I got lost a few times and even panicked. But my meanderings began to root me in the foreign soil even as the soles of my shoes wore thin from wet cobblestones and broken pavements.

Melding into our new city wasn't easy. My polite nods to strangers went unreturned; hellos and bonjours went unanswered. Passersby who didn't avert their gazes glared. Sneers rebuffed my smiles. Perhaps the reactions were reflective of any urban environment. Maybe my expectations, nurtured in America's heartland, were unreal. Maybe the friendly dispositions of most Chicagoans immortalized in Sinatra's "My Kind of Town" had spoiled me.

The cold indifference of neighbors who passed me daily on the street was especially difficult. I grappled for an explanation. Belgium was a federation of proud French, Flemish, and German speakers. Did lack of a common language and culture make Belgians suspicious and disdainful of all strangers? Were tight-knit clans and aloofness normal byproducts of a fragmented country? Did the presence of so many nationalities, languages, and cultures in the cosmopolitan city provide a barrier to human interaction? *Belge Face* was the term I concocted for the icy glares and grimaces encountered on my walks. Sarcasm was a defense mechanism. Mocking the perceived rudeness helped me cope instead of cry.

"Says more about them than it does me," I mumbled to myself, not completely buying into that theory.

Alone in a strange city with only a basic aptitude for French, I felt vulnerable, lonely. Smiles, nods, and hellos were attempts to reach beyond my small world. I had a strong desire and probably a psychological need to connect with human beings. Instead, my repulsed efforts only made me feel more alone, frustrated, angry—a permanent outsider.

"The German Starbucks lady was right," I muttered to myself, recalling the tour guide's dire warning to the Korean expat spouses. *German Starbucks lady* became mental shorthand to describe my despair.

I expected too much from strangers. Hindsight makes that very clear, but I probably understood the problem even then. Casual exchanges might soothe my wounded psyche, but they wouldn't cure it. They were merely topical salves for a more profound condition. I assumed that relief from my isolation would come from Jim's colleagues. But offers of coffees, meetups, dinners, and parties to welcome us to Belgium and acclimate us to our new home didn't come. With Jim consumed by work, I cast out on my own—*adrift*.

Bleakness and despair could have smothered me. But I didn't surrender to them, not then. I had a plan. In Chicago, I was active in two writers' groups. In addition to providing camaraderie, both pushed my writing to a higher level. In one group, writers offer up pieces of prose, poetry, and nonfiction for critique. The workshop format teaches authors how to reach an audience. Does the piece work? Are parts confusing? What might make it stronger? The second group educates writers with lectures by experienced authors, editors, publishers, and creative writing professors. Both organizations energized me and fueled my purpose to write. Parting from them left a deep void in my personal and professional life.

Before Jim and I left Chicago, an Internet search listed a Brussels-based group of English-language writers. The Brussels Writers' Circle (BWC) had an attractive website. Operating for more than a decade, the BWC promoted three sessions per week. The format mirrored my weekly critique workshop. BWC's prompt reply to my email impressed me. The prospect of connecting with people who shared a common interest appealed to me. Moreover, the idea of tapping into the creative energy of fellow authors to jump-start my own writing gave me hope, and a much-needed lifeline.

Chapter 7

With the arrival of our furniture, artwork, and other belongings, our apartment began to feel like home. The large traditional furnishings and rugs we had selected for the journey complemented the décor of the grand nineteenth-century townhouse. Our possessions—soft leather upholstery, rich dark woods, and plush wool rugs—gave the formal rooms an air of warmth, comfort, and intimacy, the fashion equivalent of pairing a silk blazer and dress shirt with faded blue jeans and loafers.

I surveyed the decorated rooms. "Our stuff was made for the place."

Jim put his arm around me. "You've definitely turned this into a home."

Making a home was an important step in putting down roots. Home has always been my refuge, a safe haven, a place to weigh anchor and escape the harsh, judgmental world. We made other strides in establishing roots. We maneuvered through our commune's town hall, wooing the indomitable department head, Madame de Ville, to begin the process of exchanging temporary visas for residency cards. We acquired a new washing machine, dryer, cable television, and home phone. Internet and a service plan for my smartphone reconnected me, albeit tenuously, with the outside world.

Settled In

Unpacked boxes down to a manageable number, I turned my attention outward. Jim's upcoming business trip to South Africa prodded me to check out the Brussels Writers' Circle. The BWC offered rescue from isolation. Jim's past trips for work had included lengthy stays in India and an entire summer internship in Italy. But they didn't stir my anxiety. In Chicago, a vast network of friends and family nurtured deep roots. In Brussels, I had nobody. Despite being relatively independent and self-sufficient, I was frightened by the prospect of complete isolation. Even a great swimmer can panic far from shore.

Unpacking a box of clothes, I turned to Jim. "I'm planning to try the writers' group on Tuesday." I wanted to test the waters not only for my own sake but also to allay Jim's concern about leaving me alone for two weeks.

He grinned, his entire body relaxing with my news. "Great. That's great, sweetie. You love your group back home."

I nodded. *But this isn't my group back home.* I left so many doubts, fears, and insecurities unspoken in those early days. Jim already had an overcrowded plate without my piling on more stress. Only time would tell whether the BWC could cure my loneliness.

I placed Jim's dinner in the warm oven to keep until he got home from the office. After putting on my coat and scarf, I patted Sadie on the head. "Wish me luck, girl."

I ventured into the rainy evening for a brisk twenty-minute walk into the historic city center, my stomach churning with the anxiety of meeting a room full of strangers. I remembered my father's twist on new, scary beginnings. Citing his childhood fascination with Robert Louis Stevenson, he encouraged me to view uncharted moments through the lens of a courageous adventurer. My father's romantic philosophy still guided me in adulthood.

As I strolled to the meeting place, sights, smells, and sounds of Brussels offered diversions to my worries. The novelty of cobblestone streets, ancient churches, bustling cafés, and medieval walls hadn't worn off. In addition, the night air teased with aromas of chocolate, waffles, and *frites.* In Chicago, my weekly journey to the writers' group was also about twenty minutes. But that was a drive through bland suburban settings of subdivisions and strip malls, not a sensory-filled adventure through a stunning urban landscape. If these new surroundings couldn't arouse my writer's muse, I doubted anything could.

Will I fit in?

My father's counsel notwithstanding, concern haunted my thoughts as I stepped into the Maison des Crêpes, the place where the BWC gathered on Tuesdays. *Hope I enjoy tonight.* I had no plan B for building a social network.

"*Je suis* écrivain," I said, identifying myself as a writer.

"*Oui. En haut.*" Pointing upward, a pretty blonde directed me to a flight of stairs through a small, low-ceilinged, timbered dining room.

Crammed at simple wooden tables, a youthful clientele drank beer and dined on inexpensive crepes. The scent of savories and hops mingled in the air. This was a setting worthy of Stevenson, ripped from the pages of *Treasure Island*.

At the top of a narrow wooden staircase, a weathered door labeled "Toilets" hinged outward onto the landing. *Charming!* The door, I noted mentally, presented a hazard capable of smacking someone in the face or even hurling them backward down the stairs. A single step forward delivered me into the meeting room. The flip of a switch illuminated a single overhead bulb and two tattered sconces, none of which produced much light.

Standing in the doorway, I snapped photos with my smartphone and texted them to Jim, appending a terse message. "I'm here—first to arrive." In reply came thumbs-up and heart emojis.

After removing my coat and hat, I moved deeper into the room. Aromas of melted butter, sugary dough, onions, roasted meat, vegetables, and warm cheese wafted up the stairs. A collage of newspapers decorated one wall, its yellow hue likely a result of age and nicotine rather than a deliberate attempt at vintage. The small room was dingy—no escaping that word. Furnishings consisted of wood and laminate-topped tables of assorted shapes—square, rectangle, circle. Padded banquettes with black leather backs and twill seats ran along both side walls. Wooden chairs with unpadded seats cluttered the remaining floor space. One chair sat off kilter, its leg disappearing into a hole in the worn planked floor. I made a second mental note not to sit there.

Two large windows looked onto a busy intersection. Neon glow from fast-food restaurants and bars supplemented the room's scant light. Although both windows were closed, street noise and pedestrian chatter produced a stifled din. Siren blasts and strobing blue lights were byproducts of the nearby central Brussels police station.

The room's condition didn't surprise me. During our short time living and dining in Brussels, Jim and I had observed tired, outdated décors in many restaurants and cafés. Most eateries operated with minimal staff. Chefs often doubled as owners. Servers did everything: greeted customers, took orders, delivered food, cleared tables—all performed without expectation of gratuity. In contrast to their American counterparts, Belgian servers enjoyed higher base wages and benefits. Spare change was a common offering, though upmarket restaurants might command tips of five to ten percent. Waitstaff showed appreciation for even the smallest of gratuities. "Spare change" was sufficient for the Maison des Crêpes.

The BWC, I learned, was lucky to have the space. Private rooms in central Brussels, especially free of charge, were hard to find. Perhaps the bar assumed that writers drank a lot—a fair bet. Even so, drinks were reasonably priced and the friendly staff was an added surprise.

The edgy ambience was a world away from the staid atmosphere of the Barrington Public Library, the venue for my Chicago-based writers' group. There, coffee was the beverage of choice. Would this new batch of writers reflect these new surroundings? Was their writing steeped in a gritty, urban milieu? Was alcohol a better muse than caffeine?

Inside the bathroom and opposite a communal sink, primitive marker scribbles identified the male and female stalls. After cautiously emerging from the bathroom, I found two guys settling into the meeting room. Each held a drink, one a can of Red Bull, the other a glass of beer. The first fellow, short and stocky with cropped white hair, was about my age. Soft-spoken, he introduced himself succinctly as a teacher with a Spanish passport. The other fellow was about the same height as the first but trimmer and a few years younger. David, I soon learned, functioned as the group's chairman and Tuesday night facilitator. He'd been the one who answered my original query.

"From Chicago, right?"

I flinched. "Wow, good memory."

"Welcome. Happy you're here." David explained that he had moved to Brussels from his native England more than a decade earlier for a position with the European Commission. "I generally start the session with a *tour de table*." Answering my quizzical look, he added, "We go around the room with brief introductions. Name, nationality, writing genre."

"Perfect. What are you both working on?"

"Not much," the teacher from Spain whispered. "A little poetry. A story now and then. You'll see." Below his dark, mischievous eyes, he flashed a smile worthy of Carroll's enigmatic cat.

David grinned. "Mine's a science-fiction trilogy."

I smiled politely despite loathing the genre. "Look forward to hearing it." *Not!*

He snickered. "I've tortured the others, so why not you too." His self-deprecating humor was refreshing, a sign of a writer who didn't take himself too seriously. "And how about you?"

"Contemporary stories, no specific genre. Just published my first novel. Working on two more at the moment." My portfolio tagged me as a serious writer in terms of aspiration if not talent. Too new to the craft, I had little confidence.

"Fantastic. By the way," he said hoisting his beer, "as a matter of protocol, people order drinks on the way in and pay on the way out."

The Spaniard raised his can of Red Bull and smiled in silence.

"I'll go fetch a beer, then. That is, if I have time?"

"You do," he replied with a shrug. "We say seven, but most people straggle in well past. We only have three readers tonight, maybe a fourth."

The room filled, becoming crowded and warm—quite the cozy affair. The *tour de table* was helpful. The dozen or so writers, a balance of men and women, were a jumble of nationalities—Dutch, Bulgarian, Canadian, Irish, Spanish, Italian, Moroccan, Danish, and English. I was the only American. Ages ranged from twenty-five to the early sixties, with an average between thirty-five and forty. Among my Chicago writers, I was "the kid." Here, I was among the more senior. A few long-time Brussels residents were in the group, but most were recent transplants like myself.

In standard workshop format, readers shared copies of their work. As the author read his or her piece aloud, others formed impressions and added comments to the manuscript. An ensuing discussion consisted of general reactions, specific feedback, and suggestions for improvement. In my Chicago group, authors took a passive role during the discussion. Feedback wasn't intended to fuel debate or spark defensive posturing. The BWC didn't adhere to that practice. Wine and beer, it seemed, loosened inhibitions and lips.

The first reader presented her piece—a science-fiction fantasy. I concealed my disappointment. The writing was sharp, her images rich. But it was still *science fiction*. The critique that followed mirrored the helpful commentary to which I was accustomed. I overcame first night jitters to contribute to the conversation. Eliciting choruses of laughter and groans, repeated blasts from the bathroom hand dryer interrupted discussions.

Handing out copies of her work, the second writer described it as a romance. My delight was short-lived. Vampires and werewolves populated her romance. As the third reader handed out his story, I took an anticipatory breath. But alas, yet more science fiction and fantasy. *Good grief. Do vampires, werewolves, fairies, aliens, and dystopian worlds monopolize the BWC literary landscape?* Many BWC members spoke of plans for science-fiction trilogies. *Aargh!* In my years with Chicago-based writers, I recalled only one piece of science fiction. I disliked that one too.

Despite reeling from science-fiction/fantasy overload, I was impressed by the writing. For most of the group, English was a second or even third language. Conversation is one thing; crafting a written story in another language is quite another. BWC writers had proficiency with grammar, spelling, and other nuances of the complicated English language. Although I've studied many languages, I couldn't string together a paragraph in anything but English. Many English speakers take for granted that the world doesn't force them to speak another language. Although a single universal tongue facilitates global travel and communication, it has disadvantages. People who never learn a second language forego cultural enrichment. Might they also be denying themselves valuable mental stimulus?

After paying for my beer, I stepped outside into the chilly January night for the walk home. My mind churned. The evening's camaraderie and stimulating conversation filled me with satisfaction and hope. Many of the writers were potential friends outside the group. At the same time, a wave of nostalgia for my Chicago colleagues swept over me. Perhaps what I felt was grief, the natural process of letting go. Would the BWC fill my emotional void, quench my craving to belong to a community? After a single night, it was too early to tell.

As I shut our front door behind me, Jim's voice called out from the living room. "How'd it go?"

"Good. It was…good."

"Doesn't sound very good."

Making my way into the living room, I found Jim and Sadie on the couch. The television was on, and Jim had a beer in his hand. I kissed Jim and patted Sadie's head. "Let's just say, it wasn't bad."

Jim smirked. "Another rousing endorsement…"

I chuckled, moving into the small area beside the couch where we kept coats and shoes. "I had fun. It's just that…"

"You miss your old group."

Back in the living room, I stared at Jim. He knew me better than anyone. "Yes, a lot. Don't get me wrong, the BWC are good people, but it's…"

"Simply not the same. I get it. I'm sorry."

I shrugged off his words with a grin. "Let me offer up two words."

A quizzical look came over his face. "Huh, what words?"

Allowing the suspense to hang in the air, I walked to the kitchen to pour a whiskey. Squeezing onto the couch beside Sadie, I hoisted my glass. "Cheers."

"Cheers," Jim replied. "Now tell me what you mean by 'two words.'"

Laced with sarcasm, my answer trickled across my lips. "Science fiction."

Although I shared my frustration with the science-fiction/fantasy concentration, I spoke also of the evening's many positives including the tremendous camaraderie.

He studied my face. "Will you go back?"

My answer came fast. I'd debated that very question on my stroll home. "Sure. Let me see how Thursday night goes."

Jim grinned. With worries about my settling in, he shared my hopes for the BWC.

Creativity is addictive. Artists inspire artists. In the past, workshop sessions stirred my desire to write. Despite the preponderance of science-fiction/fantasy, my visit to the BWC prodded me to ponder my writing.

My first novel had launched three months earlier. A mature draft of my second book needed one more polish before I sent it to a professional editor. The initial draft of a third novel was incomplete, work interrupted by our move to Brussels. Could I let my second novel languish so close to the finish line? Could I abandon my third novel altogether? I didn't have answers. Writing required passion, focus, and energy. How much of any of those I retained remained unclear. However, hanging out with other writers offered the best chance to jump-start my creative drive.

Two nights after that first BWC session, I again donned my raincoat and Blackhawks cap for the walk into central Brussels. On Thursdays, the BWC gathered at Falstaff, a restaurant near the Maison des Crêpes and adjacent to Fritland. The latter had been serving up *pommes frites* for nearly forty years. A guidebook warned against using the term "French fries." Belgium claimed the savories as its own creation. Customers who cared more about eating than debating the food's origin lined up at Fritland's takeout windows, rain or shine.

From the pavement, Falstaff looked grand, a fine example of Belle Époque design. A large red awning covered an expansive terrace reminiscent of Paris or Vienna. Whereas the Maison des Crêpes evoked images of a Stevenson novel, Falstaff begged comparisons to a Toulouse-Lautrec painting. Inside, the décor suggested a grand and gilded past—red velvet seats, marble floors, high coffered ceilings, and plenty of brass trim. Harsh lights, however, revealed a faded beauty well past her prime.

"*Je suis* écrivain," I said, repeating my words from Tuesday, "*avec le Bruxelles* Writers' Circle."

The stern-faced woman with hints of Dickens' Madame Defarge directed me to the back. "Private room," she replied in English. "In the corner."

The session mimicked Tuesday night's flow—a *tour de table* followed by four readers. Our facilitator was a spirited, redheaded Irishman with a penchant for debate. The group was as welcoming as Tuesday night's bunch, but markedly older—a few in their seventies and eighties. I counted four Americans in addition to myself.

A middle-aged American woman read first. *Unbelievable!* Another science-fiction story, the heroine some kind of half-cat, half-woman creature. David, Tuesday's facilitator, followed with his contribution. Yes, more science fiction. *Am I doomed?* Perhaps Brussels inspires only science fiction and fantasy, an urban *Twilight Zone*. The baton then passed to an older Englishman and a Scottish woman. As I listened to their readings, sipping my dark Belgian beer, a wave of contentment came over me. *At last, a respite from vampires, aliens, and zombies.*

I walked home satisfied with the experience and pleased to have options. Of the two sessions, which did I prefer? Thursday's workshop, despite a facilitator who debated every bit of feedback, felt familiar—an older crowd and a variety of writing. Tuesday's group was edgier, but the writers were less experienced, and the material focused on my least favorite genre. As for venues, Falstaff offered the quieter and more comfortable room. But the Maison des Crêpes had a friendlier staff and cheaper beer. Decisions are always complicated.

No need to decide now, I thought, walking over the cobblestones of the Grand Place. *I'll simply attend both sessions until I make up my mind.*

Chapter 8

Regular updates from our property manager informed us that unrelent-ing storms continued to pummel Chicago, piling more snow onto our house's ice-dammed roof. By comparison, Belgium's mild, snowless winter brought a welcome surprise. Still, Jim and I cleared a different kind of path—one that took us from outsiders to rooted residents. Finding our way forward proved as challenging as plowing through a snowbank.

Even Sadie struggled. She spent hours in our garden, dragging around and lounging on her security blanket. Perhaps the soft purple throw re-tained familiar scents of home. We kept waiting for her to bounce back to her pre-move self. But even after her jet lag passed, she remained lethargic, her appetite spotty. Did she need a doggie psychologist? Had our move brought on a serious illness? We were concerned. Sadie meant the world to us, a familial bond that only serious pet lovers understand.

We were researching veterinarians when a spell of nausea gave us a clue. Colorful bits of shell in Sadie's vomit informed us that our little princess had discovered an exotic delicacy, snails—escargot ab-sent puff pastry and garlic butter. Our garden crawled with the slimy little creatures. In Chicago, we suffered only drab, garden-variety slugs and even they were well-mannered enough to remain below ground. A few stomach purges cured Sadie of her cravings and restored her energy and personality. We had our girl back but wondered what other unknown menaces lurked in her new environment.

Sadie and her Blanket

Besides adjusting to a new job, boss, and office culture, Jim also found impediments outside work. Unfamiliar customs, culture, and language complicated even the simplest of issues.

As in most cities, Brussels regulated parking. Our street was no exception. Jim's car attracted a flurry of fines. He seethed as he dropped his latest ticket onto the kitchen counter. "I'll go broke if I don't find a solution."

"Sorry, sweetie," I replied. "Let's try to park the car in the garden."

The landlord had given us permission to use a paved section of our back garden for parking, "as long as the car fit." This meant squeezing an automobile through the building's front double doors, navigating the cobblestoned foyer, and finally clearing a second set of double doors that accessed the back garden. The plan wasn't without merit; the foyer originally functioned as a carriageway.

Jim perked up. "Think there's enough clearance?"

I shrugged. "Worth a shot. Worked for carriages and horses once upon a time." My theory, however, was based on my unknown and unspoken premise that nineteenth-century carriages were as wide as twenty-first century automobiles. *Only time will tell.*

Desperate, Jim agreed to try. After dinner we stepped out our front door and into the building's foyer. We combined our strength to pull open the double doors leading to the street. The second set of doors accessing the garden were easier to open though they squeaked from infrequent use.

"Okay," I said. "Now all we need is the car."

With an expression that looked as if he'd eaten a gut load of snails, Jim surveyed the pathway. "It's too narrow."

I assumed a cheerleader's grin. "Won't know till we try."

Taking a deep breath, Jim climbed into his parked car, a four-door, midsize Renault. White-knuckled, he inched the car from the street, across the threshold. He called out the driver's window, "How's it look?"

I mustered a reassuring tone. "Tight, but I think you can do it. Keep her coming."

Following my hand signals, he squeezed the car through the narrow entry, his side mirrors barely clearing the doorframe, slowly moving the car deeper into the foyer. His shoulder muscles tensed. His face looked ashen.

Although I gave an encouraging smile, my mind churned with images of Lucy and Desi's long, long trailer. Despite my forward gestures, the car came to an abrupt stop. Jim's hands lifted from the wheel.

"Are you okay?" I asked. "What's wrong?"

"Nope. Not gonna happen. I'm not comfortable. It won't fit."

He'd get no argument from me. The car was his responsibility. Besides, if we were to turn this parking ordeal into a daily ritual, one of us would end up with a tire iron in his skull while the other lived out his expat adventure in a Belgian prison. After backing the car into the street, Jim looked apoplectic as he threw a parking meter receipt on the dashboard.

I offered a sympathetic hug. "I'm sure we can get a resident sticker."

Jim groaned, his aggravation understandable. Belgian bureaucracy turned every task into an ordeal. Securing a permit meant another bumper car ride through the town hall, an odyssey that made Alice's tumble down the rabbit hole look like a summer picnic. The language barrier loomed large. Jim's visit to exchange his Illinois license for a Belgian driving permit had turned into a surreal experience. Office rules prohibited clerks from speaking English. We didn't speak bureaucratic French or Flemish. The standoff ended when a kind young woman breached office protocol. Casting furtive glances at her sourpuss boss, she coached Jim through the process in whispered English.

Aided by my smattering of French, I navigated the Byzantine bureaucracy and obtained a resident parking permit. I'd need to repeat the process once Jim's permanent car and registration plates arrived, but his broad grin when I presented the permit was ample reward. The slip of paper represented a small but highly symbolic triumph.

Jim moved beyond his failed attempt to park in our garden. Motivated by the sight of vandalized cars in our neighborhood, he rented a spot in a public garage. Even then, he had trouble squeezing in the car, changing assigned spots and garages until he felt comfortable. For the sake of our relationship, I let him find the perfect fit on his own.

Language proved problematic in resolving issues with our apartment. We obtained our landlord's agreement to let us carpet the stairwell for Sadie and hang curtains and shades in street-facing windows. Fine print is dangerous in any language, but especially in a foreign one. Seeking reimbursement for the carpet, a tidy sum, Jim learned that the landlord agreed merely to allow us to install carpeting and window coverings, not to actually pay for them.

We also had issues with the heat. After many unreturned messages, the landlord finally gave Jim the phone number of the building's handyman, a Polish fellow named Jean. Again, Jim's messages went unreturned. One evening, we huddled on the sofa. Fed up with feeling cold and seething from Jean's unresponsiveness, Jim grabbed his phone. Miraculously, Jean picked up but spoke no English. Jim spoke in English, and Jean replied in heavily accented French. Watching Jim in the fractured exchange, I didn't see how either man could possibly understand the other. Jim's face flashed with anger. His voice grew louder, bellowing into the phone, "What the fuck is wheat hour?" He disconnected before he could burst a blood vessel.

I flinched. Jim seldom swore. "What was that all about?"

Jim stared at the phone still clenched in his hand. "Hell if I know. He kept babbling on about 'wheat hour'."

My mind churned. "Hmm. Might he have said '*Huit heures*'?"

Jim flinched. "Repeat that."

"*Huit heures.*"

His brow furrowed. "Maybe. Why? You know what that means?"

I chuckled. "We'll see in the morning, but I think Jean told you that he'll be here at eight o'clock. That is, if you didn't scare him off." Surprise swept over Jim's face before he doubled over in laughter.

Despite Jim's f-bomb and hang-up, Jean appeared the next morning at eight o'clock. After several failed attempts, more chilly nights, and threats from our real estate agent to blacklist the landlord, a professional heating expert was finally called in to fix the heat.

Fitting in was to be a long, difficult process. Laughter made the ordeal tolerable. We harvested humor wherever we could, especially during those early months. *What the fuck is wheat hour?* entered our vernacular as code, a comic reminder of our struggles to assimilate.

The day before Jim's flight to South Africa, we set out from the apartment for a brisk stroll. Since arriving, we had taken many walks. These strolls blended exercise, familiarization, and exploration. Only the day before and quite by chance, we had happened upon the house where actress Audrey Hepburn was born in 1929. With Jim's extended work hours, strolls provided quality "couple time," a chance to share our weekly adventures.

Under blue skies, the sun nipped the chill from the early February air. Sunday meant empty streets and sidewalks as well as fewer trams. We walked up Avenue Brugmann, a broad and tidy thoroughfare lined with neat homes, upscale apartments, and an occasional embassy.

"Would you like to live here?" Jim asked as I pointed out handsome houses and interesting shops.

"Nope. The area may be pretty, but I wouldn't trade our location. I can walk to the Grand Place in twenty minutes. Then there's our garden. No, I love our place."

Jim stared at me, a smile forming on his lips. Although he didn't say anything, I saw his pleasure with my reply. Despite the many fitting-in struggles, I had staked claim to a piece of Brussels—our home.

When we reached Place Brugmann, a chic tree-filled square, a restaurant drew our attention. Bright décor evoked a 1950s American diner. Pink barriers and an aqua canopy delineated an outdoor dining area set with flamingo pink tables and chairs. Red neon flashed "Coca Cola" in a window and pink neon spelled the diner's name. Le Balmoral seemed as out of place as we felt.

Glancing at the posted menu, Jim sighed with delight. "American breakfast."

In Brussels, a hearty meal of eggs, hash browns, pancakes, and breakfast meats was as rare as sunshine and smiles. Although we didn't eat big breakfasts on a regular basis, the availability of such familiar comfort food pleased us.

I nodded toward the windows. "Assuming you'd like to try?"

"Hell yeah," he replied, his hand already pulling open the glass door.

The diner motif continued inside—pastel colors, aqua-colored vinyl booths, metal tables, and pink padded chairs. Our eyes widened and our lips smacked at the scent of bacon, flapjacks, and other savories frying on the griddle—aromas of home.

"Wow!" Jim's face radiated with childlike delight.

Our server had placed before him a plate piled high with plump sausages, thick slabs of bacon, juicy ham slices, and two wedges of hash browns encircling a toasted bagel topped by eggs sunny side up. My cheese omelet, paltry by comparison, was no less filling or satisfying. A bottomless cup of coffee, a rarity in Europe, rounded out the experience.

Jim took a break from his feast. "Sorry about the car, babe."

I recognized his concern at leaving for two weeks. I, too, worried about my ability to withstand the lengthy period of isolation. I affected a cheery tone. "No worries, sweetie, I can walk anywhere I need to go."

"Would be nice for you to be able to drive someplace…if you wanted to."

I shrugged. "It's okay, really. I'll be fine."

Jim's Renault had manual transmission. Jim never understood my reluctance to learn stick. A few years earlier in his attempt to teach me, we had spent a lovely Sunday afternoon circling the deserted car park of Munich's Nymphenburg Palace. Jim, I knew, had an ulterior motive. Because of time spent as a traveling salesman and a propensity to get drowsy behind the wheel, Jim loathed long drives. Ironically, he usually got stuck with the task, especially on foreign holidays when an automatic was either unavailable or outrageously expensive to rent. I, however, loved taking the wheel for long road trips. Despite the regal training ground, I remained unconvinced. I simply didn't see the value. Automatics got me to the same place without all the added work of a clutch and gearshift.

American Breakfast, a Rare Find

Jim's permanent car, an Audi, scheduled for delivery the following month, wouldn't solve the issue. His employer, citing past difficulties reassigning automatics, denied his request for one. I didn't know which of us was more disappointed.

On Monday morning as Jim prepared to leave the house, we shared an extended embrace. He whispered in my ear, "I'm worried about you."

I pulled back to look into his eyes. "Go! Enjoy. I'll be fine. I've got Sadie and my writers' group."

"I'll call every day," he added, offering a farewell kiss. "I love you."

"Love you more."

From our front window I watched Jim pull his luggage toward the garage. We exchanged a final wave before he disappeared around the corner. Although a brave front and mention of the writers' group allayed Jim's concern, anxiety stirred within me. I was alone.

Daily strolls provided diversions from the monotonous solitude. A detour off Avenue Louise put me on Rue de Bailli, a bustling strip of restaurants, bars, cafés, and boutiques. At the top of the busy street, the neo-Baroque church of Sainte-Trinité gave the neighborhood an air of grandeur despite its soot-covered facade.

On Wednesdays, the area's commercial focus shifted one block away to a pretty square that gave the area its name, Chatelain. Dozens of vendors in caravans, tents, covered stalls, and specialty trucks took over a car park. At first glance, the market seemed ordinary. Stands offered fruits, vegetables, meats, fish, breads, and cheeses. But I also observed stalls selling beer, wine, and champagne by the glass as well as an exotic buffet of aromatic delicacies. Strolling under canvas marquees, a visitor could choose from sweet and savory crepes, quiches, olive tapenades and hummus, roasted chicken, Moroccan meat pies, Portuguese sweet pies, pad Thai, egg rolls, panini, African stews, shrimp and lobster bisques, mussels, and oysters.

Marketgoers sat at tables eating and drinking in tents or under trees. The bountiful market assumed a carnival atmosphere. Chatelain was a sensory feast. Wide-eyed, I strolled through the street party. An outing to Chatelain for wine and dinner made for a fun and romantic evening. *Can't wait to share this with Jim.*

Curiosity led me to research other afternoon markets, finding that our own commune hosted one on Mondays. The following week, therefore, I set out for the Saint-Gilles town hall. From our front door, the walk took less than twenty minutes. The market transformed the town hall's bleak car park into another magical spectacle. Flickers of twilight silhouetted the branches of stately trees swaying in a breeze. Strings of white lights bathed the marketplace in a festive glow. Stalls offered the same selections of fruits, produce, prepared foods, and alcohol that I had seen at Chatelain. Many of the vendors, in fact, were the same. Making no fewer than three loops around the market, I headed home with arms hanging heavy at my sides, my hands gripping bags filled with blueberries, strawberries, apples, fresh pasta, gooey white cheeses, and warm bread. *Jim's gotta see this too!*

Each market's unique personality made it all the more interesting. Chatelain attracted professionals, young diplomats, and expat wives pushing expensive prams. Tailored suits, Italian loafers, smart dresses, and expensive haircuts prevailed. Saint-Gilles drew a more diverse crowd—artsy, bohemian, working class—its patrons more likely to sport man-buns, peasant dresses, and untamed hair. Despite disparate clientele, the markets shared the same lighthearted, convivial atmosphere.

Afternoon markets were a tremendous find. They gave me a ringside seat to a merry street party. More than mere spectator, I felt part of the spectacle. Amidst the bustle and revelry, pangs of loneliness and isolation faded away. Under its dour frowns, Brussels had spirit. For an hour or two, my mood lifted. I almost forgot I was an outsider.

Chapter 9

Had the robust vitality of afternoon markets stimulated my senses? Were the camaraderie and collective creativity of the Brussels Writers' Circle infectious? Perhaps Jim's lengthy absence forced me to ponder my path forward. Whatever the catalyst, newfound energy motivated me to act.

"Wish me luck, Sadie girl."

Throwing my manuscript into a bag, I headed out our door for the short walk to the Maison du Peuple, nicknamed the MDP. More hipster coffee house than traditional café, the MDP attracted an eclectic clientele. Among those banging away at computers, I imagined, were other writers crafting blogs, travelogues, and screenplays, or penning novels like I was.

Exposed brick, planked floors, tall ceilings, dark wood, and an open floor plan gave the interior loftlike warmth. A long wooden bar anchored the space. Tall front windows captured whatever scant natural light the Belgian climate offered. Above simple wooden tables and chairs, giant murals decorated the walls. One of these depicted a colorful, tropical scene featuring Gauguin-inspired women, palm trees, coffee beans, and a volcano. A rendering of the café's logo, its three initials outlined in purple, graced the opposite wall. The décor produced a comfortable, welcoming atmosphere.

Ordering a coffee and croissant at the bar, a three-euro special, I carried my breakfast to a front table. A small chocolate accompanied the strong, creamy concoction. Sipping from my cup, I gazed out the window where the bustling weekend market spread over the parvis. *Parvis,* as Google informed me, was synonymous with plaza, piazza, and square, but more specific to a large, open space in front of a church. The cobblestoned area served as the social heart of Saint-Gilles. In addition to the church and daily market, the parvis was home to a Metro stop, police station, and social services center. Several cafés, restaurants, and bars and a smattering of shops produced a steady parade of people.

Just outside the MDP, eager shoppers queued beside a van transformed into an Italian deli offering a bounty of meats, cheeses, and prepared foods like arancini, calzone, lasagna, and tiramisu.

Forcing my gaze from the mesmerizing market, I stared at my unfinished manuscript. Inspired by my dear friend Gia, my third novel *None Shall Sleep* told of Isabella Fabrini, a middle-aged consultant yearning for purpose. Her journey of reinvention, a struggle to realize a lofty dream, mirrored my own. Plot twists detoured each of our stories down an uncertain path.

Since I last touched the story three months earlier, my life had undergone a major transformation. My head was in a different place, literally and figuratively. A thorough review of the unfinished manuscript was needed before I could even think of completing the novel. This didn't count as "writing" in the traditional sense. I wasn't creating new material. But this "author work," nonetheless, gave me great satisfaction. As I waded deeper into the manuscript, a thought nagged at me: *you can't let this story languish.*

Reacquainted with my protagonist and her story, I left the MDP later that afternoon surging with optimism. I owed it to myself and my characters to tell the rest of the story. I'd rekindled my passion, regained my purpose.

The next night, Jim Skyped with me from South Africa. "How's it going, sweetie?"

"Great. I'm getting back to work."

"You are?"

"Yep. I want to finish my book."

"Fantastic!" His grin signaled delight and satisfaction. My happiness meant his happiness. He understood my love for creating stories. More importantly, writing promised a return to normalcy for me and, by extension, our little family.

That night, Sadie took her usual spot beside me in bed. I sank into the mattress, my mood buoyed by Jim's reaction. Worries about my well-being topped his long list of concerns. When I watched him receive my news in our Skype session, tension seemed to roll off his shoulders. Sleep came swiftly for me. After a rocky first month, I finally started to feel grounded.

Ironically, as my path forward cleared, Jim's future blurred. Challenges of a new position weren't unexpected. Neither were fourteen-hour workdays nor the frequency of travel to places like Barcelona, Warsaw, Oslo, London, and Paris. Proximity to company branches had been a primary driver for his transfer to Europe. He took the disruption and exhaustion of these business trips in stride. The project that brought us to Europe, launching a common analytical platform, still excited him. Challenges of leading a far-flung team gave him great satisfaction. Collaborating with his people to develop strategies and a tactical playbook to accomplish goals were exercises at which he excelled.

Soon after our arrival, however, Jim spoke of obstacles on the horizon. Budget cuts and wavering support by top management threatened his mission. His tone seethed with frustration and anger. "The same people who moved me here now want me to justify the project."

"What the..." I replied. We'd been in Belgium barely one month. "Unbelievable. They want *you* to justify *their* project? Shame on them. All that work should have been done before they hired you. Don't put a pilot into the cockpit and take away his fuel."

Sadness replaced anger in Jim's face. "Or tell him to fly without wings."

It was an apt metaphor. Financial cutbacks paired with leadership's mixed messages threatened to clip Jim's and his team's wings just as they took off. The gut-wrenching development blindsided him. He found himself squeezed by superiors for faster results with fewer resources while also trying to insulate his team from questions about the value of their work. He couldn't let doubts about their mission demotivate his people, thwarting their forward momentum. Shouldering the burden alone, Jim looked and sounded deflated. My heart ached for my dear partner.

I understood the situation. As a corporate executive, I'd observed and often led projects that moved from imperative to discretionary effort in the blink of an eye—resources and commitment drained away. Knee-jerk reactions, mixed messages, and shifting priorities weren't only symptoms of weak leadership; they gutted morale. By focusing on short horizons and quick wins, management stifled risk-taking, innovation, and collaboration.

The fact that Jim disclosed his frustrations was, in itself, significant. In general, both of us left job aggravations—bad bosses, impossible deadlines, childish politics, and any number of other irritants—at the office. We weren't those spouses who phoned and texted each other during work hours. Neither of us wanted to bring negative energy home, spoiling our peaceful refuge. The old iceberg theory sprang to mind. Jim probably shared with me only a glimmer of the true situation. I'd only learn the depth of his anguish later. Concern for me was one reason he held back. Seeing me only just emerge from an emotional funk, he feared a relapse. Above all and despite my protests to the contrary, he bore profound guilt for disrupting our life by moving us to Belgium. There was no easy unwinding of things, no calling it quits without serious financial and emotional repercussions. He was backed into a terrible, dark corner.

Frustration overwhelmed me. Jim's happiness was my happiness, his sadness my own. Ours was a partnership in every sense of the word. Hugs, sympathy, and a ready ear were the only salves I could offer. But although fixing his work situation was beyond my control, alleviating pressures at home was well within my power. I vowed to keep complaints to a minimum, to bear my daily frustrations in stoic silence. They were, I reasoned, petty compared with Jim's challenges. So, just as Jim kept his struggles from his team, I hid my anxieties and despair from him.

I'd discover, however, the consequences of keeping things bottled up. In the weeks and months ahead, my own emotional health would suffer. Our fates, after all, were intertwined, especially as expats living tenuously in Brussels. As Jim's future blurred, a patchy fog of uncertainty crept toward me.

Weekends were key to our survival. They provided a much-needed relief valve. Reveling in the joys of shared adventure, we found temporary escape by living in the moment. Assuming roles as wide-eyed tourists, Jim pushed aside work pressures and I suppressed my anxieties. Belgium, a country the size of Maryland, offered several interesting day trips: Antwerp, Ghent, Bruges, Waterloo, Leuven, and Liège. And just across the border: Lille, France, and Maastricht, Netherlands. The options were infinitely more exciting than Milwaukee, Springfield, and St. Louis.

Touring the country, we soon became aware of the simmering schism between Wallonia and Flanders, Belgium's two main regions. Going beyond economic and political division, similar to the red/blue state divide in the United States, stark cultural differences factor into the equation. Language explains part of the friction, as does natural regional rivalry. The split, however, goes deeper. An invisible border between Wallonia and Flanders separates the continent's Germanic north from its Latin south. Each subculture has its own history, beliefs, values, attitudes, and traditions. Harmonizing the two isn't always easy.

Although Brussels is of Flemish origin and completely surrounded by Flanders, many Flemish consider Brussels a French enclave. Indeed, much to the chagrin of the nation's Flemish majority, French became the capital's majority language in the mid-twentieth century.

For excursions into Flanders, guidebooks advised using English over French. Proficiency levels bore this out. Residents of Flanders spoke good English. By comparison, many natives of Wallonia, the French-speaking region, spoke little or no English.

A small, vocal faction has called for Flanders' independence. It's currently the wealthier of the country's two regions. Personally, I don't think Belgium faces imminent danger of splitting. Besides the complicated question of Brussels, most Belgians are content with the status quo. Divorce would be too acrimonious and too much effort.

Antwerp became a favorite destination of ours. Vibrant and beautiful, the Flemish city's historic center bustled with commercial activity, its port Europe's second largest. Art and design scenes thrive. Barely twenty-five miles from Brussels, Belgium's second largest city was less than an hour drive, a short hop by U.S. standards. People we encountered in Antwerp, however, spoke as if we traveled a great distance. "You came *all* the way from Brussels." Perhaps their perspective was influenced by culture rather than distance. "You live in Brussels? Why? It's filthy," was a common response of grimacing Antwerp merchants.

Fortunately, Jim and I didn't have to take sides in this domestic dispute. We enjoyed Brussels and Antwerp equally. Brussels had charm and international sophistication. Antwerp was clean and chic with a keen sense of style. Its Grote Markt, more triangle than square, equaled the majesty of Brussels' Grand Place. Its cathedral and churches were every bit as stunning and historically significant as their Brussels counterparts. The central train station is an architectural gem superior to the concrete bunker that serves the capital. Visits were never complete without a stop for flaky, knotted pastry, buttery gems called *strikje*, meaning "bow tie." Rubens' house and workshop, showcasing the art of the seventeenth-century master painter, became a favorite destination. At the end of every visit, however, we were happy to return to Brussels, our home.

Besides weekend getaways, out-of-town visitors created pleasant diversions. Our apartment had an ideal setup—a spacious guest room with queen-size bed plus a daybed and trundle. Guests had a separate toilet as well as a shower and sink en suite. Our central location allowed visitors easy access to the city. My walks and keen curiosity armed me with enough local knowledge to make me a good tour guide for visitors *and* Jim.

Saint Patrick's Day brought our first houseguests. Besides visiting the Grand Place bathed in green and Manneken Pis, the iconic statue of a peeing boy, attired in Irish woolens, we drove our guests to Bruges, the quaint medieval city popularized by the Colin Farrell film *In Bruges*. Jim and I never envisioned that a constant stream of overnight guests would follow. Nor did we guess that every last visitor would want to visit Bruges.

In Bruges with our First Houseguests

Weekend guests didn't disrupt my writing. My manuscript progressed toward completion. At the end of March, I read the first chapter to my writers' group. First readings were always a bit unnerving. But after attending several BWC sessions, I trusted my fellow authors and respected their critiques. Feedback was positive and helpful.

Throughout that spring my writing flourished, propelled by regained discipline and inspiration from the BWC. I even branched out from my novel. My Facebook posts with photos of our new adventures proved very popular. Blogging—a combination of travelogue, insight, and photos—offered an additional creative outlet to reach friends and family. My first post hit my website in April.

Brussels Sprouts–Musings of an American Expat in Belgium

Three months have passed since we left Chicago for Brussels. Spring brings houseguests, and for Sadie our golden retriever, lazy afternoons in our sunny garden feasting on a new treat— escargot, in or out of the shell. My head finally cleared of the transition out of our old life and into the new, allowing me to write. I completed eight remaining chapters of my third and latest novel and farmed it out to my loyal team of readers. Now it's focus, focus, focus on polishing up novel 2 for a fall 2014 release.

I leave you with 5 random insights of our new life:

- Dog poop is everywhere
- Grocery bags are not—bring your own or pay up
- Fresh vegetables and fruits aplenty in markets at reasonable prices

- Tipping is not expected although 5% to 10% is customary at a finer restaurant when pleased with service
- Awesome bread!

More to come...

Chapter 10

Writing is solitary work. And although "author" has a romantic ring, in many ways writing is merely another profession. Like most jobs, it's painstaking labor. Producing a book is a multiphase process. The path from conception to "The End" is typically a long, often lonely journey. But writing provided a crucial lifeline for me in those early months of our expat adventure. Fueling my need for purpose, it occupied my time, exercised my brain, suppressed anxiety, and thanks to the Brussels Writers' Circle, quenched my thirst for companionship.

Three months after arriving in Brussels, I completed the initial draft of *None Shall Sleep*, my third novel. Overcoming paralytic self-doubt that disrupted my creative process sweetened the accomplishment. A completed draft warranted a victory lap, but only a short one. Loads of work remained before my eager hands would hold a glossy bound book. As a first step, I sent the draft to advance readers, close friends, and family members, for feedback on plot, characters, and other story elements. Within this circle, Jim provided the most ardent support. "Not believable. Nobody would say that. Are you sure?" were typical of his feedback. His notes guided many revisions as well as a running joke. When reading a book by another author or watching a movie, I'd point to a problematic passage or scene. "See there," I'd say, "you'd *never* let me get away with that." Jim simply replied, "You're right."

Months awaiting reader feedback were beneficial. Somewhere between mind and paper, lucid thoughts can become murky. "Marinating," my term for letting the manuscript sit idle, enhanced a deep-dive edit. Distance improved objectivity. With my eyes fresh, simple errors popped out, as did more complex disconnects between creative intent and the printed word. With a heavy edit completed, off went the draft to a professional editor.

While my third book marinated, attention returned to my second novel. It had been sitting idle for sixteen months. I'd begun writing that book, a coming-of-age story set in the sixties, four years earlier. Based on feedback from readers and advice from a senior editor at HarperCollins, I knew the story needed additional material and a thorough edit, its fourth major revision. I set a goal of handing off the revised manuscript to my editor by late summer.

Whereas editing occupied my weekdays, out-of-town visitors filled many weekends. A family of five living in Munich and a Parisian couple were among our April wave of houseguests. Both sets of friends had lived as expats in Chicago. In addition to traveling for pleasure, Jim and I had worked for global corporations, he for Daimler and I for United. Opportunity and design brought a rich mix of expats and globe-trotters into our life, creating an international network of friends.

As my familiarity with Brussels grew with each passing week, showing visitors around our adopted city became easier and more enjoyable. A day trip to Bruges topped every visitor's list. For Easter, we drove our Parisian friends to the picturesque town for a delightful meal that included *moules-frites* (mussels and fries) and a bottle of white wine. Opposite the sunny veranda on which we dined stood the medieval Church of Our Lady, home to Michelangelo's Madonna of Bruges dating to 1504. The historic setting reminded us of our good fortune. Michelangelo's marble masterpiece surpassed the Easter Bunny ice sculptures of the brunch buffets back home.

Hosting gave Jim a chance to socialize, something for which his coworkers continued to show little interest. He described his office environment as cold and unwelcoming. The dearth of hospitality surprised me especially given our affinity for welcoming and befriending expats in America. I couldn't fathom why his coworkers didn't want to show off their lovely country or, at the very least, have an interest in helping us adapt to a new and daunting environment. Houseguests tempered such disappointment, but they were insufficient remedies for our isolation. Guests went home. For a more lasting solution, I turned to the BWC, a savory soup of expats, writers, and professionals. Common interests and shared circumstances helped me bond with several members.

Among these was Nick, a gregarious Englishman who took morning coffee and read newspapers at the MDP, the café where I wrote. A decade older than I, Nick spoke of current and former entrepreneurial pursuits. He had lived in Italy, working as a translator. Current projects included writing a book, a thriller drawn from his childhood in Uganda. I looked forward to our morning chats that covered an array of subjects, politics a favorite. Nick's plan to leave Brussels, however, threatened this newfound camaraderie.

Walking home from BWC sessions, I struck up a friendship with Richard, a tall, lean Netherlands native my age. He spoke of his writing project, a young-adult fantasy novel. Richard and his American partner lived with two dogs only a few blocks from our apartment. We set a playdate for Sadie, but the couple's young schnauzers proved too energetic for our senior princess. Despite the puppy playdate flop, Jim and I found the dog-owning gay couple a good social fit for our little family.

Anne-May, a woman in her early thirties, became another good friend. Also from the Netherlands, she came to Brussels with her partner, a Dutch diplomat. In addition to job-hunting, Anne-May was writing a horror romance novel. Her writing showed great promise and her critiques of our fellow writers mirrored my own. We met regularly for long walks, strong coffee, and stimulating conversation. In a way, we were discovering Brussels together. On one such outing we toured the Abbey of La Cambre. A noblewoman founded the complex in 1196 for a monastic order of nuns. Historic gems such as the abbey dotted Brussels; one merely needed to know where to look.

Like most Dutch, Anne-May was an avid cyclist. But unlike the Netherlands, where cyclists enjoy incredible infrastructure, Belgium presents a smorgasbord of hazards. Belgian drivers are so notoriously bad, motoring might be considered a contact sport. They rate among Europe's most aggressive drivers, even ahead of Italians—imagine that! Still, I looked forward to Anne-May's suggestion of a bike ride, hoping it would be the first of many. Sitting atop my bicycle, I followed the more experienced Anne-May as we navigated the busy, narrow streets of Brussels. My sense of adventure, however, quickly turned into white-knuckled fear. I felt like targeted prey, a run-in with a car or truck merely a matter of time.

I learned later that Belgium introduced compulsory driving tests as part of licensing requirements only in 1977. As both car passenger and pedestrian, I observed many dings and dents from vehicular jousts. Cars routinely careened onto sidewalks to park. The "priority to the right" rule seemed particularly dangerous. The law allows cars entering a roadway from the right to hurl into paths of other cars, pedestrians, and cyclists. My sense of danger surged one day when a fellow hobbled into the MDP with his leg in a cast, blaming his cycling injury on a collision with a Belgian driver.

Thankful to make it home alive after our first cycle outing, I turned to Anne-May. "Thanks for the tour, but I'm going to park my bike until we leave Brussels."

With a nod of understanding, she shared another story that supported my decision. "The Netherlands donated several driving simulators to Belgium," she said. "We considered it a smart investment in *Dutch* well-being."

We laughed heartily. Treasuring our time together, I selfishly hoped her job search would be lengthy.

Houseguests, writing, tinkering in our garden, and preparing dinner brought a predictable routine to my life. I was excited when *Global Connection,* a magazine for expats, contacted me. They wanted to include my story in an article featuring expat spouses, "Changing Course."

"That's great," Jim said when I told him. "You gonna do it?"

"I'll say. Free publicity for my books."

In addition to offering exposure for my writing, the attention thrilled me. I'd begun to feel like a forgotten exile, an incredible shrinking spouse. The interviewer, Maria, a former expat spouse herself, validated my emotions—isolation, loneliness, and depression. *Wow, she gets it,* I thought. *She's been there.*

"All that didn't disappear when we got back to Canada," Maria added. "I wasn't prepared for the repatriation blues. Be forewarned. Returning home is a tough transition."

With establishing roots as my focus, repatriation hadn't crossed my mind. In fact, Jim and I were hoping for a multiyear posting. *I'll worry about that later.* Still, I filed the unexpected warning away in my mind.

My piece, "Time for a New Chapter," dealt with my transition from airline executive to novelist that began five years earlier. "Business skills are highly transferable to my work," I told her. "Writing is a lengthy work in progress that requires focus, patience, flexibility, and determination. My discipline derives from lessons learned in business."

"Once Todd connected with a local writers' group," Maria wrote in the article, "he fell into a routine. He generously credits his success to his writing groups (in both Chicago and Brussels), and especially to Jim. 'This adventure,' he says, 'wouldn't be possible without Jim's love and support.'"

Although referencing the many challenges of an expat spouse and author, the article ended on an upbeat note. The optimistic outlook reflected my hope if not always my reality. "Todd has no regrets about turning the page and starting a new chapter," Maria wrote. "In fact, he feels fortunate to be able to embrace his passion. 'Writing may not be easy or pay well, but it's a joy,' Todd says. 'As the adage goes, *Find something you love and you'll never work another day in your life.*'" Three photos accompanied the piece, including a nice shot of Jim and me. The final article pleased me. I derived greater satisfaction, however, learning from Maria that my roller coaster of emotions as an expat spouse was natural and common.

Four months into our adventure, Jim and I finally took advantage of Brussels' central location to travel abroad. On our first weekend jaunt, we visited Scotland for its famous whisky festival. We rendez-voused with friends from Chicago in Aviemore, a quaint town that served as our base for touring the lovely Highlands and sampling whiskies including my favorite single malt, Macallan. A week later we flew to Munich to attend the first communion of the daughter of good friends we met when they were expats living in Chicago. The celebrant's younger sister is Jim's goddaughter. Such a quick trip—flying in Saturday afternoon and out Sunday evening—would have been impossible from Chicago. At months end, we traveled to Italy for Gia's concert. I'd met the Italian native and London resident, thirty years earlier when we were both students at London Business School. Her concert weekend was unique and special—three days of laughter, song, sightseeing, and fine wine with an eclectic mix of people in the rolling hills above Parma.

These concerts spawned a global network of friends. Gia's quest to sing inspired my novel *None Shall Sleep*. In the two years since her last concert, I'd written vivid descriptions using my memory to sketch the fictional setting of San Benedetto. Attending the actual concert gave me the feeling of stepping into the pages of my book. The glorious weekend among good friends allowed Jim and me to recharge.

A European base enriched our lives with unique experiences and allowed us to nurture new and established friendships. Weekends— day trips, out-of-town adventures, and Brussels meanderings—were the peaks of our adventure. Valleys came during the week when Jim returned to his lengthy workdays and I sank back into my lonely routine.

Although writing and the accompanying jolt of renewed purpose tempered my spells of desolation, a fog of anguish drifted toward me. Episodes occurred most often in late afternoon, when I was weary from a productive morning, before Jim arrived home from work. I didn't recognize the dark moods for what they were at first, or even for a very long time. In fact, the fog's icy fingers reached back months—the weeks before our move—those moody spells that I didn't fully understand. The excitement of relocation and non-stop stimuli provided by our new environment probably suppressed my anxieties. But my insecurities related to my new career and tenuous connection to Brussels started to awaken.

We viewed Brussels as our home for the foreseeable future. This was no adrenaline-fueled short-term holiday or weekend getaway. No calling it quits. To survive and flourish, we needed to burrow our transplanted roots deep into the foreign soil. Quite often, that task proved daunting, requiring more energy than I had.

Even something as routine as a chipped tooth, the result of non-pitted olives unexpectedly served on pizza, caused undue consternation. With no dentist and unfamiliar with both the Belgian healthcare system and our insurance, I didn't know how to begin finding treatment. I couldn't pester Jim, buried in his new job, with something so trivial. For weeks I remained silent until the tooth became sensitive. My sense of helplessness triggered sadness and anxiety.

"You haven't been yourself. What's wrong?" Jim asked one night after dinner.

"Nothing," I said, choking back a tear.

Jim caressed my cheek. "That tear isn't nothing. Something's up. What is it?"

I described my plight: the chipped tooth, my attempt to keep it from him, the increasing sensitivity, my anguish at not being able to fix it myself. "I'm so sorry."

Jim's face flashed with a mix of anger, embarrassment, and compassion. "Oh sweetie," he said. "I'm the one who's sorry. You come first, job second—*always*. We're going to get that tooth fixed right away." And so we did.

The dark spells to which I succumbed not only blindsided and confused me, they also conflicted me with guilt. How could I feel despair? How dare I claim depression? How could I expect empathy? Observers would reasonably assume that I enjoyed an enviable life of which most people only dream—every day a carnival, a magical fairy tale.

My second blog post partially addressed my inner conflict in the age of social media.

Not All Godiva and Stella Artois

Let me state upfront that our posting to Brussels is a phenomenal opportunity. We realize our good fortune to live and work in Europe. For many, this is a dream; for us, reality—one that includes access to the world's best art, food, architecture, and history. But there's another reality, a darker side that doesn't align with an idealized vision of expats in Europe.

Facebook connects us to more than 600 people who tune in for our exploits. For friends not on Facebook, I send monthly summaries. This recap, I fear, is beginning to resemble the dreaded of all missives, the insufferable Christmas letter—dense, blustering narrative framed by festive holiday bunting. I assume very few of these letters are actually read. Most are probably tossed or used as eggnog coasters. On top of copious amounts of fruitcake and pumpkin pie, only the hardiest stomach can tolerate a hefty dose of "Pinch-Us-Cuz-We're-Livin'-the-Dream Stuff."

Truth is, life isn't all Christmas cookies and candy canes. We're taught, however, to put our best foot and face forward.

The ole, "Laugh and the world laughs with you, cry and you cry alone." My monthly recap is a generous slice of "Life's grand." That's the story people want to hear, isn't it?

Don't get me wrong, our life rocks in many ways—a veritable adventure. But omitting my bouts of isolation, loneliness, and depression distorts reality. Do friends picture our life only as one of outdoor cafés, quaint little towns, and fairytale castles? Another fear grips me as a writer. Am I boring our friends to death? Perhaps my recap suffers a humiliating fate, the digital equivalent of eggnog coaster—SPAM.

What to do? Cry and you cry alone, right? People don't want to hear that the life of an expat spouse isn't all Godiva and Stella Artois, but that's the darker reality.

Chapter 11

People don't notice whether it's winter or
summer when they're happy.
(Anton Chekhov)

Not yet rooted and prone to bouts of melancholy, I welcomed summer's arrival. The season offered escape from dour moods and dreary thoughts. Darkness retreated metaphorically as well as literally. Days adjoining the summer solstice delivered more than sixteen hours of sun, double the scant amount endured in January. Prolonged doses of daylight nurtured body and spirit even in Brussels where summer was more a state of mind than climatic certainty. Imagination and a wool sweater were essential accessories for weathering the season. Still, abundant sunshine and outdoor activities pushed most worries to the fall.

Spoiled by a warm, sunny spring, Jim and I weren't prepared for summer's cool, rainy days. Narrow-banded annual temperatures differed from the harsh extremes of America's Midwest. The same black raincoat and red sports cap that served me in January were regular companions throughout summer. Even our garden suffered. After spells of uninterrupted rain, impatiens, geraniums, and daisies wilted and drowned. Soil never dried out. A rice paddy would have been a more sensible alternative to the grassy lawn we seeded for Sadie. The small plot remained a moist mess of barren earth throughout our residence.

Rain, however, didn't extinguish all the joys of summer. Tall glass doors that led from our kitchen to the garden remained open most days, perfuming the apartment with fresh aromas of soft summer rain and greenery. Mosquitos and flies were rare, and a colorful patrol of cats atop the garden walls deterred rodents. Chirping choruses of birds and tolling church bells evoked the serenity of a country retreat—that is, when wailing sirens and buzzing helicopters associated with EU dignitaries didn't disturb the peace.

Enclosed by high brick walls and dotted with trees and shrubbery, our garden was a lush retreat. Among established hedges of manicured yews and ornamental bushes, we added purple rhododendron, yellow roses, and blue hydrangea. In clear weather, with the sun lingering high in the sky until early evening, I frequently settled into the plump cushions of a wicker glider with a glass of white wine and a book. At my feet, Sadie snoozed on the cool paving stones.

Throughout the summer, the garden provided an idyllic retreat to entertain new friends from the BWC—Nick, Anne-May, and Richard and his schnauzers. With extended twilight, Jim often joined Sadie and me outdoors to wind down after a long day at the office. In this private refuge, cares lifted from our shoulders, drifted over the garden walls, and disappeared into lofty leafy limbs.

Swaying beside me on the glider one evening, Jim squeezed my hand. "We're very lucky."

"I know," I replied lifting his hand to my lips. "I only wish these perfect evenings didn't have to end."

June contained two notable family anniversaries:

Eight years earlier, in 2006, we had rescued Sadie. A proxy for her birthday, the anniversary was celebrated with steak, cake, ice cream, candles, and song. Our golden angel deserved the attention. Snails aside, she adapted well to city life and a grassless yard. Her vet was a short, high-energy man named Nick. He declared her fit for her age. Recently, Nick had conducted her annual checkup and cleaned her teeth on our living room floor. His bill for house call, exam, and cleaning including anesthesia, came to less than one hundred euros, a fraction of the cost for such services back home.

Sixteen years earlier, in 1998, Jim and I had met. In 2011, we chose the same date to register our civil union when such relationships became legal in our home state of Illinois. June 23, therefore, was the closest thing we had to a wedding anniversary. That would soon change…or so we hoped. Just three weeks earlier, same-sex marriage became legal in Illinois. For us and our community, the fight for equality had been a long, emotional battle. Over the years, we joined peaceful protests and wrote a barrage of letters to legislators and newspapers, pushing for equal rights and protections. On election night 2004 when George W. Bush won reelection on a platform that included a Constitutional ban on same-sex unions, Jim and I wept ourselves to sleep.

Now, the finish line was in sight, made possible by a June 2013 Supreme Court ruling, *United States v. Windsor*. Illinois' new law included a provision allowing civil unions to convert into marriage, retroactively. Doing so, however, would require navigating through a sea of Cook County civil servants for whom flexibility and common sense were foreign concepts.

That summer, our guest room occupancy peaked. Although we encouraged houseguests, with Jim away at his office, primary hosting duties fell to me. To give me time and space to write, I suggested escorted tours to Antwerp, Ghent, and Bruges. Buses collected sightseers at a nearby hotel. As a gentle nudge, I stockpiled brochures in the guest room beside the Wi-Fi code. For those needing a firmer push, I booked the tours myself.

In late June we welcomed a friend from my American writing group. Phyllis, a spry seventy-something, arrived for ten nights. An avid reader and masterful storyteller, she made for a fun and interesting houseguest. Our conversations never dulled. I especially enjoyed updates regarding our colleagues from the Barrington Writers Workshop.

In addition to Brussels, we visited Bastogne and the nearby memorial to World War II's Battle of the Bulge, Ypres, and Luxembourg City. During a visit to the Brussels town hall, Phyllis fell ill. Although unnerved by the situation, Jim and I kept our composure, assuring Phyllis that all would be well. In truth, we had no idea what to expect. Neither of us had experience with septuagenarian ailments. We didn't even know the location of the nearest hospital. After getting an address and hailing a taxi, we whisked Phyllis to the emergency room where a doctor diagnosed a mild infection and prescribed medication. Fortunately, one of the few pharmacies with Sunday hours was located in our neighborhood.

"I liked the doctor," Phyllis said when we got her home. "Very professional staff too. And, oh, that handsome pharmacist…almost made getting sick worthwhile." I laughed, comforted by her show of humor that suggested she was on the mend. "My only regret," she added, "was putting you two through that ordeal."

"No worries," I replied. "Glad you're okay. At least we now know the emergency room's only a seven-minute walk from our apartment… and that our pharmacist is dreamy."

After a day or so of bed rest and medicine, Phyllis recovered in time for a Fourth of July celebration. Gloomy weather didn't stop us from observing the holiday *indoors* with martinis, hamburgers, corn on the cob cooked on our new gas grill, and my late mother's recipe for potato salad decorated with American flags.

During her stay, Phyllis recommended a book, *The Guns of August*, Barbara Tuchman's account of August 1914, the first month of World War I. Violation of Belgian neutrality by German forces intent on invading France had ignited the global conflict. Living amidst the historic settings made the book especially meaningful to us.

By the end of her visit, Phyllis was anxious to get home to family. Jim and I had only five days to regroup before his Aunt Mary Anne arrived for eleven days. In addition to fetching Tuchman's book from Waterstone's, I readied the house for our next visitor, and blogged.

I created a blog post commemorating our first six months. In addition to summarizing our first impressions of Brussels, I discussed the challenges of adapting to our new city and concluded with a positive message about the meaning of home:

An American in Brussels—Six Months Later

Six months in Brussels—longest I've lived outside Illinois. I'm a proponent of the adage, "Home is where you hang your hat." Brussels is home. My husband is here as is our beloved golden retriever, Sadie. Everything else is secondary....If you were to ask about our first six months, I'd say we're having a grand adventure.

———— ((◉)) ————

Aunt Mary Anne, an energetic sixty-something, rang our buzzer. Appearing at our front door toting an enormous backpack, she toppled forward into my outstretched arms. She'd flown in from Dublin where, mixing up her flight schedule, she'd spent the night sleeping on an airport bench.

We looked forward to her visit. Eleven years before, Mary Anne was among the first family I met from Jim's father's side. Lovable and slightly eccentric, she welcomed me with warmth and love. Because she lived in California, we didn't see her often. Traveling alone didn't frighten her. Independent and single, she had spent two years in the Peace Corps in South America. Exploring on her own gave me time to write.

In addition to a Brussels city tour, which by then I could have conducted in my sleep, we drove her to Maastricht just across the border in the Netherlands. The charming university town on the Meuse River had begun as a Roman settlement. Although compact, the place buzzed with sophistication offering visitors a multitude of restaurants, cafés, and shops. A magnificent bookstore occupied a converted thirteenth-century church. I wondered what the ancient men and women of the cloth would think of the steamy romance novels stacked in the former sacristy.

A highlight of Mary Anne's visit was movie night. Civic promoters literally brought the beach to Brussels, creating a sandy playground with movies projected on a giant outdoor screen. Simple, unpretentious moments are often the most magical. Sitting on rented beach chairs, the three of us wiggled our toes in sand as we watched *Roman Holiday*. The movie, like Audrey Hepburn, retains its charm. In my youth, Hollywood's idealized version of Europe mesmerized me. Movies filmed on location in London, Paris, Venice, Rome, and so forth captivated me. And here we were, living in Europe, a dream fulfilled.

Mary Anne enjoyed walking Sadie. One morning, I planned to surprise them by popping over to the dog-friendly park that Mary Anne intended to visit. Hustling to the park, I found no trace of them. I backtracked but they were nowhere to be found.

I phoned home where Jim was working. "Have you seen your aunt and Sadie?"

"They're not here, sweetie. Weren't they at the park?"

"No. I'm worried."

"I'm sure everything's fine," he replied, though concern laced his voice.

I scoured our neighborhood with no luck. My mind flickered with terrible scenarios. Were they hit by a notoriously bad Belgian driver? A tram? Were they mugged? My phone rang. When I recognized Jim's number, my words raced from my mouth. "Are they home?"

"No! Just checking to see if they turned up. I'm going out to search."

Ten minutes later, Jim's number popped up on my screen. "Sadie's home. She and Mary Anne walked in moments ago." His tone filled with relief and joy. "They're both fine."

With his promise to fill me in, I rushed home. Jim met me at the door. "She's flustered and frightened."

"Sadie?"

"No, Aunt Mary Anne. She's freshening up in her room."

I settled onto the living room rug beside Sadie as Jim explained. As was her custom, Sadie tired and plopped down onto the sidewalk. Not budging, she began to pant heavily. Mary Anne panicked. She asked bystanders for help. A street cleaner offered to haul Sadie home in his cart. Perhaps recoiling from the indignity of being transported in a garbage cart, Sadie rose from the sidewalk and walked home. Although Sadie soon recovered, Jim's aunt spent most of that day in bed.

Numerous houseguests, visitors, and open garden doors broadcast a message of welcome. In early August, our neighbor's tiger cat—gray and tan with black stripes—appeared at our back door. Until then, the little fellow had kept his distance, strutting atop the wall that separated the two gardens. I feared Sadie might get bitten or scratched. Protective of my little family and garden paradise, I reached out to our neighbor Barbara. Weeks earlier, she'd given us her number when she and her husband appeared at our door with a request to search our garden for a missing cat. Dyed-in-the-fur cat people, they had six.

After I described my concern for Sadie, Barbara laughed into the phone. "That's just Puhi. He's harmless."

Was he, or was Barbara merely a devoted parent, blind to her beloved pet's nasty habits? There was another important consideration. Jim was allergic to cats…and pollen, mold, and practically everything carried on a summer wind. Try as I might, I couldn't shag the gregarious feline from our garden.

To keep peace in our household, I kept the cat outside. Whenever I retired to the garden, the newly emboldened Puhi dropped over the wall for a friendly visit. Honoring Jim's request to keep the cat outdoors, as Jim washed dinner dishes, I set a chair outside our back door. Taking my action as his cue, Puhi jumped onto my lap, often falling asleep with his head resting in my palm. After observing this nightly ritual from the window, Jim conceded, "Puhi's adorable. Can't take that away from him." *Hmm,* I thought, *is that a chink in Jim's anti-cat armor?*

Attention and affection from the precocious stranger touched me. I stared into Puhi's kind green eyes. "You're the friendliest Belgian I've met, even if you are a cat."

In mid-August after another set of houseguests from London and more American visitors, families on summer holidays, time came for us to get away. A long weekend to Copenhagen was our anniversary gift. The Danish capital was wonderful—pedestrian zones filled with shops and street artists, legions of bike riders, the colorful and iconic Nyhavn neighborhood, and numerous castles, parks, and palaces. We found a good Mexican restaurant, satisfying our craving for a cuisine impossible to find in Brussels. Copenhagen earned Jim's seal of approval, which he pronounced with his customary terse declaration, "I could live here."

In late August, excitement mounted as we prepared to visit the U.S. Embassy to set our marriage in motion. I'd spent weeks negotiating with the Cook County Clerk's Office for approval to convert our civil union to a marriage, remotely from Brussels. "Same rules for everyone," their emails read. "You must show up in person."

I bellowed at my computer screen, "F###! It's only a paper exercise. An administrative formality."

Pecking at the keyboard, I typed a toned-down reply. "With all due respect, this is the twenty-first century. We have Skype and video conferencing. The IRS accepts electronic tax returns and digital signatures."

The office remained unmoved, agreeing to an exception only after

I escalated my request to the Cook County Clerk himself. In addition to a standard application, our special protocol required separate, notarized letters from each of us, requesting the conversion. All of the original materials had to be expedited back to our contact in the Clerk's Office.

On a fine summer day by Brussels standards, Jim and I strolled to the U.S. Embassy. Not only did Jim take time off from work; unlike our civil union ceremony at which he appeared in blue jeans, this occasion got him into dress trousers.

We had no march down the aisle, tuxedos, carnations, vows, ring exchange, or crowd-pleasing kiss. Our "marriage" was officiated by a stone-faced bureaucrat behind a window with an ink pad and stamp. Rather than offering congratulations, the embassy clerk merely asked each of us, "And how would you like to pay the $50 notary fee?"

The milestones of our relationship—Jim's taking my surname, our ring exchange, a domestic partner filing, the "I do's" in our civil union—happened piecemeal over many years, in private without witnesses or fanfare. Still, the act of filing our paperwork filled us with joy. We marked the occasion with a drink at an outdoor café on the Mont des Arts with panoramic views of the town hall's fifteenth-century Gothic spire and the iconic silver spheres of the 1958 World Fair's Atomium. We felt as if we were on top of the world. Perhaps we were.

Jim hoisted his glass. "To my handsome husband."

I winked. "And to *my* handsome husband. I love you to pieces."

"I love you more."

"Nope," I replied with a grin. "Love you more."

Although traditional marriage rituals eluded us, we were content. Our relationship always centered on our collective journey, one characterized by unconditional love and mutual respect. That our "marriage" would become official at an unspecified time by a second bureaucrat's stamp in some office four thousand miles away was irrelevant. We were already married in our hearts, where it mattered most.

That night, we booked dinner at a favorite restaurant. Our friend Janice, a flight attendant on layover, joined us. "Why didn't you tell me?" she said after we disclosed our news. "I'm honored to share this special moment with you." She seemed to appreciate the significance of the event more than we did. A photo she took of the two of us at dinner has become one of our favorites—our wedding photo of sorts.

Marriage at Last

As summer drew to a close, the most mirthful of all seasons had a perfect finale—a road trip and marriage celebration. A former work colleague of Jim's from Daimler invited us to her wedding. Usually, Jim and I loathed attending weddings. Our feelings had everything to do with the fact that marriage was denied us. But with legal advances and our own marriage now in some stage of approval, our perspective had changed. We looked forward to the festivities, which in some small way served as a surrogate for our own celebration.

A quaint church in Germany was the venue for the ceremony, and an Alpine lodge nestled atop a picturesque Austrian hill hosted the reception. The German bride and groom donned traditional apparel. In fact, many of the male guests wore lederhosen and the females, colorful dirndl dresses. The setting and costumery were reminiscent of a scene from a Franz Lehár operetta. The happy occasion brought together many of Jim's former colleagues who, after years of separation, remained good friends. Showered with affection and camaraderie, Jim radiated joy.

The spectacular wedding couldn't have been more different from our low-key nuptials. But neither of us minded that so much…this time. After all, this was the first wedding we attended at which we could boast being husband and husband.

Attending an Alpine Wedding

On our drive home, we overnighted in Würzburg, Germany, a quaint university town on the Main River. Once again, we passed up fine local fare for the rarest of all Brussels' cuisines, Mexican. We arrived home September 1, our first Belgian summer over. Impressed by European work-life balance, I confessed my envy in a blog.

Vacation Envy
Fermé, Conges, Vacances d'Ete

Signs started sprouting up in late July. We've seen the zeal with which neighbors, businesses, and service people in Belgium embrace public holidays and Sundays. Cram all your shopping into Saturday as few stores are open on Sunday. Don't enter a shop or museum within 10 minutes of closing or you'll face sneers from staff and risk being trampled by them as they make their exit. Several stores were closed for one or two weeks over Easter. But nothing prepared us for summer holidays. Our favorite restaurant closed on July 31 with a sign announcing its reopening on September 1. Many businesses shuttered for all or most of August. The country takes a collective summer vacation.

Americans measure vacations in hours and days. Lucky Europeans do so in weeks and months. In Belgium, the legal workweek is 35 hours. Employees required to work 40 hours are compensated with an extra vacation day per month. This, on top of 20 annual vacation days most employees receive from the first day on the job. Belgian workers enjoy substantially more time off than the American drone!

Yet, studies show Americans and Belgians to be equally productive. Seems our parents were wise to send us outdoors to play. Perhaps they understood the many benefits to soul, psyche, *and productivity*, of frolicking in the grass. If you're an American worker who believes in reincarnation, pray in your next life you come back as a European.

"Traveling is a fool's paradise." Emotional baggage, Emerson opined, travels with us. We may awake in Naples, Rome, or any other exotic locale rather than in our own bed, but we can't escape sadness, problems, and anxieties that haunt us at home. The same might be said of summer. Concerns that dog us through winter and spring might hide amidst summer's joyous intoxication, but they reemerge, coming into stark focus in sober autumn.

Chapter 12

Fortunately, two highly anticipated sets of September houseguests deferred Jim's and my reckoning with sober reality for one more month. Keeping their stays to five nights each, both couples also visited Paris, a short train journey to the south. First to arrive were Barbara and Michael, Jim's mom and stepdad. Barbara had never traveled beyond North America. Michael, who had completed a European grand tour after college, was eager to share a romantic adventure with his wife of twenty-seven years.

Their visit allowed us to show them our new life as well as relieve Barbara's maternal anxieties. News of our overseas move had rattled her. She responded with a mix of emotions: happiness for her son's success and opportunity, sadness at being parted by such a great distance, and fear of terrorism.

Her concerns had merit. Newspapers labeled Belgium the jihadist capital of Europe. On a per-capita basis, Belgium contributed more ISIS fighters than any other European nation (*CBS News*, January 25, 2016). Federal prosecutors accused forty-six members of the group, Sharia4Belgium, of belonging to a terrorist cell that, among other things, brainwashed young men into fighting a holy war in Syria (*Reuters*, September 29, 2014). An ongoing trial in Antwerp created sensational headlines.

Four months earlier, a French national of Algerian origin had attacked the Jewish museum of Brussels, killing four people. My twice weekly walks to the BWC took me past the museum where flower tributes lined the sidewalk. Patrolling the cobblestone streets around the museum and the nearby Great Synagogue, camouflage-uniformed soldiers carrying machine guns were somber reminders of the constant threat. Although the heinous attack as well as news reports of radical indoctrination were disturbing, Jim and I didn't live in chronic fear. Most of the world, we reasoned, faces risk of deadly, random violence. I offered a stock reply to American friends and relatives who asked if we were scared. "In the United States, you can be killed in a grade school, high school, church, theater, or marathon, or simply riding in a car. Merely a different kind of violence." That was the sad, honest truth.

The morning Jim's parents arrived brought great excitement and a flurry of activity. Our house, garden, and car were preened. Even Sadie got groomed for the occasion. At Gare du Midi, Jim and I waited on the platform for the high-speed train from Paris.

Jim glanced repeatedly down the track. "Still no sight of it."

I caressed his back and laughed. "Train won't get here any faster, sweetie."

He took a deep breath. "I know. It's just…"

He didn't have to explain. These were very important visitors. Jim not only loved his mom, he had great respect and admiration for her. Barbara had raised him virtually as a single parent. She and his father divorced when Jim was only five years old. Jim wanted everything to be perfect. He'd even cashed in miles and paid hefty surcharges to upgrade his parents to business class for their flight home. He'd fretted over every detail of their visit including the driving route from the station to our apartment.

"First impressions are important," he said. "Don't want my mom to see the grungy part of town. Not at first anyway."

"Good luck with that. Might work to our advantage that they

visited Paris first. Eyes clouded by leftover enchantment from the City of Love."

Jim shook off my words with a glare. "I'm thinkin' blindfolds until they reach our apartment."

His concerns weren't unfounded. Contrary to the popular idiom, books are judged by their covers. The area adjacent to Gare du Midi was typical of any urban train station. Seedy bars, run-down hotels, and derelict apartment blocks would stoke Barbara's fears. My BWC friend Nick was mugged in the neighborhood. An indirect route through upscale Place Louise, Place Stéphanie, and along the Chaussée de Charleroi was preferable.

I nodded down the track. "Here it comes."

The sleek, maroon engine of the Thalys train glided toward us, its aerodynamic design reminiscent of a serpent's head. Jim jumped to his feet. I handed him a rose, a substitution for the lavish flower bouquet we forgot at home.

I gestured down the platform. "There they are."

Jim sprang toward his parents. Next to a grinning Michael, Barbara's expression turned somber. She began to sob. "Awww," Jim said, pulling her into a hug and holding the embrace until his mom calmed.

As we settled in for the drive home, Jim chose speed over show. He took the swift and seedy route. It didn't matter. Never averting her gaze from her darling Jamie, Barbara didn't notice the shabby streets out the car windows.

The strong bond between mother and son was forged by shared struggle and sacrifice. The pair could disappear into a corner of a room and chat away even at a large, noisy party. I had the same kind of close relationship with my mom. It saddened me that she was no longer alive, having died from pneumonia thirteen years earlier, only five weeks after my father succumbed to cancer. Mom and Dad would have relished every detail of our European adventure. No doubt, their love of travel inspired my wanderlust.

At home, Sadie greeted Jim's parents with tail-wagging exuberance. Dropping onto the floor, Michael roughhoused with our princess. "You remember us, don't you, pretty girl?"

Wide-eyed, Barbara scanned our apartment. "Wow! It's so beautiful. Oh my God, I can't believe I'm here." Jim put his arms around her as she fell into a cycle of grins and tears. "Oh, oh," she added, "Got something for you. Michael, where is it?"

Michael retrieved a large bundle from their suitcase. "Here you go, my dear." He turned to us with a smirk. "We've been carting this—correction, *I've* been carting this—all over Europe."

Barbara swatted her hand in the air toward Michael. "Oh, come on, it's not that heavy." Grabbing the bundle, her expression changed. She giggled. "Well, maybe it is."

With a flourish, she unfurled a large quilt crafted with orange, brown, and crimson fabric. Several years before, she'd given us a lovely quilt in yellow, blue, and white. Her superb workmanship reflected pride in her craft as well as love for lucky recipients.

I inspected the quilt. "I love it."

Jim kissed Barbara. "Thanks, Mom. It's beautiful."

"Now your new home will have a piece of old home…back home. Oh, you know what I mean," she said.

I pulled my phone from my pocket. "How about a photo?"

Jim took time off from work. Warm, dry weather allowed us to spend time in our garden and tour Brussels without umbrellas. We took his parents to Ypres, and of course, Bruges. Our outdoor markets wowed them. The four of us spent a lovely afternoon at Chatelain enjoying wine, cheese, and bread. Puhi visited frequently. Still banned from the house due to Jim's allergies, the impish tiger cat stood on his hind legs to peer into our kitchen window. He struck the pose at our garden doors, mournfully watching us exit the building.

Barbara was astounded. "Will you look at him? I've never seen a cat do that."

"He adores Todd," Jim replied. "Hates to be away from him."

Michael added, "He's saying, 'Can Todd come out and play?'"
Jim groaned. "More likely, 'Let me in!'"

It pleased me to see Jim unplug from the office. His job was becoming a simmering exercise of attrition. Internal politics, shifting priorities, budget constraints, and conflicts with his boss over approach and strategy were wearing him down. I'd never seen him struggle so much. It wasn't the amount or type of work that frustrated him, but rather the assault on his integrity and leadership values. He sustained battle scars protecting his team from unfair criticism and unwarranted attacks. "They're scapegoats," he complained, "for flawed strategy, ill-conceived tactics, misaligned leaders, and insufficient resources." Time away from that toxic environment in the company of his parents soothed his wounded spirit.

Jim's Parents Go to Market

For their farewell dinner, we took Barbara and Michael to Le Chou de Bruxelles, a favorite restaurant in neighboring Ixelles. Actually, it was more my favorite than Jim's; he loathed fish and seafood. This was *the* place for *moules-frites* in Brussels. Against a continuous musical loop of Jacques Brel, Le Chou served perfect fries and offered more than thirty unique preparations of mussels.

Like many things Belgian—*pommes frites,* Smurfs, Tintin, saxophones—the tiny country doesn't always get the credit it deserves. I thought Jacques Brel, the singer-songwriter of classics including *Ne Me Quitte Pas,* was French. Actually, the talented musician was born in the Brussels commune of Schaerbeek in 1929 and only died in France, forty-nine years later.

"Oh, Jamie and Todd," Barbara said as we dined in the restaurant's back garden. "Everything here is so beautiful…your home, garden, *everything.* I love Brussels. It's just like Paris." Jim and I exchanged knowing glances. Paris was a stretch. "*La* Ville *en Rose,*" perhaps? But Barbara's rose-colored sentiment informed us of the visit's rousing success.

Next morning brought teary goodbyes and last looks around the apartment. Sadie got tummy rubs and Puhi received farewells shouted from the garden door. At the airport, the four of us huddled with hugs and kisses.

"Jamie, Todd," Barbara said, "I'm *so* happy. I got to see your apartment, garden, neighborhood, the market…all the places in your life. I'll picture them more clearly now when we Skype."

"Okay, Mom," Michael said as Barbara chatted away. "Time to go. The plane won't wait. Not even for us business-class passengers."

Responding with rolled eyes and giggles, Barbara gave Jim a final embrace. "Love you guys," she added. Tearing up, she and Michael walked toward security.

My budding relationship with mussels was the subject of a lengthy blog post. If the excerpt below whets your appetite, read the full post in the appendix.

Mussels in Brussels–*Moules-Frites*

If you think of mussels merely as shellfish in a bucket, a gastronomic tour of Belgium will convince you otherwise. I arrived in Brussels unimpressed with the bivalve mollusk. In the States, I avoided the dish, wrinkling my nose at what looked like merely a pile of dark blue shells sitting in a puddle of lukewarm water. Why would I eat that? Looks like more work than it's worth. I couldn't possibly fill up on the tiny, rubberlike morsels. And those gritty grains of sand…no thank you.

Then we moved to Brussels. "Heck," I thought, "I'll give mussels a shot." And why not? The food known as *moules-frites* is, after all, the national dish of Belgium….

———◈———

Less than a week after Jim's parents departed, friends George and Jerry arrived from Chicago. They planned to visit Paris after Brussels. Jim and I were eager to join them there. Four years earlier, the four of us had traveled to Paris for George's sixtieth birthday.

Together for thirty-five years, the couple were friends as well as role models. During our sixteen-year friendship, we shared countless activities and loads of laughs. Among their gags were hilarious parodies of Martha and George from Edward Albee's play *Who's Afraid of Virginia Woolf?* and Blanche and Jane Hudson from the film *Whatever Happened to Baby Jane?* The couple supported my writing, reading drafts and offering encouragement. Their stay promised laughter, sarcasm, dry wit, and irreverent commentary on just about any subject.

When George appeared at our door parroting the officious TSA agents who processed them through O'Hare Airport security, barking, "*Shoes off, belts off, computers out…*" he set the riotous tone for their stay. Aware of my laments about unfriendly neighbors and repellent glares, the couple made a game of pointing out prime examples. "Get a load of that *Belge Face*," George would say with a head gesture before mimicking the dour expression.

Fair weather held, and Puhi scaled the garden wall again. Jerry wasn't impressed. "I'm with Jim. Don't let that cat in the house." Caressing our princess's golden fur, George concurred, "Sadie wouldn't like it."

After taking time off for his parents' visit, Jim had to get back to work. He managed to drive us to Antwerp and Maastricht, but he spent most of our Antwerp visit inside his parked car on conference calls.

Sitting in our dining room, George gazed at the high ceilings and classic décor. He sighed. "Makes me want to move to Paris."

Jerry declared, "All in all, we approve."

I rubbed Jim's shoulder with my own. "We're here, sweetie."

Jim grinned. "Very exciting, my love."

A mere hour and twenty minutes on the high-speed train had delivered us to Paris Gare du Nord. Dr. Johnson's famous quip about London could easily apply to the City of Light. Only a man tired of life itself could tire of Paris. The city of superlatives inspired great artists, musicians, and writers. A visit was ideal for celebrating Jim's birthday.

Paris held a special place in my heart. Three trips with my parents and two prior romantic getaways with Jim covered a span of thirty-five years. Walking the grand boulevards, strolling along the Seine, meandering through manicured parks, and gazing upon iconic landmarks rekindled vivid moments. Images flickered through my mind like an old-fashioned newsreel. On my first visit as a wide-eyed nineteen-year-old, the city held magical delight for my parents and me. Two decades later, with my heart bursting with new love, I shared the charming city with Jim. Now, fifteen years after our first visit, Jim and I returned as seasoned adventurers, our relationship matured and mellowed like fine French wine.

Having already seen the top attractions, Jim and I could simply eat, drink, and soak in the sensual city. Grabbing chairs in Tuileries Garden was a favorite activity. Beside the Grand Basin with its sweeping views of the Place de la Concorde and Arc de Triomphe, we absorbed the city's beauty while marveling at our good fortune.

George and Jerry had arrived in Paris several days ahead of us. They rented a place in the Marais, an area with large Jewish and gay populations. Ethnic bakeries, falafel stands, gay bars, and chic boutiques gave the area an eclectic charm. For those savvy enough to know one arrondissement from another, it was the 4th. Our friends offered us the sofa bed in the living room of the small, but centrally located apartment. Rue des Rosiers, the bustling commercial street in front of the building, had a large presence of military police who looked fit and handsome in SWAT uniforms. The street had a tragic history. Thirty-two years earlier, in 1982, Middle Eastern terrorists attacked a restaurant. Their grenades and machine-gun fire killed six people and injured twenty-two others.

Our arrival coincided with Yom Kippur, the Jewish Day of Atonement. The Jewish community prepared also for Sukkot observance. Standing at makeshift street stands, boys sold four items, traditional symbols of the celebration—a citron, leafy boughs of myrtle and willow trees, and lastly a frond from a date tree.

On Jim's birthday, we attended a performance of *La Traviata*, Verdi's popular opera based on a novel and play by Alexandre Dumas. Hollywood adapted the story into the film *Camille*, starring Greta Garbo and Robert Taylor. Surprisingly, supra titles projected above the stage were in English. A packed house enjoyed a classic production set in nineteenth-century France.

"Shh," I said turning to Jim. He'd launched into a fit of giggles during the dramatic final scene. I squeezed his thigh for emphasis. "I can't take you anywhere."

With George & Jerry in Paris

"Oh my." My hand flew to my mouth to stifle my own snickers. "Will the poor woman never die?" The consumptive Violetta kept springing up from her deathbed. Opera fans generally agree that the death scene drags on. My snickering continued until the heroine expired with a final trill.

Jim leaned over, a smirk on his face. "Can't take you anywhere either."

"Touché."

We celebrated into the wee hours at Le Curieux, a bar in the Marais. George and Jerry knew the gregarious proprietor very well. They had introduced us to him four years earlier. We ate, drank, laughed, and chatted with other patrons, the proverbial *joie de vivre*.

Jim blew out sparklers on his dessert. "A birthday to remember always." To be sure, another special Paris moment to treasure.

On Sunday, Jim and I organized a brunch for two sets of friends, former colleagues from United and Daimler who were among our first houseguests in Brussels. One of these families had only recently moved to Paris from Munich. We'd hosted both families previously at our Chicago home. Reunions with friends in foreign locales were special treats. They made the world seem smaller, accessible, and a heck of a lot more fun. Friends often tell us, "You guys know people everywhere."

After brunch, we strolled to the area around the Centre Pompidou, the iconic building that houses a vast collection of modern art. I'd visited the museum with my parents in 1980, only a few years after it opened. On this afternoon, the three young girls in our party pulled us to nearby Stravinsky Fountain. The large, shallow basin of water featured sixteen whimsical sculptures inspired by the composer's work in vivid colors.

Jim's six-year-old goddaughter squealed before him. "Pick me up, pick me up."

As Jim lifted her into the air, her eight-year-old sister ran to me. "Twirl me, twirl me."

Group Hug

I lifted her. Pain shot through me. "Ouch," I said, releasing her grip. "Sorry, honey, can't play today."

Flashing a look of disappointment, she quickly recovered and dashed to her older sister who stood at the fountain's edge. The sharp pain wasn't unexpected. Due to medical phobias, I deferred repair of a hernia, maybe even two hernias, for many years. But surging pain and chronic discomfort suggested my days of avoidance were numbered. Even more compelling than the pain were the physical constraints brought on by the condition. I wanted to play with our young friend; I wanted my freedom.

After a chilly evening cruise on the Seine through the heart of the City of Light, we were off to bed. Another perfect Paris weekend was over. The next day Jim and I boarded the train for Brussels. After snapping a selfie, I leaned over and kissed his cheek. "As Bogey says, we'll always have Paris."

Shortly after returning home, I blogged about the marvels of European train travel.

Paris by Train

"What did you do last weekend?" It's a common Monday morning question in most offices....In Brussels, options are endless....Three world-class cities are a quick nap away. High-speed, efficient rail takes passengers to London in two hours, Amsterdam in one hour and forty minutes, and Paris in just one hour and twenty minutes. No traffic snarls or cramped airplanes to contend with either.

Getting to Paris quickly, unstressed by highway or airport congestion, allowed for more time, more fun, and more romance in the City of Love. Trains, at least in Europe, are civilized modes of transportation. By the way, what are you doing next weekend?

How long would the enchantment of Paris last? Jim returned to a stressful job and I faced probable surgery, my first ever.

Chapter 13

"Go ahead, try it, sweetie. It's pretty good if I say so myself." Standing in the narrow galley of our kitchen, I handed Jim a spoon and stepped back from the stovetop.

With his eyes widening at the invitation, he plunged the spoon into the pot. "I'll be the judge of that." He blew on the steamy scoop of meat, beans, and peppers before slipping the mix into his mouth.

"Good?" I asked.

"Very good."

"Hope they like it. Not sure they've ever tasted American chili."

Preparing a pot of chili was a Halloween routine dating back to the earliest years of our relationship. Other traditions included home-made scarecrows, carved pumpkins, and hand-decorated sugar cookies in shapes of witches, pumpkins, ghosts, and monsters. Back in Chicago when the weather cooperated, Jim and I cozied up on our front porch glider with bowls of chili and bottles of beer to await trick-or-treaters. We carted out a TV and showed scary movies. Trick-or-treaters loved our approach as well as our full-sized candy bar treats. In recent years we had moved the party inside, hosting friends for chili and liquor tastings. Blind tastings taught us that all alcohol paired rather well with chili—beer, wine, vodka, whiskey, and martinis. The annual event was a hit.

Our first Belgian Halloween party, however, made me a bit nervous.

The bulk of our guests weren't American. I wasn't without optimism. Over the summer, I had served up an Italian-themed buffet for Jim's Brussels-based staff and their spouses. Our guests, natives of the Netherlands, Colombia, Flanders, and India, showered compliments on my cooking. Recalling the clean plates and second helpings from that earlier party boosted my confidence as I prepared for Halloween.

With the holiday falling on Friday night, we decided to test how our American tradition translated in Belgium. We invited our small social circle: our Slovenian neighbor, residents of our building, BWC acquaintances, and Jim's work peers. An overlapping visit by a former boss was serendipitous. Our houseguest, Jane, brought us chili spices unavailable in Belgium.

As the party date neared, Jim and I fell into a familiar and comfortable groove. Experienced hosts, we had designed our Chicago house for entertaining. For several years, we hosted an annual summer party that drew as many as 150 guests. We threw birthday and retirement parties, baby showers, and receptions welcoming overseas visitors and sending off friends and colleagues moving away. Parties were our specialty. A house, I believe, absorbs the warmth, laughter, and love of its human occupants. Together, we'd created that aura in Chicago. The question remained whether we could recreate that magic in Brussels.

Party planning and an additional houseguest distracted me from health concerns. Around doctors, my heart races, blood pressure spikes, and I break out in a cold sweat. The prospect of being poked, prodded, and pricked makes me nauseous. Aversion has grown with age. *No, I don't need to see the vials of blood extracted from my arm. I can verify my name without your waving the tube under my nose.* Subscribing to a theory that when you dig for problems, you usually find them, I'm content imagining that my body is working just fine. Similarly, when I'm in an airplane, I don't dwell on the thousands of parts that keep engine turbines moving. No peace comes from either line of thought.

My anxiety, perhaps even phobia, grew more acute after my

parents' illnesses. It pained me to witness their final weeks dying in the hospital. No fewer than nine specialists including doctors of the lung, blood, heart, brain, and every other vital organ tended my mom as she waged a courageous battle with pneumonia. My dad's battle with cancer lasted three years, and he spent the final two months bedridden in the hospital. My fatalistic view, I fully understand, may even kill me some day.

After arriving in Brussels, chronic pain in my groin intensified, aggravated by the physical exertion of our move. I'd recently learned of a friend's husband who avoided treatment for an inguinal hernia. His prolonged neglect resulted in emergency surgery that required removal of a portion of his intestines. I didn't want that…not in Belgium.

I started the quest for treatment after our trip to Paris and the painful flare-up. Jim found a list of doctors on the U.S. Embassy website. Criteria for making the list weren't stated, but English proficiency was a prerequisite. The office of one doctor of internal medicine was a five-minute walk from our home. He needed to examine me before providing a surgical referral. On my first attempt, the doctor answered his phone. His English was good.

Walking to my appointment, as my heart pounded and my breathing stalled, I pondered my entry into the world of European medicine. Would the Belgian system be the paragon of universal healthcare that progressive Americans hold up as a gold standard? Or was it a quagmire of bureaucracy and overstretched resources that other Americans decry as pitfalls of socialized medicine? Making my way to Boulevard de Waterloo, I easily found the office, the tallest building on the block. Though clean and well maintained, the narrow five-story structure of concrete and small windows lacked the grandeur and charm of its neighbors; with bright sunshine reflecting off facades of white stucco and brick, they looked more like townhouses than offices.

Stepping onto a small stoop, I rang the bell. A male voice crackled over the intercom. I waited for the garbled noise to stop before announcing myself.

"Yes, yes. Come in." The entry buzzer sounded.

The foyer was as clean and sterile as the exterior. Up a few steps, a frosted glass door opened to a small waiting room. I exchanged nods and soft bonjours with a middle-aged woman who sat reading a magazine. There was no receptionist or check-in window, standard features in American medical offices. The dusty whitewashed room was cluttered with chairs, a children's play area, and two end tables piled high with magazines. A construction skeleton shrank the room. Planks supported by two-by-fours anchored to the floor spanned a white plaster ceiling. Was this a doctor's waiting room or a mineshaft? I soon understood the reason for wooden reinforcements. Loud, rapid-fire pounding of a jackhammer reverberated overhead. Plaster powder sprinkled to the floor. *No mood-mellowing stimuli here.*

Choosing an issue of *National Geographic*, I noted that it was ten years old. All the reading material was similarly outdated. After several minutes of nerve-wracking waiting, an inner door opened. An elderly woman said adieu to a tall, slightly disheveled man whose white smock suggested that he was the doctor. He called a name and my sole companion in the waiting room rose and disappeared through the open door.

"Apologies. An emergency," the doctor said, nodding toward me. His accent was Flemish. "Won't be long."

American and European health systems had one thing in common—excessive waits to see the doctor. Thirty minutes later, the prior patient left and Dr. Jacobs summoned me. After short introductions, he ushered me into his inner sanctum. *Here goes.* My blood pressure spiked; my body perspired. The room was both office and examining room. Stacks of charts and files cluttered his desk. File cabinets, bookcases, consultation chairs, and an examining table packed the limited floor space.

Dr. Jacobs directed me toward a chair. His manner was calm and his face kind. "Sit, please." Taking a seat behind the desk, he asked for my resident and insurance cards before launching into a battery of routine questions: name, address, birthdate, and so forth. As he entered my responses into a computer, his desk phone rang.

"Pardon." Picking up the receiver, he pushed a blinking light. As the interruption repeated, it became clear that he didn't employ a nurse or other staff. Alternating among French, Flemish, and English, he answered patients' questions, set up appointments, gave referrals, and provided lab results. Dr. Jacobs was the medical equivalent of a one-man band.

Paperwork complete, he directed me to disrobe. I stood naked in front of his desk. Continuing to field calls, he occasionally glanced up at me. *What do I do with my hands? Where do I focus my eyes?* Uncomfortable, I imagined myself auditioning for an adult movie in front of a distracted casting director.

Returning his attention to me, he directed me onto the examining table. "I see the bulge. Does it hurt?" he asked, pressing my groin.

I winced. "Yes. But not always. However, the frequency's increasing."

After I disclosed my anxiety, he offered me eyeshades as he took blood samples, my blood pressure, and an EKG. "The tests," he explained, "will certify you for surgery."

Again clothed, I returned to the consultation chair and waited for the doctor to get off the phone. "I'll call you with the blood test results, but everything looks fine for surgery. Vitals are good." My muscles relaxed. "Oh, but there is one thing," he added, concern flashing across his face. I tensed. *Oh my God, it's cancer, isn't it?* "Are you planning to apply for a mortgage?"

I bristled. "Huh?" *This guy really is a one-stop shop. Is he a financial planner too?*

"Your weight," he added, "is fine...give or take. But you're carrying a bit too much around the middle."

My eyes narrowed.

His expression signaled understanding of my confusion. "Belgian lenders peg mortgage rates to health factors. Yours are all fine except your waistline. It's only a few millimeters, but it's enough for them. Just cut down on beer and chocolate."

I'd heard of jumping through hoops for a home loan, but I couldn't imagine the indignity of a mortgage rate pegged to one's pants size. With beer and chocolate, not to mention waffles and *pommes frites,* as staples of the local diet, Belgian mortgage lenders undoubtedly enjoyed very high interest rates indeed.

Dr. Jacobs handed me a piece of paper. "Here you go. A fine surgeon. Good reputation and English speaker. Good luck. I'll be in touch about the blood test."

The surprisingly reasonable cost of the visit—under $40—offset the dire prospect of surgery.

With another doctor's appointment and surgery on the horizon, our party and having Jane as a houseguest were timely diversions. Our circle of friends remained small after ten months in Belgium. At some point, the tide of houseguests and visitors would ebb. With our mindset that Brussels would be home for the foreseeable future, a broad network of friends was necessary for us to feel rooted. I viewed the Halloween gathering, therefore, as an important bellwether of our social progress. I awaited RSVPs with great anticipation.

The number of positive replies from my writers' group encouraged me. They fit the perfect party-guest profile—an eclectic mix of people who were never at a loss for words. Barbara from next door as well as our new upstairs neighbor, a professional woman from Paris, also replied yes. Jim's work colleagues, however, were enigmas. Many didn't respond to his invitation, and most who did declined without explanation. Only two of his peers responded yes. I better understood Jim's isolation at the office. His colleagues' refusal to engage socially both saddened and angered me. *Why don't they like us? Why won't they help us settle in?* Jim and I were doing our very best to make Belgium our home. How successful could we be without Belgian friends?

Despite the lackluster response from Jim's workmates, the list of confirmed party guests offered great promise. Jane, smart and engaging, would be mingling with people from Spain, Ireland, Bulgaria, the

Netherlands, England, Sweden, France, Denmark, Slovenia, Canada, and Belgium.

Jim and I had brought terra-cotta pumpkins, decorations from our annual display, with us from Chicago. I set the trio of grinning jack-o-lanterns on the raised terrace at the back of the garden. Candles illuminated their exaggerated features. The alien creatures transfixed Puhi. He spent hours sitting and staring at them.

Guests received a tutorial on chili—ingredients and accompaniments: sour cream, shredded cheese, and oyster crackers. Many people returned for seconds and thirds until the pot was empty. Homemade guacamole and cheese quesadillas, vegetarian alternatives, vanished as well. Although poblano peppers and Mexican spices were unavailable, I found a Latin American grocer that sold *queso fresco*, the key ingredient of quesadillas.

The party was a turning point in our relationship with Puhi. He took advantage of an open back door kept ajar to give guests access to iced beverages. Sneaking inside undetected, he roamed room to room scoping out the apartment that had been, until that night, strictly off limits. Sadie quietly observed him with suspicion.

"Puhi!" Barbara, the cat's owner, exclaimed. "You shouldn't be here." She turned to me with wide, mischievous eyes, her giggle stifled by her hand held to her mouth.

A young Irish woman looked at me earnestly from the sofa. She was petting Puhi, who purred his satisfaction. "You mean this isn't your cat?"

Barbara and I exchanged amused looks before I shrugged. "He thinks he is."

For the remainder of the evening, the precocious imp mingled with party guests. A cat, I figured, whether black or not, was an ideal Halloween accessory.

Sarah, a BWC poet who attended with a new beau, enthused, "Simply fabulous party. An authentic American Halloween, pumpkins and all."

Jim's colleague was the last guest to leave at about one o'clock in the morning. He was exuberant as well. "Great party! Never met such intriguing people."

The apartment was empty of guests except the cat. Jim, Jane, and I tidied up.

"Fantastic party," Jane said. "Maybe the best I've ever been to. You two have so many interesting friends."

After shooing Puhi out the door, we turned out the lights. Jim and I settled into bed. The satisfaction of hosting a great party was a familiar feeling. The lively evening brought us closer to making Brussels home. And despite the fact that nary a single trick-or-treater showed up at our door, our entertaining style and classic American chili translated well.

Jim leaned over and gave me a good-night kiss. "Great job, love."

"Thanks sweetie. And you're okay with Puhi?"

Jim snickered. "He is a cute cat. Can't take that away from him."

Score!

Sarah sent a note of thanks. Having sold two books of her poetry at the party, she was ecstatic. She included a poem, adding, "Apropos, I think."

Halloween

Think spiders, cobwebs, pointy hats,
Broomsticks, witches, rats, black cats
Enormous pumpkins carved with care
Turned into lanterns everywhere
An eerie glow on window sills
Flickering candles ward off ills
Ghoulish masks, the Devil's kin
Evil walks abroad—stay in!

But who now thinks what this may mean
The revelry of Halloween
When Dracula and Batman faces
Pop up in unexpected places?
Legends and religion try
This Pagan vestige to apply
Fear of Darkness—the Unknown
Better not go out alone.

In America it is "trick or treat"
As hordes of children walk the street
Attired as ghosts in flowing drapes
Or wizards swirling round in capes.
Doorbells ring, each neighbour greets
These tiny visitors with sweets;
Who now remembers the bell tolls
To commemorate "All Souls"?

(c) Poet in the woods 2013
(Reprinted with permission of the poet, Sarah Strange)

Chapter 14

"What would you say about a quick trip to Chicago?"

Jim's dinner fork stalled midway between his plate and his mouth. He stared across the table at me. His mind churned. "Could work... uh-huh...yeah, might be nice...very nice."

I grinned. "Thought you'd say that. We could use the break. *Both* of us."

Jim and I had plunged into our European life with a spirit of adventure. Most expat friends enjoyed at least one annual employer-paid flight home to visit family, tend to business matters, or simply reconnect with their social network—a tap into one's roots, so to speak. The fact that our expat package didn't include home visits was more nuisance than aggravation. Chicago would always be there. We intended to explore. Brussels blessed us with easy access and proximity to places like Stockholm, Nice, Lisbon, and countless other bucket-list locations.

But despite our intent to wander, we needed to recharge, plug into close friends and family back home. Job stress including frequent skirmishes with his boss wore Jim down. His confidence waned. He began to doubt whether his leadership style translated to his new circumstances. Self-doubt undermined his sense of purpose, shaking him to his professional core. In the past, he had known only success. Familiar surroundings, I hoped, might lift his sagging spirit. A hug from his mom couldn't hurt.

Jim's well-being wasn't my only concern. My own bouts of lone-liness and depression returned with disquieting regularity. Perhaps the rapidly fading light of the Northern latitude and bites of chilling night air triggered the emotional flare-up. Upheaval, new surround-ings, limited social connections, impending surgery, and Jim's unhap-piness had already frayed my emotions. Even without those stresses, the onset of autumn gripped me with wistful nostalgia. This was a familiar pattern. Somber anniversaries dotted the calendar from late October to year end—deaths of my parents and all four grand-parents. Autumn represented deep personal loss. The episodes that afflicted me in Brussels that fall, however, were rawer, deeper, more frightening.

I longed for my parents. How or why those feelings surfaced, I didn't know. This was neither fresh grief nor a delayed response to their deaths; they had died thirteen years earlier. The profound yearn-ing was new. Had feelings of isolation stirred it? I couldn't expect Jim to understand my emotional needs when I didn't understand them myself. And I couldn't ask for his help, adding to his burden when he was battling his own demons. Despite Jim's abiding and steadfast love, I was missing the unconditional love of my parents, and maybe I too needed to return to a place associated with love, comfort, and emo-tional security.

Although understanding the strange, toxic mix of feelings re-mained beyond my grasp, I began to recognize its approach. Like a creeping fog, a thick veil of depression edged toward me. Powerless to stop its encroachment, I waited for it to blanket me. Once it was upon me, I felt languid, numb, listless, drifting. I was tired—spinning my wheels, running in place—exhaustion with nothing to show for it. Maybe I even began to lean into these spells—something familiar in an unfamiliar world. Did I surrender to these paralyzing episodes or actively embrace them? Did it matter?

My refuge was our bedroom. Reclining on the bed to rest my heavy limbs, I succumbed to a steady stream of dark thoughts and despair. At best, I had fitful slumbers.

I miss you, Mom and Dad. Please come and take me away. "Please," I cried aloud.

Eventually and on its own terms, the fog lifted...temporarily.

Loneliness and isolation were common themes. Two of my Brussels friends were moving on to new adventures. Nick the Englishman was relocating to Alderney, a remote island off the coast of Normandy. He'd spoken of escape and grand schemes from the moment we met. Whatever he was looking for, Brussels, his home for several years, didn't provide it. "Chalk it up to a mix of rootlessness, restlessness, and opportunity," he gave as an explanation for leaving. His departure would end our morning chats over coffee at the Maison du Peuple. Anne-May secured a job with an advocacy group that advanced the interests of Dutch institutions of higher learning. I was excited for her but saddened that our long walks and talks would end. The loss of two close confidantes taught me that solid footings were impossible in Brussels. By definition, expats were as transient as shifting sand.

A quick jaunt to Chicago, therefore, would be therapeutic for both of us. Avoiding peak holiday traffic, we set a travel date of early November. We limited our stay to four nights. Two close friends, United Airlines retirees, had flight benefits. They designated each of us as eligible companions. We could travel home cheaply...with one catch. Seats were standby. Although that gave us a chance to snag first-class or business-class seats for practically nothing, we faced the possibility of getting no seat at all. To enhance our chances, we planned prudently, choosing flights with fewer bookings. Similar prudence guided our choice of return flights. We'd start the journey back to Brussels on Friday. That gave us three days to get seats before Jim needed to be at work.

Many friends offered to host us. Although downtown Chicago

held great appeal, most of our business and social commitments were in the suburbs. We split our time—two nights with Jim's parents and two nights with a couple who lived near our home. Jim wanted to check the repairs of the prior winter's damage to our roof. He also wanted to meet our tenants.

"Want to join me?" he asked.

I shook my head. "Nope."

"How about a drive-by? You wouldn't even need to stop or come in."

Again, I shook my head. "Nope," I repeated. "I don't want to see *that* house." My reaction was emotional, even irrational. I remained angry with the house for hounding us in Brussels, giving us headaches and unplanned expenses. In addition, perhaps after seeding a new life in Brussels, I didn't want to disturb those tender roots. "I can see selling the house."

"What?" Shock flashed across Jim's face. A decade earlier, he had left the city to live in my suburban family home. It was a major concession on his part. And as much as he admired our house, I loved it more. "You don't mean that."

I shrugged. "Sure do. Especially if we stay in Europe. We won't need the house. Besides it's been nothing but trouble."

Instead of debating, Jim let my outburst silently fade. His sideways glance and smirk suggested he was somewhat incredulous. At the same time, however, we both recognized my response as a major pivot.

Mine was no snap decision. *Never look back* was a motto of mine. During my professional career, I experienced triumphs and disappointments. With each promotion gained or lost, I moved forward. When I left United after twenty-three years, it was my choice—perhaps somewhat forced, but ultimately my decision. A financial-operations guy, I had no appetite for a job in Human Resources. I gave up a hefty paycheck, enviable travel benefits, enhanced financial security, and in a way, my independence and identity. "No regrets," I told people on my way out. "Always look to the future."

Despite my aspirational credo, the rearview mirror often tempted me. Frequently finding myself adrift in Brussels, I had endless hours to ponder the choices I made. Perhaps those unproductive ruminations fueled my lapses into depression. Or, were they symptoms of drifting? Did it matter?

The standby gods smiled on us; Jim and I made it to Chicago.

"One night has to be Mexican food," I said.

Jim grinned. "And you know what's on my list?"

"Portillo's?"

Jim nodded. "Yep." According to him, the Chicago institution served up the best cheeseburgers and Italian beef sandwiches in the world.

Running errands to fetch favorite products and brands unavailable in Brussels, we were struck by the customer service. Super-friendly and smiling store clerks freely offered assistance. One clerk went out of her way to find us discount coupons.

After piling shopping bags into the rental car, Jim climbed into the passenger seat. "I forgot how friendly Midwesterners are."

"You can say that again."

That level of service didn't exist in Belgium, not on a regular basis anyway. The positive experience carried us away. We had to buy a suitcase to carry our purchases home.

"Hope Belgian Customs doesn't stop us," I added. "How would we explain a dozen cans of pumpkin, boxes of pancake mix, and bottles of maple syrup?"

Four packed days flew by. We had breakfast and lunch dates and spent each night with a different group of friends and family. We basked in the genuine and hearty welcome receptions. Jim got several hugs from his mom.

Recharging in Chicago

Fortunately, we got seats on the first flight home via Newark—business class. We toasted our good fortune with wine.

Across the plane's aisle, Jim looked content. "Great trip, sweetie."

I clanked his glass. "Sure was, sweet pea."

"Can't wait to see our Sadie girl."

"And our little Puhi," I added with a wink.

Jim rolled his eyes before turning his attention back to the in-flight movie menu.

Back in Brussels, I blogged about our trip and the real meaning of *home*. Here's an excerpt. The full post can be found in the appendix.

There's No Place Like Home, or Is There?

Where is home? As expats are wont to do, we traveled back from whence we came—Chicago, or more specifically, the Village of Arlington Heights. Ten short months ago, Chicago was "home," Brussels a pretty flirtation....Slowly and almost unnoticeably, Brussels claimed a piece of our hearts....

Can you go home again? Of course! But where is "home"? Ten months of grand adventures and simple moments have transformed Brussels from a shallow flirtation into a promising new partner. Toward the end of our visit, we looked forward to going *home. We* meant Brussels. Home may be where you hang your hat, but more importantly, home is where you share a life with the person you hold most dear....

Perhaps the best definition of all—*Home is in your heart!*

⸺ ((◊)) ⸺

We returned to Brussels with our little family facing two medical concerns. My hernia surgery was less than one month away. Although I was anxious, the ailment was defined and the remedy straightforward. Sadie's health, on the other hand, fell into the category of fear of the unknown. A well-informed diagnosis would require surgery.

Toward the end of summer, a lump had formed on one of Sadie's hind legs. Our dear girl was prone to cysts. Over the years, vets advised that they were most likely harmless fatty cells. Whereas fur camouflaged prior growths, this one was hairless and unsightly. The bulbous pink mass looked raw. Recommending removal, the vet set a surgery date for late November, two days before Thanksgiving. "Routine," he said, allaying our concerns about the surgery. "We'll know what we're dealing with once it's removed."

We didn't think the procedure would upset our holiday plans. Klaus, Jim's former boss at Daimler, and his wife Kathrin invited us for a long Thanksgiving weekend. As fellow dog lovers, they included Sadie in their invitation. They lived near Stuttgart, a five-hour drive from Brussels. I looked forward to the trip, reciprocity of sorts for our welcoming expats and others without family into our home for the holidays. Kathrin, a patron of the arts, asked me to read an excerpt from one of my books after dinner. The gesture was positive affirmation of my fledgling vocation. Jim would benefit from a good dose of confidence and camaraderie. He loved working for Klaus, and Jim's years at Daimler were among the happiest and most fulfilling of his professional career.

Yippee! I thought. *We won't be alone on Thanksgiving.*

First, we simply had to get through Sadie's surgery. As experienced pet owners, we were familiar with the sinking feeling of dropping off a furry family member for surgery. We spent several anxious hours at home awaiting the vet's call. The phone rang at about two o'clock.

"Sadie's fine," the vet said.

"And the cyst?" I asked, relaying the vet's words to Jim who sat at our desk.

"Most certainly benign. Everything looks normal." I felt a great swell of relief. "You can pick her up this evening. She's sleeping now."

Jim and I drove our still-groggy Sadie home. A four-inch incision stitched up as tight as a stuffed turkey kept her immobile. Incapable of taking the stairs to our bedroom where she usually slept, she also needed help getting up to go outside to relieve herself. With her recovery slower than anticipated, Jim and I relocated our bedding to the first floor to keep our family together. Throughout Wednesday afternoon, Sadie remained lethargic.

That evening, Jim stared down to the living room floor where Sadie rested. "I think we better call off our trip."

I sighed. "Let's wait a little bit. Maybe she'll rally."

Although I hesitated, the answer was clear. We couldn't subject our dear girl to a five-hour drive and a strange house filled with people and another dog. When we're sick, we want to be in our own home and bed. Still, I held out hope that she'd rally.

But on Thanksgiving morning, Sadie remained weak and

immobile. We couldn't leave our princess with a pet sitter when she needed us most. We spent the day housebound and alone. Even Puhi moped about the garden, banished from the house as Sadie recovered. Frustrated, I retreated to our bedroom in a deep funk.

Late afternoon, Jim came downstairs. "I booked a table for dinner."

"I'm not up for it," I replied from the bed.

"We have to eat. Sadie's fine. We'll only be gone a few hours." He talked up the restaurant, L'Auberg'In. He'd dined there for a business function. "Come on, I'm sure you'll enjoy it."

Begrudgingly, I got up from the bed and changed. I couldn't ruin Jim's Thanksgiving. His efforts to salvage our spoiled holiday and coax me from my funk were sweet and endearing. And although he didn't show it, he too felt the sting of disappointment of our canceled trip to Stuttgart. He held his former boss and mentor in great esteem. Visiting Klaus would have allowed Jim to revisit a happier time when he was most satisfied professionally. Klaus was probably his best boss ever—a stark contrast to Jim's current boss and situation, which left him frustrated, deflated, and questioning his value. Jim probably would have asked Klaus for advice for working with his difficult boss, the type of delicate conversation that was best had face-to-face. Now, that coaching and counseling session wouldn't happen.

Although I remained silent and distant in the car, I warmed once we reached the restaurant. I found the ambience classy and romantic, an ideal spot for a special occasion. With no turkey on the menu, I settled for sea bass. No fan of turkey, Jim happily dined on lamb chops. For dessert, creme brûlée and ice cream topped with meringue and raspberry sauce replaced pumpkin pie. The food, service, and entire experience were terrific. Friendly staff sent us home with warm wishes for a Happy Thanksgiving.

Over the weekend, with our spirits still dragging, we found an ideal diversion: shopping for a Christmas tree, the magical stuff of childhood and family traditions. For our very first Christmas together sixteen years earlier, Jim and I had dragged a tree over sidewalks to his Chicago apartment. As our relationship matured, we established new traditions. A twelve-foot Fraser fir customarily graced the great room of our rehabbed home. I strung lights and draped ribbon. Jim added the angel. With holiday movies as background, we hung ornaments and dined on pizza and red wine. These traditions, like prized ornaments, were precious.

After we scoured two nurseries looking for an acceptable tree, Jim pronounced them scrawny and unacceptable. An Internet search guided us toward a garden shop in Wemmel, a town on the opposite side of Brussels. There we found the perfect tree. When we asked for twine, the nursery worker shot us an odd look. After an extended wait, he returned, handed us a spool of twine, and studied us with great curiosity as we hoisted the tree onto the car and secured it to the roof for the ten-mile ride home.

"Very exciting," Jim said, driving the car from the lot. "Our first Belgian tree. And such a beauty."

"Reminds me of our first Christmas. Ah, those were the days.

Christmas Tradition

Jim squeezed my thigh. "We're very lucky."

We drove a few more miles singing along to a Christmas CD when we slowed. Stopped in traffic, I glanced out my side window. "Sweetie," I said. "People are staring at us."

Jim scanned the sidewalk. "You're right. Kinda odd."

"Must be the tree."

"Hmm. It's pretty big. Guessing that's it."

I shrugged it off, but more pedestrians gawked, laughed, and snapped photos with their phones. We were a spectacle, but why? I quickly rolled down the window to check the bindings. They were still taut; the tree was secure. We arrived home safely. Weeks later, I learned that most trees were delivered by van. The quaint tradition of hauling Christmas trees home on car roofs was uniquely American.

I pulled ornament boxes from the storage rack. Jim ordered pizza, opened a bottle of wine and popped a holiday movie into the DVD player. Sadie hobbled onto the rug at our feet. As Sadie gradually returned to her old self and as our splendid tree took shape, Jim and I recovered from the disappointment of our canceled trip. Even Puhi made an appearance. To our surprise, he ignored the shiny ornaments. Instead, he plopped down onto the velvet tree skirt for a snooze. All things considered our Thanksgiving wasn't a catastrophe after all.

An eventful week that included Sadie's surgery, missing an authentic American style Thanksgiving, and purchasing of our first Belgian Christmas tree inspired another blog post.

Thanksgiving Blues

Thanksgiving used to be my favorite holiday. Free of commercialism, gift-buying frenzy, and hype, Thanksgiving was a peaceful lull before the Christmas juggernaut. When family settled down to dinner, calamity was limited to gravy splattered on the linen tablecloth. Each year I yearn for that simpler time. But it no longer exists. I'm not a child, a passive celebrant whose sole task is to show up at the table and eat....

In Brussels, it's just another Thursday. Turkey, *dinde* in French, is seldom found on Belgian menus or in grocery stores. Our golden retriever, Sadie, is our only family in Europe. Suffering bouts of loneliness, we were thrilled when friends invited us to Stuttgart for a large, festive gathering that included a Thanksgiving dinner of turkey with all the trimmings....

But responsibility, that chunky albatross around the neck of every mature adult, reared its ugly head. Dear Sadie had a cyst on her leg. Recommending immediate removal, the vet scheduled the procedure for the Tuesday before Thanksgiving. Thankfully, the procedure went well, Sadie's prognosis excellent. But would she be well enough for the 5-hour Thanksgiving drive?

The right answer was difficult to accept. Depression, a frequent companion in our adopted country, took hold. My funk lingered. I wasn't mad at anyone and certainly not angry with Sadie. Dashed were my hopes for an old-fashioned Thanksgiving....

Black Friday, the day most Americans gorge on doorbusters, Jim and I bought a Christmas tree. Each hung ornament had a unique story of our life together. By the end of the weekend, Sadie was back to her old self and our towering tree was magnificent. Our little family was together in our warm, beautiful home—healthy, happy, and most thankful for our bountiful life.

Perhaps by chance, I'd stumbled upon the real meaning of Thanksgiving.

Chapter 15

We headed into December with Sadie on the mend. But my operation loomed on the near horizon. On one hand, I wanted it over. On the other, I was scared. If Sadie could be brave, I reasoned, so could I. Setting up our Christmas tree, adding holiday decorations to the apartment, and busy weekends eased my anxiety. But I kept my eye on the calendar. Each passing Wednesday brought the procedure one week closer.

The surgeon recommended by Dr. Jacobs impressed me. Shortly after returning from our visit to Chicago, I traveled by Metro to his office inside St-Michel Hospital, a private facility in Etterbeek. The surgeon had a Flemish surname and a confident demeanor. My first impressions were positive. A well-tailored suit spoke to his success, graying temples indicated experience, and a strong physique suggested positive self-image and good discipline. When I confessed my fear of doctors, he didn't flinch and offered only a soft nod.

The procedure, he explained, required two small incisions near my navel, one for a camera and the other for surgical equipment. The incisions would allow access to my damaged groin area by burrowing down between my outer skin layer and abdominal wall. Inserted mesh would keep the bulging intestine in place.

"Not at all what the Americans do," the surgeon said. "Less invasive. Heals faster. You can return to activity almost immediately." He had a very effective sales pitch. He made the surgery sound simple and straightforward. *I can do this,* I thought, nodding my understanding.

Unlike most U.S. protocols, this wasn't an outpatient procedure. I wasn't thrilled. I'd avoided hospital stays since birth. "It's for the best," the doctor said, no doubt sensing my tension. "Relax. Enjoy the care. Staff will watch you. It's only for one night."

Again, nodding my assent, I must have looked like one of those bobblehead dog novelties displayed in car windows. *Whatever you say, doctor, whatever you say.* An image of being carted to the curb in a wheelchair gave me a fleeting moment of delight—*just like TV and the movies.* I recalled my late father's rave reviews about hospital food: "Best Jello in the world."

"Preferred room?"

"Huh?" I asked, recovering from my trance.

"Single, double, or triple? Your choice. There's a surcharge for private rooms although I don't know what it is."

"Double I guess." With U.S. prices as my only guide, I figured a single room supplement would be thousands of euros. For one night, I could rough it…*within reason.* A triple, more ward than room, multiplied risks of such nasty things as germs, noisy visitors, and disagreeable roommates. A double room, I also reasoned, might be a rich experience to flavor my writing. A roommate's sad saga of woe might inspire a compelling plot line. Meals might aid in conjuring up vivid descriptions of food trays to give authenticity to a future scene set in a hospital. An irascible aide might inspire the next Nurse Ratched.

The doctor opened his calendar, fingering through several pages. "Okay then, let's look at schedules. I've got openings starting early December," he said with a smile. "What would you like?"

Like? A loaded word if I ever heard one. I was about to seal my fate—the point of no return. "How about January? Could even do the first half," I added, proud of my mustered courage. *Gives me one more Christmas on earth.*

The surgeon flashed a shaming scowl. "What? You want to wait until the new year?"

I swallowed hard. *Maybe I'm not so brave after all. Okay, okay, you win.* "Let's go with December...*mid*-month." It sounded much further away than *early* December. I studied his face.

A firm nod signaled his approval. "Fine, fine. How about the tenth? It's a Wednesday."

I stifled a gasp; my stomach soured. Technically, the tenth was mid-month, but only by the slimmest of margins. I shrugged, forcing a brave smile and, again, bobbled my head. "Okay. Sounds good."

"That way you'll be nearly healed by Christmas."

Oh boy!

As he entered my information into his calendar, I silently assessed my fate. If I had to go under the knife, Wednesday was probably the best day to do so. I drew an analogy to an oft-repeated warning from my youth that advised consumers to steer clear of cars assembled on Mondays and Fridays. Allegedly, quality suffered on days bookending the weekend due to worker fatigue and distraction. Similar advice, I assumed, applied to surgeons. Yes, a midweek hernia repair was best.

Choosing to walk home from my appointment, my head swirled with a mix of emotions. I was attempting to bolster my confidence. *Has to be done. The right thing to do. The adult thing.* "Yep," I muttered aloud, "I can't wait to tell Jim."

When Jim got home from work, I briefed him on my visit. Grinning, he pulled me into a firm embrace. "I'm so proud of you, my love. I know it's not easy for you. I'll add it to my calendar right now. What's the date?"

"December 10, a Wednesday." Basking in his pride, I saw no need to confess that my first choice had been January.

"Fantastic. You'll get over it before Christmas."

I nodded, forcing a smile. "So the doctor said."

The Sunday before surgery, Jim executed a brilliant tactical maneuver. He booked us a tour to the Cologne Christmas market sponsored by the Expat Club. Two favorite things—travel and Christmas—offered an ideal diversion. We took a two-and-a-half-hour journey on a comfortable bus through eastern Belgium, the Netherlands, and western Germany.

The prospect of seeing Cologne again and sharing the pretty city on the Rhine with Jim filled me with excitement. Recollections of my earlier visit flickered through my mind. I had visited Cologne with my parents and sister thirty years earlier, one month before I started business school. The four of us had embarked upon a two-week driving tour of Germany with side trips to Strasbourg, France, and Salzburg, Austria. Travel, shared experiences, and prized memories bonded us as a family.

As I recalled that earlier trip, I considered my personal journey over those three decades. My academic degrees, a dozen jobs in two decades at United, my parents' deaths, my coming out, meeting Jim, his advanced degree, our house renovation, marriage, travels, my writing, and our move to Brussels. I'd lived a life that would have pleased my parents.

Approaching Cologne Cathedral, my head filled with images of that prior visit. Family photos snapped before the impressive church whose twin spires soar more than five hundred feet into the heavens. As depression blanketed me during that autumn, I felt my parents near. Now here I stood on a spot that held a special memory from my past. With my arms folded across my chest, I stood silently, playing parallel tracks from my life…images of then and now.

Jim sidled up to me, putting his arm around my shoulder. "What is it, sweetie?"

"Quick trip to the past, that's all. Memories of my folks."

He looked into my eyes. "Oh, how they loved you."

My lips pursed into a smile. "That, they did. I miss them."

"I know you do, my love."

Brushing the past from my mind, I pulled my phone from my pants pocket. "How about a selfie, sweetie?"

Visiting Cologne Cathedral

A highlight of the trip was meeting two couples. Pat and Bob, expats from New Jersey, joined us for the short Rhine River cruise. Fellow Americans in Brussels, they shared many of our same experiences and impressions. At lunch, we met Europeans Cecilia and Tom, a dentist and a physical therapist with established practices in Brussels. We exchanged contact information with both couples, who became good friends.

Monday and Tuesday, final countdown days, I stayed close to home comforted by Sadie and Puhi. Surgery day arrived. Waking long before dawn, Jim and I showered. Before we headed out the door for a two-block walk to the Metro I gave Sadie a kiss. After a single transfer, we arrived at Merode station followed by a short stroll to St-Michel. Walking felt good, an effective way to calm my nerves.

After a quick check-in, a pleasant clerk directed us to a private room. There, a nurse instructed me to disrobe, put on a gown, and wait: "Shouldn't be long." Calmness settled in. I was still anxious but no longer scared.

"How ya doin'?" Jim asked.

"Fine. Just want it to be over."

But two and one-half nerve-wracking hours passed. As dawn broke outside the window, I was tempted to put on my clothes and run. But I persevered, breathing deeply. I rid myself of nervous energy by moving back and forth between a chair and the bed. Two attendants finally arrived and tucked me into the movable bed.

With his hands on the bed rails, Jim leaned down and gave me a kiss. "Love you."

"Love you more, sweet pea."

"I'll see you soon," Jim added as the orderlies wheeled me away.

They parked me at the end of a long line of patients, the row of beds resembling an auto assembly line. *Good thing it's Wednesday.* Twenty minutes later, my doctor appeared. After joking about the un-fashionable hairnet he handed me, he wheeled me outside operating room number 7. *Lucky number.* "You're next." His words sounded as if I were at a bakery counter.

Several more minutes passed. Surgical staff walked by as if I were not there. At last, a nurse arrived to roll me inside. As the operating room doors opened, I took a deep breath. *Oh boy, here we go!*

After scooting onto the operating table, I stared up at the tiled ceiling interrupted only by an occasional appearance of the nurse's hairy nostrils as he set up. The table was cold, hard, narrow. My shoulders extended over the edges, my toes popped out from the blanket, my arms drooped over the sides. *I'm a big guy, but really? Why can't I stay in the warm, comfy bed?* The nurse swaddled my arms to keep them from dangling to the floor. Like a newborn, I was imprisoned in my blankets.

The anesthesiologist was a cheerful little chap. After introducing himself, he asked where I was from.

"Chicago," I replied to the ceiling.

"An American? I'm honored to be operating on an American."

Perhaps it was polite banter intended to calm me, but how do you respond to that? "Well, I'm honored to have a Belgian anesthesiologist."

His green-masked face peered down at me, his dark eyes focused. "No, seriously. Americans have very high standards for anesthesiologists. To practice over there, you need to take an exam."

Was that supposed to make me feel better? If I hadn't been swaddled like a mummy, I might have bolted.

"Take a deep breath," he added. "You're about to go to sleep. It's the same stuff Michael Jackson's doctor used."

…and we all know how that turned out. *Blackout!*

My surgeon met me in the recovery room. "Everything went well," he said. "You actually had *three* hernias." I always was an overachiever.

In a regular room, nurses hooked me up to IVs through which I received antibiotics, anti-inflammatories, hydration, and low doses of pain medication. Another tube drained my incision. A therapist periodically arrived to administer respiratory treatments. As I remained on my back, the thought that the surgery was performed as an outpatient procedure in the United States stupefied me. Which was the better healthcare system?

Although my doctor and his assistant spoke perfect English, most staff did not. Basic French got me through menus and markets. Hospital and medical terms proved challenging. My roommate and his wife, an older working-class couple, were polite. But they didn't inspire intriguing characters. They spoke only French, a fact that precluded me from adapting their story. I understood less than a quarter of their conversation. Although I explained to the wife that Jim neither spoke nor understood French, she kept trying to converse with him.

The nurses, pleasant and proficient, didn't speak English. Charts weren't kept in patient rooms, nor were names exchanged as in American hospitals. My imagination ran wild. Would they mix me up with another patient? Could I be sedated and awaken missing a leg? Pain medications and sleeping pills ended my fretting.

My surgeon visited early next morning. "You're doing fine."

"So, I can go home?"

He smiled. "Yes, but only after my assistant comes. He'll review the next steps."

"How much longer…er…I mean, when can I expect him?"

He looked at his watch. "About an hour from now."

An hour! Yippee! Homeward bound. I texted Jim at work, putting him on standby to pick me up.

Three hours passed. Still no assistant. I kept Jim updated. Thirty minutes later, three nurses arrived. "Here to change your bedding and hospital gown."

"*Pas necessaire,* no need," I replied with a smile. "*Je vais bientôt.* I'm leaving soon."

The nurses shot me a perplexed look. One pulled some paper from her pocket. Shaking her head, she said, "*Aujourd'hui?* You think you're leaving today?"

I nodded. "*Oui. Maintenant!*"

She offered a condescending smile. "*Désolée,* sorry. That's not on our paperwork."

C'est ridicule! That's ridiculous! Panic set in. With a fading phone battery, I quickly texted Jim: "May need your help. They don't know I'm leaving."

Wasn't this a *Twilight Zone* episode? Suppressing the anxiety in my tone, I mustered my finest accent as I addressed the nurse. "*Je pense que c'est necessaire appeler le docteur.*" Sensing my duress and—perhaps, my intent to flee IVs, drain tube, dressing gown, and all—the nurses humored me. Two left the room. The remaining nurse readied me for departure.

Another hour and one-half passed before the assistant showed up. I had an urge to scream, "Where the hell were you?" But reason prevailed. I wanted my freedom and didn't want to bust a stitch.

Having called my doctor's office, Jim arrived on the heels of the assistant.

I gasped. "Boy am I glad to see you. Take me home!"

As I changed and Jim pulled my things together, he recounted his conversation with the front desk. After reviewing my account, they alerted him to a mix-up in the precertification process. "This might cost you," they had said with pained expression. Steeped in American prices, Jim braced for bad news. "Could be as much as…a thousand euros," they added timidly. He almost burst into laughter. Obviously, they had no conception of American hospital sticker shock. He pulled out his credit card to pay, but they waved him off. "Go, get your husband home. We'll catch up with you. In all likelihood, you'll only owe a fraction." His jaw dropped. On a hunch, he asked what the charge would have been for a private room. "About fifty euros," was the reply. Again, which is the better healthcare system?

Overall, my experience was excellent. The bulge in my groin and my chronic pain were gone. The surgeon and nursing staff were professional. Care and treatment, as they should, took precedence over cost. On the downside, no Jello and no wheelchair ride to the curb. After I dressed, Jim walked me down the hall. A farewell wave to nursing staff, chatting away in their lounge, went unnoticed. Without as much as an au revoir, I was out the door, in our car, and on the road to recovery.

With the ordeal behind me, I called my decision to seek treatment timely. With rolled eyes and a scoff, Jim called it sheer dumb luck that my abdomen wall held for so long. That's the beauty of a healthy relationship—a good mix of candor, compassion, and humor. And while I joked that three hernias proved that in our marriage I did the heavy lifting, Jim replied that they were merely signs of a weak membrane.

Jim is the world's best cheerleader. Lucky me. For when it comes to doctors and hospitals, he needs enough bravery for the two of us.

Chapter 16

With my hernias repaired, angst surrendered to pain-free days and restful slumber. Recovery, as the surgeon predicted, was swift. I didn't require a single painkiller. The double incisions near my navel were stitched and bandaged. Until my January appointment to remove the sutures, the area needed to be cleaned, inspected, and dressed on a regular basis. Understanding my innate queasiness with anything medical, Jim played nurse.

"Aren't you curious?" he asked, inspecting my stomach.

"I'm not interested in gaping wounds," I replied, my eyes directed to the ceiling.

"Sweetie, what you call gaping wounds are two tiny pinpricks."

"I don't care. I'm not looking...not until you replace the bandage."

Other than stitches and minor lifting restrictions, I felt fine. I had yet another reason to celebrate. After years of effort including rewrites, edits, title changes, and a good share of hand-wringing, my second novel launched. My publisher sent notice of the book's release while I rested in the hospital.

Publication gave me great satisfaction. The book represented a tangible end to a fluid process, physical evidence of my reinvented self, and a healthy boost to my self-esteem. For authors, such milestones are few and far between. Writing isn't a sprint; it's a marathon. The idea for the story had come to me five years earlier as Jim and I vacationed on the Greek isle of Mykonos. Now, four years after writing the first chapter, I crossed the finish line. The list of emotions was long. Elation, validation, hope, and pride were simply the few at the top. For a moment, those at the bottom, self-doubt, disappointment, dejection, and frustration scattered to the margins.

Jim grinned when I shared the news. "I'm so proud of you."

He remained my biggest fan. His encouragement and faith in my abilities kept me writing even when self-doubt and frustration blocked my path. In a small way, I viewed the new book as my contribution to our relationship. It might not supplement our family finances, but it represented a joint investment nonetheless. Each new book represented a smidgen of hope that my writing might reach a larger audience.

In that regard, the timing was terrible. Launches close to Christmas get lost in holiday noise. Unfortunately, my publisher had dropped the ball and delayed the editing. As an independent author, I simply had no choice but to adapt. Lowering expectations regarding promotional opportunities also was necessary. Living in Brussels complicated such efforts. My target market was American. The novel *Jell-O and Jackie O* was a coming-of-age story of a middle-class suburban boy who discovers Jackie Kennedy on the cover of *Life* magazine just as his flamboyant aunt, a prodigal daughter of sorts, returns to the family fold. Although Jackie O was an international icon, Jello was a uniquely American dessert. Unlike my debut novel, this one would have no launch party or local selling blitz. The celebration would be small and private. None of that, however, dampened my enthusiasm. I eagerly updated multiple social media platforms with news of the book. Congratulatory notes and good wishes poured in. First reviews were encouraging.

Arrival of the Christmas season further buoyed my soaring spirits. Despite the absence of snow, Brussels embraced the holiday. From late November to New Year's Eve, a sprawling market extended from the Grand Place to the Bourse to Place Sainte-Catherine and the Marché aux Poissons. In the shadow of the Black Tower and above the ruins of a Franciscan convent, both dating to the thirteenth century, scores of stalls offered food, beverages, and a variety of gifts and trinkets. Aromas of candied almonds, roasted chestnuts, mulled wine, and savories such as *tartiflette* and sausages swirled in the chilly air. The vibrant market drew a colorful crowd. Jim and I especially enjoyed watching the whimsical carousel on which grinning children squealed atop giant squid, flying ostriches, bobbing seahorses, and other exotic creatures. The spectacular contraption looked as if it were ripped from the pages of a fairy tale.

Greeting cards flew across the Atlantic in both directions. Each envelope from the United States represented a precious piece of home. Our cards were holiday scenes of the Grand Place. Writing personal notes and carrying addressed envelopes to the post office became a labor of love. Far from friends and family, I reveled in a holiday tradition that kept us connected.

Our Christmas tree became a neighborhood spectacle. Passersby on Rue d'Ecosse stopped to peer through our windows. Decorated with tiny white lights, gold ribbons, shimmering tinsel, and shiny ornaments, the huge tree invited admiration. Entire families shaded their eyes and pressed their noses to the glass for a better look. They didn't notice us working at the desk or sitting on the sofa, or simply didn't care. The attention pleased us, as if we were suddenly part of the neighborhood, sharing good cheer and brightening the holiday. For months afterward, neighborhood regulars commented about the tree.

As the holiday spirit swept me up, news articles began appearing on the Internet for the seventieth anniversary of the Battle of the Bulge. The battle, one the most famous in American military history, took place in eastern Belgium in December 1944. As a student of history and son of a proud veteran, I appreciated the event's significance. As an American living in Belgium, the topic seemed fitting for a Christmas blog. To commemorate the battle and honor my patriotic father, I penned a piece. The post, "Nuts & Nutcrackers, Christmas in Belgium," can be found in the appendix.

One week before Christmas, Jim and I grabbed coffee from

Starbucks and took seats on its outdoor terrace within the crowded Grand Place. The loud din of spectators softened to a droning murmur as the opening notes of Borodin's Polovtsian Dance plunked through the night air. The familiar melody rose in volume, echoing off the fifteenth-century town hall and gilded facades of the gabled guildhalls dating from the seventeenth century. Accompanying the music, a light show illuminated the magnificent square in hues of green, red, pink, blue, and green. A towering Christmas tree glittered in the center of the grand square.

Jim scooted closer to me on the bench. "This is amazing," he whispered. "And we're right here to enjoy it."

Tears welled in my eyes. The breathtaking spectacle triggered an emotional surge. "I know it sounds funny," I replied, "but I feel my parents' presence."

Jim squeezed my hand. Unlike the numbing fog of depression that had blanketed me throughout autumn, my parents' love, warmth, and security enveloped me as music reverberated through the square. *If only they were alive to see my life.*

A few days before Christmas, a box arrived. Ripping it open, I found copies of my new book. "Beautiful!" I muttered aloud. The cover, which Jim and I had helped design, exceeded my expectations. An eager-eyed boy in the back seat of a cherry-red Mustang convertible gazes adoringly at the carefree driver, his flamboyant Aunt Ver who doubles in his mind as Jackie O. With my book in hand, doubts, insecurities, and fears related to my writing melted away. In that moment, I felt as successful as any *New York Times* best-selling author.

Most of our acquaintances, including my writer friends, left the city for Christmas. In Chicago, Jim and I had made room at our holiday table for those away from family. Since we didn't receive invitations from European friends, we improvised, inviting our neighbor Barbara for Christmas. With the exception of her six cats, she was alone. Her husband, a diplomat who worked for the European Commission, had returned to Slovenia to spend the holiday with his aging parents. Barbara's commitment to her furry friends kept her tethered to Brussels. She was happy to be invited, especially with my promise of holiday cocktails.

She replied to my invitation with an impish grin. "Manhattans? Fantastic."

In addition to Barbara, we had another guest—Puhi the cat. By this time, there was no keeping the clownish feline out of the house. From his perch on the garden wall, he watched, waiting for me to appear in the kitchen window. Bolting into our garden, he stood on his hind legs peering in, meowing and scratching the door until we let him in. The gray, tan, and black tabby continued to ignore our Christmas decorations and showed no interest in climbing the tree. Puhi melded into our family. Even Sadie grew accustomed to his visits.

Christmas dinner began with colorful cocktails, manhattans for Barbara and me and a cosmo for Jim. In homage to Jim's and my upbringings, I prepared a traditional Polish meal, substituting, as a treat for Jim, beef for ham. Although I had ordered prime rib from the butcher, something got lost in translation. Unwrapping the package, I found a simple roast, a tough one at that. Sauerkraut, fruit-filled pierogi, and mashed potatoes satisfied Barbara's vegetarian diet. For dessert, we served a chocolate Yule log, a *bûche de Noël*.

At the end of the evening, Barbara gave us warm hugs and the three cheek kisses customary in Brussels. "*Merci*. How can I ever thank you? The Arkenbergs, including lovely Sadie, made my Christmas very special. Everything was delicious. And oh, those manhattans," she added with a giggle. She gazed under the tree to her snoozing cat. "Come on, Puhi. Time to go home to number 6."

I couldn't let our wonderful Christmas pass without a blog post, a holiday card to friends and family.

Merry Christmas from Europe

Shiny ornaments, glossy wrapping paper tied with shimmering ribbons, greeting cards filled with friendship and love. Familiar songs that stroke the strings of our hearts, beautiful carols that awe and inspire, shrieks of delighted children, voices of those we hold dear. Delicious meals painstakingly prepared with love. The sights, sounds, and mouthwatering aromas of Christmas are what we remember, what we carry in our hearts....

Christmas helps us recall the magic of love and the wonders of our amazing world. But Christmas is there every day of the year—it's merely a bit harder to spot without twinkling lights, brightly wrapped packages, squeals of joy, and lilting melodies of our youth. The spirit of Christmas is in the smiles of strangers, the kindness we impart to others, and the warm embrace of those we hold dear....

From our new home in Brussels, Jim, Sadie, and I wish you all a very Merry Christmas! Friends, family, and all who extend to us great kindness truly make ours *A Wonderful Life!*

———— ((●)) ————

Two days after Christmas, we awoke to gray skies and more than a mild dusting of snow. Our garden assumed a seasonal serenity. Fresh white powder on evergreens and shrubs looked like a classic snow-globe scene. Although less than an inch, the accumulation represented more snow than had fallen during the entire prior winter.

As I let Sadie out for her morning constitution, I inhaled crisp, clean air. "Reminds me of our yard back home."

"It's pretty," Jim replied. "I'll give you that. But I'm not a fan."

I laughed. "Oh, come on. By Chicago standards, it's nothing."

"All the better for our drive."

Chilly air nipped our faces as Jim and I lifted Sadie into the back seat of the Audi just before 6:00 a.m. We were both excited at the prospect of a rendezvous with good friends from Paris in Annecy, a holiday destination in the French Alps. Jim even agreed to make an exception to his road-trip parameters. He loathed being behind the wheel for more than four and one-half hours. We usually split the driving chores, but the car's standard transmission put the entire burden on him. Perhaps holiday spirit inspired Jim to accept the long drive.

I mustered a cheery tone. "GPS says seven hours."

Jim sneered. "Closer to seven and a half."

"Fair enough, but we should get to Annecy in time for a nice lunch." Jim's dour expression informed me that he wasn't convinced. "Look," I added, holding up a baggie, "I've brought snacks."

Without turning, Jim extended his arm. "Hand me a cookie."

The early Saturday hour and the fact that many foreign residents were away on holiday allowed for an easy drive out of central Brussels. GPS guided us east toward the Ardennes, the same densely forested hills and low mountains of eastern Belgium and Luxembourg where seventy years earlier American troops repulsed Nazis in the Battle of the Bulge.

I studied our route. After a short transit through Luxembourg, our drive would take us south into France past the French cities of Metz, Nancy, and Dijon. Near the town of Mâcon, our path turned east toward Geneva, Switzerland, before the short final leg south to Annecy. Before Annecy, the terrain became irregular. Near the Italian border, mountains reached greater heights. In this picturesque setting were the French ski resorts that hosted prior winter Olympics—Chamonix in 1924, Grenoble in 1968, and Albertville in 1992.

"Can't wait to see the Alps," I said. "Bet they're stunning after the snowstorm."

My exuberance made him smile. "This will be fun."

An Alpine holiday was a treat, a combination of romance, adventure, and friendly camaraderie. And with Sadie in the back seat, our little family was together. An hour into our drive, Jim nodded to the windshield. White, open fields and banks of trees rolled onto the horizon. "Lot more snow than in Brussels."

"It's beautiful." I glanced to the car's tracker gage. Our elevation was a thousand feet higher than Brussels. "Doesn't look too bad for driving, though."

A few minutes later, our speed slowed.

"Hmm," Jim muttered. "Red lights ahead."

We soon came to a complete stop along with hundreds of other cars as far as the eye could see. We were both used to Chicago traffic where clogged roadways were more the rule than the exception. This looked far worse.

I pointed out the front. "That's not a good sign." Men exited vehicles to relieve themselves in ditches. Obviously, they'd been parked for a long time. Thirty more minutes passed without our advancing a single inch.

"Odd," Jim said. "The other side of the highway is empty. Not a single car."

We soon learned why. A battalion of plows, side by side, advanced up the deserted roadway in the wrong direction. Clearing snow from the empty motorway, they disappeared over the forward horizon.

I shook my head. "D'ya suppose those are the only snowplows in Belgium?"

"Don't doubt it," Jim replied. "Might explain why we're not moving."

We surmised that the same plows clearing the westbound lanes were now somewhere far ahead of us, backtracking to clear our eastbound roadway.

"Plow drivers probably don't start work until eight in the morning," I said, adding a sarcastic chuckle. Jim groaned in sympathy with my frustration and anger.

On the westbound motorway, a trickle of cars soon became a steady flow. Occupants stared across the median at our clogged roadway.

Their sympathetic expressions should have been a clue as to our fate. Another thirty minutes passed before we moved again.

With the roadway clear, traffic flowed swiftly through Luxembourg into France. "What the…"

"What's wrong?" Jim asked.

"Must be a mistake…"

"What is?"

I motioned toward the GPS. "Our drive time just adjusted upward."

"How much?"

"Four and a half hours. Says we'll arrive at 5 p.m."

Jim shrugged. "Must be a mistake. With that snowplow stunt we've lost at most an hour."

With a sinking feeling in my stomach, I kept my eyes glued to the GPS. Somewhere around Metz, the drive time spiked again. I gasped. "Now it says 11 p.m."

Jim glanced at the GPS. "That can't be right. That would mean a…"

"Seventeen-hour drive." I cringed. *Disaster!* "Impossible, right?" *Oh God, I hope so.* With Jim's dislike of driving, I didn't know which would give out first—his patience or my bag of snacks.

We both dismissed the GPS estimate as a mechanical glitch or, at worst, the result of a bad car accident on the road ahead that would soon clear and lower the expected drive time. Indeed, our estimated arrival time did fluctuate wildly. However, it never dropped below 7 p.m., meaning, at best, a thirteen-hour journey. That was six hours more than planned. Sadie remained patient, Jim too. But how much longer would either of them tolerate being cooped up in the car? We stopped at a service oasis. After trips to the toilet and purchases of coffee and water, the three of us climbed back into the Audi.

Halfway through our journey, somewhere between Nancy and Dijon, traffic slowed. Unlike our earlier experience, these were intermittent stops. Our progress, however, was never more than a crawl. Tired and cranky, we plodded forward.

We finally pulled into Annecy around 8:30 at night. Jim had been behind the wheel for fourteen and one-half hours, ten more than he preferred and seven more than the scheduled journey. Our friends had already arrived. Although they had hit traffic just outside Paris, they were locals, and knowing the back roads and detours kept them from the worst of the clogged motorways.

Apparently, the snow that dusted Brussels intensified over the Alps. The first major storm of the winter season hit on a peak travel day. Hundreds of thousands of holiday travelers made their way to Alpine ski resorts. From across Europe, a solid line of cars created gridlock as they neared the Alps. Drivers clogged roadways, stopping to install tire chains for the climb to higher elevations. Tens of thousands of cars and their passengers spent the night in gas stations and rest areas. Despite our ordeal, we considered ourselves lucky to get through, especially with Sadie.

Jim was exhausted, frustrated, and hungry—rightfully so. But we didn't let the miserable journey ruin our holiday. In a way, the drive was a perfect metaphor for the first year of our expat experience.

With the Alps as stunning backdrop, Annecy sits at the northern end of a crystal-clear lake that shares its name. With origins dating to the Romans, the old town is a medieval masterpiece. A river and canals meander through the town center. A twelfth-century castle sitting on an island in the middle of the river gives the town a fairy-tale feel.

After a good night's sleep, we lunched at a restaurant with a sweeping vista of town, lake, and mountains dusted with snow. A delicious and beautifully presented multicourse meal proved the restaurant worthy of its Michelin Star. A dinner of fondue, one of the region's signature dishes, was a scrumptious mixture of Comte, Gruyère, and Beaufort cheeses. A market in the heart of the cobblestoned old town featured cheeses, cured sausages known as *saucisson*, and sweets.

As I paid for some cheese, Jim put his arm around me. "Sweetie, would you like a vinshod?"

I scrunched my face. "Huh?"

"A vinshod. It smells good."

"Show me." Following his extended arm to a wine stand, I laughed. "You mean *vin chaud*."

He scrunched his face. "Huh?"

"Your vinshod is pronounced *vin chaud*, hot wine."

"Oh brother! Vanshow," he replied exaggerating my French accent.

"Whatever you call it, *oui*, let's get *deux*." I held up two fingers to avoid any more confusion. Pulling him to the stall to buy two glasses of warm, mulled wine, I laughed with him about his French: vinshod, wheat hour, and the ongoing challenge with locals not understanding his pronunciation of "Saint-Gilles" and "Rue d'Ecosse."

Those lovely few days spent with good friends amid spectacular scenery were therapeutic. Fresh mountain air, good food, fine wine, and healthy bouts of laughter capped off one of the most eventful years of our life together.

After returning to Brussels, a pleasantly uneventful drive, I blogged about our gastronomic experience. The post, "Comfort Food, Alpine Style," can be found in the appendix.

We spent New Year's Eve quietly at home. As usual we were in bed by midnight. Somewhere beyond our closed curtains, the sound of fireworks reverberated through the city. Sadie snoozed on the bedroom floor.

I turned to kiss Jim. "Happy New Year, sweetie."

"Happy New Year, my love."

"Certainly has been an amazing year. Wasn't always easy…but we made it."

"We sure did," he replied.

"Think next year will be just as good?"

Jim squeezed my hand. "Let's hope so."

I chuckled. "Maybe you'll even learn a little French…vinshod, wheat hour, Rue—"

Jim interrupted my litany with merciless tickles until we embraced in a fit of giggles.

III

New Growth:
Our Second Year Begins

*The last step in a successful transplant process is patience!
In most cases, it takes a year or so for trees to shake off
transplant shock.* (blog.davey.com)

Chapter 17

The blank slate of a new year offered great promise: a chance to move beyond failure, dismiss guilt of procrastination, and gaze into the future even if those forward-looking glasses were tinted rose.

Surviving our rookie year gave us hope that we were on track to become seasoned expats. We gradually melded into the continent's rich and vibrant culture. If Jim worked in Europe for five years, he could apply for permanent residency. That status included full employment rights within the European Union. The idea of unbridled possibilities filled us with optimism. For me, new, exciting countries to inspire my writing. For Jim, professionally rewarding companies for which to work.

Were prospects of a bright future merely a mirage, hopes inflated by an adrenaline surge of having survived our first year as well as the halo of holiday optimism? Or had our transplanted roots burrowed deep enough to instill confidence that we could flourish in our adopted home?

Despite first-year hiccups, Jim and I had moved beyond simple survival mode. In many ways, we thrived. Having accepted the fact that duplicating an extensive social network such as the one we enjoyed in Chicago was unlikely, we nurtured friendships with couples, straight and gay. Seeing other same-sex couples rooted and prospering in Brussels comforted us. Among these were Philippe and Laurent, connections through Jim's work colleague. The good-natured couple provided glimpses into the guarded world of native Belgians.

New friendships replaced those of writer colleagues who left Brussels or moved on to other pursuits. Klavs, a tall, affable, gay Dane was a writer about my age. An avid rower, he worked for the Council, the policymaking body of the EU. We began meeting monthly for lunch. Usually choosing a restaurant near the EU campus, Klavs tutored me in the intricacies of EU bureaucracy. Our conversations were lively, stimulating, and fun, covering an array of topics. Klavs grew most animated when discussing his writing. Whimsical fairy tales and stories of two elderly South African lesbians were among his pet projects.

At the same time, I got closer to our neighbor at number 6, a relationship nurtured by our mutual fondness for Puhi. Barbara had the air and giggle of a lovable imp. Her small, blue Mazda convertible complemented her free-spirited personality. Her husband, the Slovenian diplomat, worked long hours. When Jim traveled on business, Barbara and I scheduled dinner at a Thai restaurant on nearby Chaussée de Charleroi. An extensive menu satisfied her vegetarian lifestyle and allowed me to sample an exotic cuisine that Jim shunned.

Passion for animals drove Barbara's diet. Sensing my sympathies, she tried various means to influence me. These included emailing stories about the intelligence of pigs, photos of adorable lambs, and examples of environmental damage caused by beef production. Her conversion efforts weren't successful, but I admired her for them nonetheless. Jim's unyielding love of meat rendered him a lost cause. Barbara's advocacy knew no bounds. For an entire week, she scoured a local forest in the middle of the night, flashlight in hand, to search for a missing cat. She traveled to nearby countries rescuing dogs from high-kill shelters by bringing them into her extensive foster network. She sponsored dogs in Serbia. The possibility that donations intended to feed Balkan boxers might have lined the pockets of a Belgrade conman never entered her generous mind.

Domestic management of her six cats fascinated me. To keep peace among her felines, two of which were antisocial, she created a complex schedule that gave the two feral cats access to the garden. Sleeping on the living room sofa in order to shuttle cats in and out of closed rooms throughout the night was merely one sacrifice that showed her devotion. When I called her crazy, she simply giggled. Kind, funny, and idiosyncratic, the Slovenian sprite was the perfect guest for cocktails, tea, and neighborly chitchat. Socializing with a European who held positive views of Americans was refreshing. "Americans are always so nice," she said. "They're so open about everything." She also validated my observations about aloof locals. "Want to know why the Belge don't invite you into their homes?" she asked with mischievous grin. "Because their houses are filthy, that's why."

I burst into laughter at the notion that sloppy housekeeping might be the source of unsociable Belgian behavior. Humor continued to be my preferred device to cope with the cold detachment of locals. In that regard, Puhi's arrival into our lives was serendipitous. His antics, lovable nature, and persistence in befriending us brought smiles to our hearts.

Puhi, our Intrepid Visitor

Although we hadn't purchased a litter box or permanent food dish, the green-eyed tiger cat made daily visits. I usually kept the door to our garden open, which meant Puhi came and went as he pleased. His tentative visits grew more confident. He never failed to cheer me up. Our ever-patient Sadie probably cringed, especially when she sustained the cat's occasional swat to her bushy, gold tail. Most evenings when Jim's key rattled our front-door lock, Puhi took a seat beside Sadie in our entryway to await his entrance. After dinner, Puhi jumped onto the couch between Jim and me. The Scottish wool throw on which he sprawled became known as "Puhi's blanket." When we switched off the TV and turned out the lights, Puhi exited into the garden, but usually not without a bit of prodding. For his final nightly farewell, Puhi wandered down to the ledge outside our bedroom window.

"Good night, Puhi," we said, drawing the curtains. "See you tomorrow."

Absent rain, a day didn't pass without that ritual. As our second year began, the domestic routine at Rue d'Ecosse 4 purred like a kitten. To commemorate our first anniversary, I created a blog post that included scores of photos culled from our rookie year.

Measuring Our First Brussels Year

Last January, we packed away our old life and moved to Europe....The expat experience can be daunting, even depressing at times, but mostly it's exhilarating. We consider ourselves lucky to have this chance to enrich our lives....

But how best to measure our first year? Broadway fans know one answer: 525,600 minutes. That calculation, however, seems bland and, ironically, lifeless. What one does with those minutes is what matters.

We could measure our annual consumption of mussels, *pommes frites,* chocolates, beer, roasted chickens, waffles,

etc...The calculation would reveal a staggering caloric intake....
Selfies might capture our year. Oxford Dictionary named
"selfie" its 2013 Word of the Year. The following year brought
the selfie stick, an annoying device now seen regularly in the
Grand Place.

We could count adventures.

Another yardstick might be the best of all. A cavalcade of
houseguests and visitors popped into Brussels....Houseguests
numbered twenty-five, spread out among fourteen separate
visits....

Yes, time spent with family and friends, old and new, is the
best way to measure a year. Given the number of people we
hosted or with whom we connected during our first twelve
months in Belgium, I'd say Jim, Sadie, and I had an exceptional
525,600 minutes. We're looking forward to an even better
second year in Belgium.

***

A second year in Brussels didn't mean that our honeymoon was
over. However, the possibility of permanent residency brought practical concerns.

"If we're going to remain in Brussels," I said to Jim, "I may as well
learn the language." Although I communicated basic needs adequate-
ly, responses from strangers delivered in rapid-fire French stymied
me. *Please limit your reply to the smattering of words I actually know,* I
thought, glaring blank-faced at the speaker.

"Wish I could do the same," Jim replied. "I simply don't have the
time."

He learned one phrase: *Parlez-vous anglais?* Do you speak English?
Purely rhetorical, Jim continued in English even if the response he got
was "*Non.*"

"They know English all right," he said as justification. "They only *said* they didn't." Even he laughed at his stilted logic, a sign of growing frustration with his inability to communicate. He had proficiency in Spanish. Unfortunately, that hadn't been very valuable in Belgium since the sixteenth-century court of Hapsburg Emperor Charles V. "If we'd been posted to Madrid," Jim lamented, "I'd be fluent by now." Humoring him, I merely nodded.

Although many expat friends had employers who supported language enculturation with time off and financial reimbursement, responsibility for adapting to Belgian life was exclusively ours. In mid-January, I visited the Alliance Française, an organization that promoted French language and culture around the world. A receptionist gave me course and fee schedules and instructed me to take an online placement test. Courses were pricey, but we considered them an investment in our expat future.

Passing out of the beginner course, I found a class starting in March. Timing was perfect. In late January, I was flying to Lisbon to join Jim at the conclusion of a leadership meeting. In February, we planned a London weekend to offer condolences to a friend whose mother had recently died. Although every trip was reviewed against our budget, such jaunts made us sound and, to be fair, feel like posh jet-setters.

In fact, at Jim's suggestion we compiled a list of places to visit before our posting ended. "I'd like to finish off Scandinavia," I said. "Last year Copenhagen, this year Stockholm. Perhaps Norway next year. Iceland and Finland would be good too." *What a life!*

To us, Brussels was home. Besides language courses and travel wish lists, we spoke of new furniture and draperies for the apartment. Taking a long view, Jim looked at real estate. Although two years remained on our lease, Jim dragged me to brokerage windows to review residential listings.

"When our lease runs out, where do you want to move?" he asked. "You always say you like Ixelles and Uccle."

I offered a stock answer. "I love our apartment. Location and garden are perfect. I can walk anywhere. Sadie likes it, and of course there's Puhi to consider."

Our apartment didn't only feel like home, in my mind it *was* home—perhaps not perfect, but comfortable and reflective of our personalities. We took great pride in it. So much so that a steady deterioration in common-area upkeep distressed us. The building's cleaning woman had virtually disappeared. My test of a candy wrapper placed on the staircase drew gentle ribbing from Jim. But the cellophane remained untouched for weeks.

Vindicated, I texted the building manager. Perpetually tanned, fur-vested, and adorned with wrist bangles, the stylish blonde hadn't proved responsive in our first year. After several texts, Madame Goosen finally telephoned. As was our protocol, she spoke to me in broken English and I replied in broken French. That system worked most of the time.

"I don't understand," Madame Goosen said over the phone.

"The foyer is dirty," I replied, uncertain whether she misunderstood my French or my message. "I can't tell you when I last saw Anna. At least six months, maybe longer."

"That's what confuses me," she replied. "Can you hold on?"

After a couple of minutes, she returned to the phone. "I have Anna on the other line." *This ought to be good.* "Claims she was there last week. Every week as a matter of fact."

Spontaneous laughter burst from my mouth. I may have even snorted before describing my candy wrapper test. I offered to text several time-stamped photos as proof.

"Hmm. Okay." Madame Goosen apologized, said goodbye, and promised to resolve the issue. Her tone suggested an epiphany: Anna had duped her.

Presenting the Evidence

Oh boy, I can't wait to tell Jim. We had our own history with Anna. When we moved in, we hired her as a housecleaner. She already cleaned the common area and had keys to the building. More significantly, she was Madame Goosen's personal cleaning lady. With such a rock-solid reference, we even gave her a key to our apartment. Jim was pleased that he could communicate with her in Spanish, a language close to her native Portuguese. Anna was pleasant, her cleaning adequate.

"If you visit the States," she said to me on one of her first workdays, "could you buy me an iPhone? I pay you. They're so much cheaper there."

"Sure, sure," I replied, though I had no intention of getting into the electronics business.

Soon I began noticing things disappearing from the house: an outdoor chair cushion, then a potted flower from the garden. "I don't get it," I said to Jim. "Surely this stuff is too small for Anna to want, and of too little value to jeopardize her job."

He nodded. "It does seem absurd." We were in agreement. Missing items were too petty to mention.

Several weeks later, packing for a trip, I grabbed underwear from a drawer in our walk-in closet. The same drawer held a stash of U.S. dollars in large and small bills. I counted the money out of habit, though having only recently taken cash to insert in a birthday card, I knew the exact amount. "What the…" Instead of two fifties on top of the pile, only one remained, a clever way to conceal the theft. Timing of the discovery was fortunate, occurring before the first visit of a new house and pet sitter. Only one person had access—Anna. Our former iPhone conversation sprang to mind. In the same closet, I'd tucked away my old phone in its original box. The box was in its customary spot. As I grabbed it, my heart raced. It was too light. Opening the lid confirmed the obvious. Empty. *What else has she taken?*

We felt violated. We had put our trust in Anna. She had to go. But how? She had the key to our apartment. Whatever our action, she'd continue to have keys to the building to clean common areas. Her duties also gave her access to our private garden for a hose to wash down the foyer. For all we knew, she still cleaned Madame Goosen's house. How tight was their relationship?

I shook my head. "It's all terribly complicated."

Jim groaned. "I'd like to nail her ass, but we probably should tread lightly."

I sighed. "For all we know of Belgian law, our accusation could backfire. Anna probably would sue for defamation. End up retiring in our apartment…on the settlement money."

We hatched a plan.

The following Saturday, Anna's scheduled cleaning day, Jim and I remained at home. Normally, we left to give her space. Nervous, we felt as if *we* were the guilty ones.

"What should I tell her?" Jim asked. "I mean, the reason we're dismissing her. I could come up with some story—"

My glare interrupted his stream of consciousness. "Keep it simple. We don't owe her an explanation. 'Your services are no longer required' should suffice."

Jim reluctantly agreed. "Okay, but let's lock the closet before she gets here."

"Unless she's stupid, that'll send a clear message," I replied. "She'll know we're on to her. Maybe she'll panic, fear we'll call the police."

"We can only hope."

As Anna worked around us, we remained in our living room. Two hours passed. If she noticed the locked closet, she didn't let on. Wearing her coat and carrying a purse, she entered the living room. "Okay, all done."

Jim and I stood up. Anna eyed us cautiously. Our anxiety probably showed. "Great. Thanks. Here you go." Jim handed her the customary fee. "By the way," he added as she took the cash, "we're not going to require your services any longer."

Good boy! Short and simple. He glanced at me and I nodded my approval.

"Ahem," he added clearing his throat. "A friend of ours has a sister who needs the work…and…well…you know how that goes." *Oh brother! Where'd you pull that whopper?* "I'll take the key," he added quickly, thrusting out his hand.

Anna glanced from him to me as if deciding whether to say anything. With only a shrug, she dropped our key into Jim's outstretched palm.

Now, several months later and learning that Anna stopped cleaning the common areas, we assumed that she was embarrassed or too frightened to return to the scene of her crime. We never knew what happened to Anna although we speculated that she may have been connected to an eerie incident of a stranger making her way inside our apartment. Quietly reading on our sofa, I heard rattling at our front door shortly after houseguests departed for the afternoon. Neither they nor Jim were expected home. Sensing something amiss, I walked into our entryway. A strange woman stood inside our apartment. Initially dumbstruck at my appearance, she stammered a dubious excuse in French about looking for a friend, a former tenant. She apologized before making a hasty exit. I was more bemused than scared.

Soon after my conversation with Madame Goosen about the missing Anna, an elderly woman and her son assumed the building's cleaning chores. Jim and I cycled through three cleaning people before finding a capable and congenial Polish girl. However, we never again surrendered our house key.

On the professional front, Jim began year two confident that despite shifting priorities and a boss with whom he often sparred, he found a path forward. Writing continued to give me purpose. My latest book launched with great reviews, bolstering my confidence. After a brief hiatus fueled by the prior autumn's healthcare demands as well as bouts of depression, I found my way back to the BWC.

Our second year thus began with our roots burrowing deeper into our adopted soil.

Chapter 18

As we settled into our second year, two events dangerously close to Brussels shocked the world and shook our sense of security.

In early January, two brothers burst into the Paris offices of *Charlie Hebdo*, a French satirical magazine. In a torrent of automatic gunfire, they murdered twelve people and left nearly the same number injured. Video shot by an amateur photographer showed assailants shooting a policeman in the head at point-blank range. The brothers, born in Paris to Algerian immigrants, were the focus of a massive manhunt before being killed by police. During the manhunt, a co-conspirator attempted to aid the fugitives by initiating his own shooting spree in the French capital. Before being killed by police, the Paris-born man of Malian descent killed a policewoman, murdered four hostages in a Jewish market, and wounded several other people. The subsequent investigation led to Belgium. Authorities announced that the terrorists had obtained their weapons from an arms dealer in Charleroi, a Belgian city forty miles south of Brussels.

Ten days later, a news bulletin flashed across the television: "Belgian police involved in shootout with suspected terrorists in Verviers." Grabbing my computer, I searched the Internet. Two suspects were dead and a third arrested. According to media reports, the targets of the raid in the city sixty miles east of Brussels planned attacks on law enforcement. Across Belgium, authorities were on high alert. Police stations fortified against attack.

Both events spawned sensationalist headlines and news coverage around the globe: "Terrorists Strike Heart of Paris" read the *International New York Times;* "BARBARIC, Bloodbath in Paris," *The Daily Mail;* "Freedom Assassinated," *Le Figaro.* The phrase *Je Suis Charlie* became a symbol of solidarity, unified resistance against terrorism. Signs popped up in windows throughout our neighborhood. Friends and family sent messages of concern. Although appreciative of the notes, we were realists. The atrocities and plots that had occurred in Paris and Verviers could have happened anywhere. The United States had a growing litany of mass slaughter: an elementary school in Connecticut, a movie theater in Colorado, a college in Virginia, a navy yard in Washington, a military base in Texas. Jim and I didn't feel any less secure living in Europe. Future attacks were inevitable, *anywhere* on the globe.

The specter of terrorism didn't shackle our lives. In tandem with the launch of my second book, I oversaw the revision of my website with updated content and a new design and color scheme. I created an author Facebook page. My professional brand was coming together piece by piece. In addition, my first memoir took shape. By the end of March, I reached the midpoint of the manuscript. The BWC continued to play a major role in my professional and personal life. I began offering up my memoir for critique. The camaraderie, friendship, and professional enrichment of the group nurtured me.

Blogging proved another outlet for creativity. The free-form medium combined my love of storytelling and photography. Posts presented our adventures in an entertaining and informative manner. My blog became a personal archive, a digital journal preserving memories and capturing reflections of our exploits.

About this same time, Jim began to signal unexpecting news—the likelihood of our returning to the States sooner than planned. His comments were especially significant given his customary reticence concerning his job. Usually, he insulated me from worry and stress.

"Not sure how much longer I can hold on," he announced with a sigh. "Getting tired of battles, especially with my boss."

"It's not fair," I replied, "to move you here only to pull the rug out from under you."

The project that brought Jim to Europe had moved from corporate imperative to organizational elective. With central funding eliminated, any group wanting to adopt the common analytic platform had to allocate funds from its own budget. Jim's "mandate" crumbled along with his morale.

"Part of it's a test. I know that," he added. "But I'm whipped. If only something could go right."

"Your team," I said. "Be proud of your team. You pulled them together...even if your boss won't give you credit. *People* simply aren't something she understands."

A faint smile crossed his lips. The mention of his team usually lightened his mood. "I'd like to think I've made a difference with my team. Actually, I know I have." He shook his head. "I'm sorry, sweetie. Don't worry. I'm sure things will work out."

He didn't abandon all hope, not then. But even the gentlest drop of rain sends ripples across the glasslike surface of a lake. The horizon suddenly rushed forward. Instead of years, did we have only months in Brussels? What would become of our home? the lovely garden I restored? our travel plans? our new life and friends? And most importantly, Puhi the cat? The lovable imp staked a growing claim to my heart. I tried to shake the concerns from my head. I didn't want worrisome thoughts of immediate repatriation to consume me.

The temporary posting of Jim's boss to Australia put a bit of welcome distance between them, though they continued to butt heads remotely. Despite the stressful situation with his boss and a crazy workload, Jim volunteered to launch his company's European Pride, an advocacy group dedicated to European-based LGBTQ employees. Utilizing his strong organizational and leadership skills, Jim harnessed the talents of an enthusiastic team. He derived great fulfillment advocating for respect, dignity, and visibility for a maligned minority group still without legal protections in much of Eastern Europe. Failure to secure the prior expat posting because of legality issues surrounding recognition of our same-sex union also fueled his desire to drive change. Discrimination's sting is a powerful catalyst for action. Overhearing his conference calls led from home, I loved how his voice filled with confidence and great satisfaction.

"Normally it's always cut, cut, cut…people, projects, scope, timelines," he said to me, a sparkle in his eyes conveying contentment. "I love creating something for a change."

"I'm so proud of you," I replied, offering a hug.

Travel and visitors, a common thread of our first year, continued unabated. Away from work, Jim relaxed. He deserved to have fun. In early February we boarded Eurostar at Gare du Midi for the two-hour train journey to London's Saint Pancras. Our friend Gia met us at the station and walked us back to her Bloomsbury flat where we readied ourselves for afternoon tea. Visiting London and spending time with Gia were always special—afternoon tea, icing on the cake.

Our lovely weekend prompted a blog post. Here is an excerpt. The full post, a primer on afternoon tea, is included in the appendix.

Afternoon Tea & Friends

We set up the date weeks ago. The purpose, a condolence call. Dear friend Gia, an Italian woman living in London, lost her aged mother in November. Jim and I were in the States at the time and couldn't attend the funeral. But our friendship is precious and the occasion too important not to acknowledge. We proposed afternoon tea, the most sensible and civilized of all English traditions. Gia was keen on the idea….

Afternoon tea isn't about cost, venue, or even the eponymous brew from which it takes its name. An afternoon away from angry work tussles and monotonous routines is special—rejuvenation without massage, refreshment without alcohol, relaxation without sleep. Teetotalers aren't the only fans squeezing into uncomfortable chairs at low tables—champagne is also offered....

That's a traditional English tea—*never, never, never high tea.* But just as Lewis Carroll's mad tea party wasn't about tea, our afternoon wasn't really about cucumber sandwiches, scones and clotted cream, sweet cakes, or even tea. Much of life plays out below the surface in subtext, shorthand, and rich, unspoken passages. Our lovely Saturday at Brown's Hotel did the same. Conversation glided over a thirty-year landscape—shared experiences, personal joys, triumphs, tragedy, and loss. Discussion piloted toward the horizon—hopes, worries, dreams...friendships nurtured over time by admiration, respect, concern, and yes...tea!

⸺ ◦《●》◦ ⸺

Even with our plentiful hosting duties and my hours dedicated to writing, I made time to read. A good writer, as the saying goes, is a good reader. I devoured books at a rate of more than one per month. I kept returning to the pages of Tuchman's *Guns of August,* which my friend Phyllis had recommended during her visit the prior summer. The history of August 1914, the first month of World War I and Belgium's focal role in those pivotal first weeks, transfixed me. Not only did the events occur exactly one hundred years earlier, the scenes of battle and locations mentioned in the book surrounded us. I felt close to history, so close as a matter of fact that we could touch it.

As most students of history know, on August 4, 1914, two days after Belgium refused Berlin's request of unhindered transit through the country, Germany invaded. Violating Belgian neutrality, the Kaiser's

⸺ 182 ⸺

army crossed the border at Gemmenich and advanced to Liège, a fortified city on the strategic Meuse River. Two weeks later, the Germans were in Brussels. By month's end, they reached their ultimate goal, France. The opposing armies got bogged down in trenches. As a result, much of the Western Front remained in Belgium or just across the frontier in France. The conflict became a war of attrition, static lines, and a strategy of wearing down the enemy. Churchill observed, "The war will be ended by the exhaustion of nations rather than the victories of armies."

Fierce Belgian resistance surprised the invaders. Retaliation by the Kaiser's army cost hundreds of civilian lives and destroyed many Belgian towns including Leuven and its priceless library. Germany occupied Belgium for the duration of the war. Barely twenty-six years later, in May 1940, Germany invaded Belgium again, occupying the country for nearly five years.

Despite a history of war, invasion, and occupation, Belgium emerged in the late twentieth century as a first-world nation, its wealth, as ranked by per-capita GDP, among the world's top twenty-five countries (*USA Today*, November 2018). Headquartering NATO and institutions of the European Union, contemporary Belgium is a global center of peace and multinational cooperation.

With Tuchman's book fresh in my mind, an invitation to join an intimate tour of World War I battlefields excited me. The organizer was someone we met on our visit to Cologne's Christmas market. We looked forward to socializing with her and her husband again as well as meeting their friends including, coincidentally, another of our upstairs neighbors, a young American woman from the East Coast and her French fiancé.

The tour of Ypres and its environs occurred in February. Cold, gloomy weather seemed appropriate for visits to military cemeteries and battlefields. By contrast, our little company of sightseers was warm and friendly. Visits to three breweries complemented the primer in World War I history.

Our experience inspired a lengthy blog post. Here is an excerpt. The full post is included in the appendix.

Battlefields & Breweries of Flanders

Jim and I recently joined a small group of expats for a tour, aptly called Trenches & Trappistes. The itinerary featured two things for which Belgium is known—battlefields and beer. The country is awash in war history and sudsy splendor. An odd mix, perhaps, or maybe a perfect pairing.

Our day took us to the flat Flemish countryside, the area of Belgium abutting France and the North Sea. We joined our tour in Ypres (Ieper), ill-fated site of three World War I battles. Befuddled by French and Flemish pronunciations, English-speaking troops simply called the town "Wipers."

Ypres' current charm belies the fact that at war's end, the medieval town stood in ruins. Artillery reduced its thirteenth-century Cloth Hall to rubble. Between 1933 and 1967, pains-taking efforts restored the historic structure. It's now home to In Flanders Fields Museum, which offers a great introduc-tion to WWI. The town's Menin Gate honors more than fifty thousand Commonwealth Troops killed in the war whose final resting places are unknown. Each night...as it has for nearly 90 years, Last Post sounds for fallen warriors....

Our tour guide also promised beer. After steeping in the tolls of war, not one of us refused a sample of Belgium's best. I won't attempt to review the beers. Blogs too numerous to cite fill the Internet....We had time for three visits. With some alcohol contents drifting above 12%, that's probably all our systems could bear....By the end of our mellow afternoon, we were hopped up on hops. Not even a missed train for our two-hour journey back to Brussels deflated our buzz.

Over the centuries, Romans, French, Burgundians, Spanish,

English, Austrians, Germans, and others overran the land that comprises modern-day Belgium. With such an embattled history, who wouldn't drown sorrows with beer?

———— ((()) ————

As gray skies and drizzle of winter surrendered to gray skies and drizzle of spring, our situation remained unchanged. Jim and his boss waged their own war of attrition. For the time being, we remained entrenched in Brussels—no retreat. While each of us held out silent hope for some miracle advance, life went on.

In the middle of March, we trekked to our town hall for new resident cards. Among other uses, the photo ID, a national identity card, had to be presented for all medical services including pharmacy prescriptions. For Jim, the card represented a tangible symbol of accomplishing his goal of working overseas. However, the card reminded me of my subordinate status as a nonworking spouse. Belgium allowed me residency only in conjunction with my spouse. A qualified residency was only one irritant. Plenty of others had popped up during my expat journey to remind me of my inferior standing.

Visits to the town hall proved that regardless of jurisdiction or country, the wheels of bureaucracy turn at a snail's pace, a surly slug at that. Obtaining our original resident cards fifteen months earlier wasn't without incident—confusion, unanticipated paperwork, and a machine that couldn't read my fingerprints. As much as the idea tempted me, skipping the renewal process wasn't a good option. An expired card would create difficulties with healthcare, travel, and financial matters to name but a few.

I anticipated problems, but Jim sailed through the renewal process. After handing him a letter as proof of residency until his new card arrived, the clerk bid us good day.

My heart raced. Pushing my expired card and passport under the glass partition, I asked the stone-faced man in broken French, "And me? What about my renewal?"

"My husband," Jim added, responding to the clerk's glazed look. "He's my husband. His card expires as well. They should be together."

The man shrugged, appearing simultaneously perplexed and bothered, a look mastered by clerks behind glass partitions.

I pushed my card and passport deeper into his lair. "*S'il vous plaît.* Please."

Begrudgingly, he collected my documents signaling the futility of my request. As he compared ID photos with my actual face, I did my best to smile and appear calm. Then, with a technique used globally by counter clerks and agents, he banged away at a computer, his expression inscrutable. The agonizing wait lasted only moments, but it seemed hours.

The keyboard clacking stopped. The man slid my passport toward me. "*Non,* we have no record of your application."

My shoulders sagged; my stomach soured. *I knew there'd be problems.* "What does that mean?"

"Come back when you've applied."

"B...but how—"

Sensing the onset of a meltdown, Jim intervened. With his arm around my shoulders, he told the clerk and me that it was obviously a slip-up by his employer. He'd talk to his HR department for resolution.

"Come on, sweetie," he whispered to me. "Nothing more we can do here. I'm so sorry." His words and hug offered little comfort. I seethed with humiliation.

I held out my palm. "Fine. I'll take my card back, please."

The clerk bristled. "*Mais non,* I can't give it back to you. It's expired, no good."

I trudged out the town hall with my head bowed, a man without a Belgian identity, an outsider once again. The ominous warning to expat spouses by the German woman overheard in Starbucks came flooding back to me: "You're basically set *adrift* in an unfamiliar sea— no friends, no contacts, no lifelines. Practically *invisible.*"

Although my lapsed residency proved only temporary, the incident stung, hitting a nerve gnawed raw by prior incidents and primed by chronic bouts of loneliness and depression. Doubting my self-worth was a common theme of my despair. Whatever the trigger, shots to my confidence launched a series of desperate, existential questions that knew no bounds. Who was I? What was my purpose? Was being a writer a true calling or a foolish waste of time? Would my books ever find a larger audience? Would objective literary professionals ever validate my work?

My experience at the town hall was the catalyst for an emotionally laced blog. The hits, likes, and comments showed that the piece resonated with readers.

Invisible Man: The Tale of an Expat Spouse

"Perhaps to lose a sense of where you are implies the danger of losing a sense of who you are."

—Ralph Ellison, *Invisible Man*

When my spouse told me that his company wanted to transfer him to Europe, I knew what I was getting myself into—well, sort of. In retrospect, not really....

The first clue that I'd soon find myself an invisible man came when Jim and I visited a branch of ING bank to establish accounts and apply for euro-based credit cards. When we picked up the credit cards, the clerk handed us only one—for Jim. With no "local" income, I wasn't eligible. However, I had to sign a document granting the bank authority to seize my assets should Jim default. With the emotional stress of giving up my established life in Chicago, downsizing a lifetime of possessions, and the physical exhaustion of the actual move, I teared up. I was nobody. "Not to worry," the bank lady said. She'd be happy to authorize a pre-funded card such as the ones parents give college-aged children. In so many words, I told the bank what they could do with their *f'ING* card.

I brushed the experience aside. We were too busy setting up our new home, an incredible townhouse in the heart of Brussels. But the lease and all utilities were in Jim's name. Even our car has manual transmission that I can't drive. My distinct identity began to fade.

Finding new friends wasn't easy. Jim's company doesn't go in for camaraderie….As far as his company is concerned, I am invisible.

Walking on the streets of Brussels was yet another lesson in invisibility….

In the initial weeks and months after we left Chicago, we got cards and notes from friends and family….The flow of notes has slowed and, in some cases, disappeared altogether….Out of sight, out of mind? Invisible?…

I experienced the same phenomena dealing with our expired resident cards….The town hall had processed only Jim's paperwork. I didn't exist. With an expired resident card and renewal lost in a sea of bureaucratic red tape, I truly am *adrift*….

Jim and I are fortunate to live in a vibrant, European capital—culture, history, and exciting experiences within easy reach. Most people see only party balloons and glitter of our new life. I share blame because of my social media posts. In my defense, it's hard to post a picture of an invisible man. But behind the romantic stories, if you look really hard, you can see the blemishes. And it's not one thing, but many little things that wear you down, chipping away at your identity, confidence, and self-esteem, rendering you invisible.

Chapter 19

Spring arrived wrapped in winter's fraying cloak. Long stretches of drizzle, steely gloom, and nipping chill lingered as the old season slowly slipped away. Begrudgingly, rain surrendered its icy sting and metallic odor, softening into gentle, fresh-scented showers. Inching northward, the sun reacquainted itself with pasty faces and hands yearning for warmth. Celestial blue skies dotted with wisps of playful clouds floated above a lush green landscape in which new growth and florals perfumed the air.

Unlike Chicago, where summer kicks winter to the curb in the same week, Belgium treated us to a proper spring. Having never popped as much vitamin D as we did that dreary winter, Jim and I were anxious for finer weather and more hours of light. An open kitchen door brought fresh air, birdsong, and frequent visits from Puhi. Sadie sauntered out to the terrace with her velvet blanket to lounge in the sun, or maybe she did so to assert her dominion over the bold neighbor cat. With a bit of cleanup, our garden returned to its former splendor. Rhododendron and roses planted the prior summer bloomed in shades of pink, purple, and yellow.

In early spring, we traveled to Paris for a baking class. For Christmas, Jim had gifted me a lesson in creating French desserts. And as one good turn deserved another, I reciprocated with the same gift for him on Valentine's Day.

"Cool!" he exclaimed upon opening the card. "I love it."

"Way more fun to take the class together," I replied.

Nothing compares to an adventure shared with my best friend. Both of us subscribed to Audrey Hepburn's view that, "Paris is always a good idea." A short eighty-minute train ride made the charming French capital very accessible.

Our anticipation and excitement surged as the high-speed train approached Gare du Nord. The City of Light and Love promised a magical backdrop for a magnificent weekend. The *Charlie Hebdo* massacre was more than two months in the past. By all appearances, the city had bounced back from tragedy. Humanity is too resilient to collapse under the weight of terrorism.

After checking into a boutique hotel in the Marais, Jim and I made our way to the cooking school. From prior visits, we knew the central arrondissements well enough to stroll without a map. There are worse things in life than getting lost in Paris. Under the tutelage of Chef Pino, we prepared *and sampled* four desserts: Paris-Brest, a round of choux pastry resembling a bicycle wheel, sprinkled with almonds and filled with praline cream; an intoxicating Baba au Rum; a flourless chocolate tart; and a creamy Pear Charlotte. Buttery pastry dough, chocolate, whipped cream, and warm almonds produced heavenly aromas, surpassed only by the desserts' varied textures and rich flavors—a veritable culinary orgasm. Despite a fellow baker who peppered every reply with the same annoying phrase, "*Oui, absolument,*" we had a splendid time.

A visit to the recently reopened Picasso museum, shopping for eyeglass frames for me, and dinner with good friends rounded out our weekend.

As we settled into our seats for the quick trip home, I observed a subtle change in Jim's disposition—a dose of Sunday night dreads as our lovely weekend wilted in anticipation of Monday. I didn't miss the onset of workweek blues.

Mastering French Patisserie

I squeezed Jim's hand. "Thinking about work?"

"Sure. But it is what it is," he added with a forced smile.

"I know, but I wish things were better."

"It's fine."

"So you say, my love, so you say."

"Nothing I can't handle."

"I know. It's just that…well…" Lacking any better words of comfort, I rubbed his shoulders. "At least we'll always have Paris."

"*Oui, absolument*," he replied with a giggle-faced smirk. Laughter punctuated our conversation.

Paris provided Jim much-needed escape from emotional pressures and stress. Although his boss was eight thousand miles away, I felt her presence in our daily lives. I don't think Jim realized how much her spirit had invaded our home. With changes in funding priorities, Jim had to sell his initiative to reluctant organizations by convincing skeptical managers to reprioritize their own objectives and resources. Without central funding to induce cooperation, and absent a stick to compel participation, he felt powerless. Faced with constant conflict and uncertain of his group's future, he did his best to protect and motivate his team. He expended great energy to bolster their morale but had only me to do the same for him.

With head held high, Jim navigated the crosscurrents and choppy waters. From my perspective as a supportive and, admittedly, biased spouse, his boss set him up to fail. She neglected to understand, or simply chose not to see, the impact that turf wars, internal politics, and inconsistent messaging were having on him. She dismissed the shift in enterprise priorities as mere semantics. Yet when poaching his best people for other initiatives, she used the diminished status of Jim's project as justification. Quicksand offered more support.

In heated conversations, Jim and his boss volleyed back and forth, arguing whether the company had sufficient resources to support the initiative. With smoke-and-mirrors reasoning, his boss argued, "It's not that it's *not* in budget, it's simply no longer a distinct line item."

I ached for my husband. With growing frustration, I offered my opinion. "Oh brother. She can't have it both ways. Either your project's in the budget or it's not."

He was unable to get a straight and clear answer to that simple question.

I had experienced similar frustrations in my career. Years earlier, my company's Chief Operating Officer tasked me with changing the corporate culture. His earnest declaration rebuffed my healthy skepticism, "It's not a question of *if* this initiative succeeds, it *must* succeed for the airline to have a future. I rest my career on that." His clear and consistent directives sparked eager cooperation throughout the company. My work crested on this early enthusiasm. One short year later, however, when oil spiked to $147 per barrel, consultants were summoned. My budget and staff were slashed. Project justification became my focus as division heads were presented a choice: support cultural change efforts by sacrificing their own budgets or scuttle my work. Self-preservation was a forgone conclusion. The tilted process and expected result were symptoms of the very culture I'd been tasked to improve. Declarations, however earnest, can be deceiving.

Silos, fiefdoms, and political posturing are symptomatic of murky leadership. Instead of *leading* from the top with clear, consistent messaging, division heads expect mid-level managers to *influence* up, down, and sideways from the middle. That was my take on the situation in which Jim found himself.

Offering a sympathetic ear and frequent hugs, I kept our home a refuge from stress and worry. It was the least I could do. Despite turmoil and uncertainty, however, neither of us surrendered. Both of us hoped to remain in Brussels at least through the expiration of our initial lease term, a year and one-half in the future. Should Jim's current assignment end, I believed some astute division would snare him for another role. His European experience and leadership talent were too valuable to squander. Perhaps I suffered from clouded optimism.

Although I didn't abandon hope, I pulled back—slowly at first and, quite possibly, unaware of my actions. I abandoned the idea of French lessons and we postponed home improvement projects indefinitely. We adopted a "wait and see" strategy.

Jim began working from home more often. Although I welcomed his transition, I also understood the negative implication. He'd abandoned hope of garnering collaborative energy from office interactions. That was his way of pulling back. His launch of the company's LGBTQ group, however, remained a source of pride and motivation. Those efforts were his refuge.

My refuge continued to be my writing and our large walled garden. Yard and garden always meant tranquility and satisfaction, a place to make order out of chaos, create beauty, find peace, relish tangible accomplishment, and feel a deep connection. In addition to providing a bountiful metaphor for life and writing, gardening comforted body and soul. Dirtying my hands was therapeutic.

Dotting our garden with annuals meant trips to nurseries with Jim. Like bookstores and libraries, garden nurseries are a place where I can dawdle for hours. Learning from the prior summer's soggy failure, we shopped for hardy flowers and loamy potting soil that could withstand long rainy spells and cool conditions. Potted hydrangeas, New Guinea impatiens, and stalwart geraniums topped my list. I picked the varieties; Jim chose the colors. In addition to providing joyous and purposeful toil, my urban oasis gave me a place to read, write, and recharge, usually with Sadie at my feet and Puhi at my side.

With our garden taking shape, the prospect of returning to Holland's magnificent Keukenhof—acres of tulips and other spring flowers—pleased me. An organized coach trip with our Expat Club made the visit easy. Our neighbor Barbara accompanied us.

Spectacular Keukenhof

Hundreds of photos later, and buoyed by spectacular natural beauty, I wrote a blog post. It spoke of comparisons between writing and gardening. Here is an excerpt. The full post can be found in the appendix.

It's a Bulb's Life: Nature's Lessons for Life

Inspiration, sweat, patience—almost everything I've attempted in life comes down to those three ingredients. A combination of head, heart, and simple body mechanics. Inspiration is the seed, or for that matter bulb, of an idea or desire. Sweat is the effort—physical, mental, spiritual—that turns thought into action. Patience is the will, whether powered by passion, duty, faith, or sheer discipline, that keeps us marching forward.

This past Sunday, Jim and I visited Holland's famed Keukenhof where master planners and a small brigade of gardeners plant seven million bulbs annually. Each spring for eight short weeks, the gardens inspire and delight one million visitors. After their splendorous moment in the sun, bulbs are dug up and destroyed. The fleeting spring spectacle should remind us to seize upon our own brief moments in the sun—*carpe diem.*

On our first visit six years ago, I'd just begun my journey to become a writer. On this second visit, whiter at the temples and, hopefully, a bit wiser, parallels between Keukenhof and my experience as a budding author came into focus....

Enticed by fairer weather, the stream of houseguests and other visitors continued unabated that second spring. Our calendar filled with dinners, drinks, coffees, and other social outings. Taking great pride in our home and adopted city, we became pros at the houseguest routine. We didn't over-plan, smother, or ignore. A well-stocked refrigerator and bar were essential ingredients. We appreciated houseguests who welcomed opportunities to explore Brussels on their own. With a bit of guidance and access to our trove of guidebooks and brochures, the savvy traveler had a grand time.

However, we never got used to the regular exodus of friends. Brussels is a way station of sorts, especially for those rooted elsewhere. Dear friends, expats from New Jersey, came to the end of their stint. Our friendship bloomed after we met them five months earlier on an outing to Cologne. Their circumstances, attitudes, and temperaments mirrored ours. A common expat experience of life among the Belgians provided good conversation, support, and quite often great humor. We knew we'd miss the wonderful camaraderie.

Before they packed up for a return trip to the Jersey shore, we agreed to a farewell outing, the Expat Club's day trip to Champagne, France. The trip seemed appropriate—a farewell toast with champagne.

Our Trip to Champagne

My detailed blog post about our journey included a primer on champagne. Here is an excerpt. The full post is included in the appendix.

Champagne: A Name Bubbling with Joy

Champagne, one of those rare words that triggers an explosion of sensory neurons. The name conjures up images of celebrations, coronations, christenings, and myriad other happy occasions. Champagne is most often paired with smiles, laughter, and joy. Movies brim with references to champagne. No other prop has a cachet that immediately conveys class, refinement, sophistication, wealth, and a zest for life. Think Cary Grant, Audrey Hepburn, Julia Roberts, Leonardo DiCaprio. Many consider champagne all glamour and giggles. However, there's a dark side. The sparkling wine is under immense pressure (pun intended) to pop consistently with delight. Most of us would shatter under such lofty and unrealistic expectations. Besides a chic reputation, how much do we know about the drink we call Bubbly?

Recently, Jim and I had the pleasure of traveling 170 miles from Brussels to Champagne, a region in northeastern France. The trip was bittersweet. We toasted a safe farewell to friends who, after eight months in Belgium, are returning home to New Jersey. With its large international community, Brussels is full of farewells, lives in constant motion like bubbles in a flute of champagne....

This final excursion with our friends couldn't have been more delightful. We saluted them with champagne wishes and caviar dreams. Life, like champagne, is meant to be consumed, not stored away till it's too old to enjoy. Seize the day. Share a bottle of bubbly with those you love. You never know how long someone will be in your life....

———————

The next weekend an encouraging email arrived. I read it three times before I believed it. Independent Publishers awarded a bronze medal to my second novel, *Jell-O and Jackie O*. At last, the objective affirmation I craved. Perhaps I could write something of merit after all. Jim tried to convince me of my talent for years, but spouses, I knew, were prone to bias or blinded by love. In the world of independent publishing, the IPPY, as the award is known, is a big deal. Honorees would receive awards in May at a ceremony in New York.

Jim cheered the news. "We're definitely going to New York."

"I don't know. It's only a month away. It'll be a lot of money."

"No ifs, ands, or buts about it, mister. We're going, and that's settled."

"B...but."

"I have spoken," he added, clamping his fingers shut to end the debate.

Like Paris, New York is always a good idea. The news called for bubbly. We'd carted a bottle of Pommery back from our tour. However, I settled for red wine. Despite our recent immersion in the luxurious world of sparkling wines, one truth remained. Jim hated champagne. *Cheers!*

Chapter 20

The month of May brought a bounty of public holidays: Labor Day, Ascension Thursday, and Pentecost Monday, the latter two rooted in the country's religious past. Like much of Western Europe, however, Belgium has increasingly secularized. According to a March 2017 WorldAtlas.com article, only 6 percent of Belgian Catholics attend church regularly; 27 percent of the population identifies as atheist or agnostic. On these religious holidays, it's a fair bet that cinemas, cafés, and North Sea beaches draw bigger crowds than churches.

National holidays gave Jim and me an excuse to explore Belgium and points beyond. Playing tourist was easier than our role as expat residents. Comfortable jaunting across the globe, we'd visited six continents. With dozens of interesting countries and a rich history, Europe was our favorite. Perhaps we felt connected to immigrant ancestors and family traditions. Between us, our roots extended to Ireland, Poland, Italy, Germany, and Greece.

Many Americans never get to Europe. If they do, it's frequently late in life when they have ample time and resources. Beyond London, Paris, Rome, and a handful of other notable cities, few ever see secondary towns and remote villages. A pity, because roads less traveled are often where one finds authentic, memorable adventures. One such undertaking held great allure for me—finding my German roots. Germany provided my surname. Jim's too. A dozen years earlier, on our fifth anniversary, he'd legally changed his name to Arkenberg.

Researching family genealogy in my twenties, I found "Arkenberg" on an old library map. My namesake village lies in northwest Germany between Bremen and Hannover, on the Weser River. Arkenberg still exists. After Jim's name change, his German boss at Daimler Financial surprised him, sending an eager intern into the German hinterland in search of a meaningful souvenir. A photo of the town's marker, a yellow sign spelling "Arkenberg" in black letters, soon graced both of our desks. Not only a great conversation starter, it was a source of pride. Who can boast of an actual town named after them?

"It's just a hamlet," the intern later told us. "A few houses, not much more."

Although appreciative of the intern's effort, I was jealous that he'd been to Arkenberg. The photo served as a constant reminder of an adventure not yet taken. I recalled my earliest weeks in Brussels seventeen months in the past—the short, gloomy days of early January before our things arrived from the States. Fatigued by our move and frustrated with my failure to connect with our new city, I retreated to the stiff rental couch inside our cold and spartanly furnished apartment. With no friends or contacts, and Jim's long hours at the office fueling my sense of isolation, I tapped into my family history. Reviewing my roots gave me comfort, context, connection. That wasn't the first time I turned to genealogy. Five years earlier after leaving my two-decade career at United, I clutched my family tree to feel grounded. With a base in Brussels making the trip easy, I was more determined than ever to find Arkenberg, to plant my feet in soil over which my ancestors had tread. Growing uncertainty of our future in Europe served as a catalyst for the pilgrimage. I might never have the chance again.

I casually laid out my plans to Jim as we strolled passed a line of Zipcars parked in Place Stéphanie. "Perhaps I'll rent a car, pack up Sadie, and head out in search of Arkenberg." Because our car had a standard transmission, a rental was my only option.

Jim's brow furrowed. "What?"

"We could go during the week…while you're at work."

He studied me; his head cocked. "You and Sadie?"

I nodded.

"You *and Sadie*," he repeated. Detecting disappointment in his face, I wondered where his questions were leading. He didn't take long to be direct. "What about me? What if *I* want to go?"

So that's it. I'd underestimated his interest or maybe I simply figured he didn't have time, given his all-consuming job. "Fantastic, sweetie. Didn't want to force you, drag you someplace where you didn't want to go. It's not gonna be that glamorous of a trip."

"Well, if you wanna go with only Sadie, who am I to stop you?"

I laughed, pulling him into an embrace. "I'd love nothing better than to visit Arkenberg…with *you*."

"Well, I am an Arkenberg too." His expression and tone softened. "We definitely can bring Sadie."

I chuckled. "She'll be very happy. Sadie's an Arkenberg too."

On Ascension Thursday, we hoisted Sadie into the back seat of the Audi. The total trip distance was 400 kilometers, about 250 miles. GPS quoted a travel time of a little over four hours. Despite being at the upper limit of Jim's acceptable drive time, the journey was within range to maintain domestic harmony. GPS routed us northeast toward Maastricht. After a short transit through the Netherlands, we crossed into Germany, passing on the outskirts of Essen and Münster before reaching Damme, our destination for the night.

I'd studied place names on maps for many years. Like Arkenberg, Damme is in the German state of Lower Saxony. Although Damme lay fifty miles west of the dot labeled "Arkenberg," we chose it based on a wider selection of tourist amenities. Pet-friendly Europe meant Sadie was also welcome.

The weather was ideal for mid-May—sapphire-blue skies dotted by puffs of cottony clouds. A rolling landscape covered by fields of golden canola was breathtaking. Towns through which we passed looked prosperous, marked by typical German cleanliness and order. The environs made a nice area to claim as an ancestral home.

Throughout our adventure, excitement and fulfillment pushed aside my chronic worries. Disappointment with aloof Bruxellois, anxiety over my writing career, concerns about Jim's work situation, and our precarious future as expats vanished. The journey of discovery was exhilarating. Although my ancestral branch had abandoned the area two centuries earlier, I connected to the place. The inherent sense of belonging required neither proof nor residency card.

As we neared Arkenberg, I asked Jim to stop the car at the edge of a canola field. "Looks like a great place for photos."

He slowed, pulling the car onto the shoulder. "Sadie could probably use a break too."

With clear blue skies, the sun radiated heat. There were no trees, just endless fields of green and gold. A series of photos captured the moment. Even Sadie smiled for the camera.

Precious Sadie

I pointed to the horizon. "Arkenberg's just over there."

Returning to the car, we traveled back and forth across a single road. It seemed to be the extent of Arkenberg—a few houses, a couple of farms, fields, and not much else. Our visit wasn't complete, at least in my mind, without a stop at the Arkenberg town marker. Retracing the decade-old steps of that eager intern, we took a series of photos. Arkenberg may have been a mere speck of a place, but it represented a link to my tribe's deep, enduring roots.

Finding our Roots

Every place we visited that magical weekend, the name Arkenberg was met with smiles and goodwill. I blogged about our adventure, eagerly sharing a link with family back home. My cousin, the family genealogist, distributed the post to the greater Arkenberg diaspora. Here is an excerpt. The full post is included in the appendix.

Finding Arkenberg

What's in a name? Surely an identity: a way for the laundry to track your shirts, the pizza parlor to match your order, an inventory system for people—Bueller, Bueller...A surname identifies your tribe and is usually a source of pride. Sometimes, families change their name, the British Royals among the most notable to do so. At the outbreak of WWI, they quietly replaced German-sounding Hannover with the very British Windsor. Royals, however, like Cher, Charo, and Bono are so important they don't need a last name. Hollywood manufactured glamorous names: Kappelhoff became Day, Sherer became Hudson, Morrison became Wayne. Literature gives us pen names: Twain from Clemens, Eliot from Evans, Orwell from Blair. Prisons take your name and give you a number, the ultimate humiliation.

A spouse who shares not only your life but also your name is the ultimate validation. On our fifth anniversary, my spouse legally changed his name. Now, we're both Arkenbergs, as is our pooch, Sadie....

About six years ago, I started to get more serious about family genealogy....I traced back five generations to my Great, Great, Great Grandfather and Grandmother. Bernard and Mary Arkenberg were born in or near Damme, Germany in the late 1700s. Their son, my Great, Great Grandfather, Ferdinand Heinrich Arkenberg, was born in Damme in 1822 or 1823. The family migrated to Ohio with several other residents in 1831....

I was curious to see these roots firsthand....Turns out, the Arkenbergs who remained did very well for themselves.... Perhaps the Arkenbergs who sailed from Bremen to Baltimore two hundred years ago to make new lives in America did a big favor to those left behind, giving them room to grow and prosper.

I satisfied with my search? Although Jim, Sadie, and I
meet any German Arkenbergs, we got to spend time in
the land of my forefathers seeing, breathing, and listening to
the world from which I came. Yes, that was worth it. In addition, I spent time with the most important branch in my family
tree—Jim & Sadie....

<hr />

With an open weekend before our New York trip, I suggested a
day trip to the coast. The French seaside town of Dunkirk, twenty-five
miles east of Calais, was hosting an event of historical significance and
great interest to me—a commemoration of the seventy-fifth anniversary of the Dunkirk evacuation.

In the early months of World War II, the Nazis stormed across
Europe. England stood alone to stop Hitler from gobbling up the entire continent. (The United States didn't enter the war for another year
and one-half.) The German juggernaut pushed hundreds of thousands
of English and allied soldiers to the continent's edge, trapping them on
the beaches of the northern French port. Their rescue and the entire
English war effort depended upon the heroism of ordinary citizens.

On June 4, 1940, the final day of the Dunkirk evacuation, Prime
Minister Winston Churchill delivered a blistering warning to Hitler
and the Nazi menace. His words rallied a beleaguered nation, "We shall
defend our island whatever the cost may be. We shall fight on the beaches, we shall fight on the landing grounds, we shall fight in the fields and
in the streets, we shall fight in the hills. We shall never surrender."

Dunkirk's relative proximity afforded us another rich opportunity
to experience history firsthand. I also viewed our attendance as a tribute to my late father. A veteran of World War II, my dad spoke of the
war and troops with great reverence. I recalled his poignant pilgrimag-
es to Pearl Harbor, Normandy, and Bastogne. He wouldn't have cared
that Dunkirk didn't involve Americans. He considered the Brits allies,

the heroes of Dunkirk fellow soldiers in a common cause.

I submitted a blog post on what was Memorial Day in the United States, recalling the many years that Dad and I attended the local parade honoring our nation's casualties of war.

Dunkirk: Heroism Fades into History

My father, a veteran of two wars, loved a parade. He taught me to love the flag and honor the men and women of the armed forces. Memorial Day doesn't arrive without my recalling the many parades that he and I shared. Cherished memories.

As a tot in the 1960s, I regularly saw veterans of WWI, WWII, and Korea march in parades to honor fallen comrades. Later, vets from wars in Vietnam, Desert Storm, Iraq, and Afghanistan joined the ranks of marchers. WWI vets are all gone, and veterans of WWII and Korea are in their late eighties, nineties, or older. Soon, they too will fade into history.

Living in Europe this Memorial Day, I found a unique venue to quench my thirst for a parade and honor the treasured tradition that my late father and I shared. I read in *The Times of London* about a commemoration of the 75th anniversary of Operation Dynamo, the flotilla of Little Ships that evacuated over 338,000 English, Belgian, and French soldiers from Nazi clutches. In 1940, from May 26 through June 4, nine hundred vessels, civilian and naval, shuttled soldiers from Dunkirk to England. The mission was no easy feat. Small boats, today known as Little Ships, had to cross forty miles of open sea under constant risk of Luftwaffe attack. Brave souls rescued cornered soldiers from death or capture by the advancing Germans who were only weeks away from securing the surrender of France.

The sailors of Operation Dynamo rescued over a third of a million men. Another ninety thousand weren't so lucky. They were killed or captured. In wartime Britain with the London blitz raging and the nation facing a continent disappearing to the Nazi menace, the daring rescue was a boost to morale. Dunkirk became a rallying cry.

My earliest knowledge of the heroics of Dunkirk came from Hollywood. I love black and white movies. One of my favorites is *Mrs. Miniver*. The 1942 movie starring Greer Garson and Walter Pidgeon won six academy awards including Best Picture, Best Actress for Garson, and Best Director for William Wyler. The movie tells the story of the impact of the early months of WWII on one rural English family. In a memorable scene, Mr. Miniver is called to captain his small pleasure craft to the Thames estuary. There, he learns of his mission— Dunkirk. Released six months after the attack on Pearl Harbor, *Mrs. Miniver* is credited with rallying American support for the war. The inspirational film catapulted Garson to become a top seller of war bonds.

Fast forward decades later—my chance not only to see some of the mission's Little Ships, but also to witness some of the last living souls who took part in the evacuation. Survivors are well into their nineties. A few journeyed from England to Dunkirk by sea. The Grand Marshall of the parade was a 95-year-old veteran. He didn't ride in a vintage automobile. That spry gentleman of nine and a half decades *walked* the parade route. He and the remaining heroes of Dunkirk will soon live only in history books.

Jim and I enjoyed our time rubbing shoulders with living history in Dunkirk. I couldn't help but recall my dad. With flag waving and tears welling in his eyes, he would have loved the parade.

To all who served including my dad, and to those who made the ultimate sacrifice, we remember. Happy Memorial Day!

Dunkirk's Little Ships

Chapter 21

As our flight to New York neared, my excitement surged. I eagerly shared news of the IPPY with friends, family, and writer colleagues in Brussels and Chicago. A fellow author replied with enthusiasm, "Now you can call yourself an award-winning author." *Great idea*, I thought, immediately appending the epithet in social media platforms. Validation was exhilarating. After seven years of toil, disappointing responses to agent queries, and minimal success with submissions, the IPPY news filled me with gratification and hope. *Perhaps I can make a go of this writing thing.*

Revitalized, I turned my attention to my third novel *None Shall Sleep*, contracting with the same editor of my second novel. I set a goal of sending her a polished manuscript by summer's end. With a busy travel schedule ahead of us—four continents in three months—four months seemed necessary to make that happen.

In late May, we flew to New York for the IPPY awards ceremony. The trip, a three-night stay, was affordable thanks to the same airline colleagues whose "designated companion" tickets had taken us to Chicago in November. Once again, seats were standby, but we didn't care. Risk made our trip romantic, a spontaneous adventure. The standby gods smiled; we got first class. As always, watching Jim sink into his sleeper seat, play with every button, then launch into a movie marathon from takeoff to landing made me smile. Laboring hard at his job, he deserved pampering. As for me, reading and monitoring our flight's progress on the digital map filled my time.

Our flight to Newark arrived the afternoon before the awards ceremony. "Welcome home," the immigration agent said as he stamped our passports.

We aren't home. Despite my initial thought, some sense of "home" did, in fact, stir within me. But why? This was New York, not Chicago nor, for that matter, Brussels. Obviously, living in Europe had clouded my notion of "home." Perhaps the familiar sound of American accents triggered some innate mental receptor.

Blistering hot and humid, New York seared under a cloudless sky. We booked a hotel in lower Manhattan, a favorite location. Over the years, we grew to prefer edgier and hipper neighborhoods such as SoHo, Greenwich Village, East Village, Tribeca, and Nolita away from the glitz and unaffordable glamour of Midtown. Our hotel, moderately priced by New York standards, was expensive when measured by the square foot. Located at the corner of Broome Street and Bowery, the hotel provided easy access to Chinatown, Little Italy, and other favorite neighborhoods.

After checking in, we explored the vicinity. A block away we happened upon an iconic red firehouse, a vintage building that predated the automobile. I imagined a brass fire-wagon pulled by a team of horses bolting out the narrow archway over which "55 Engine 55" was proudly displayed. Closer inspection revealed that the bronze plaques flanking the red doors were tributes to company firefighters killed on September 11, 2001. I recalled Paris. *Je Suis Charlie* placards could just as easily read, *Je Suis New York*, or simply *Je Suis xxxx* (fill in the blank). Terrorism knew no bounds.

Leaving the station, we zigzagged through charming streets lined by trees and iconic brownstones. To me, the area had a livable appeal, built to a human scale as opposed to the apartment blocks and shimmering condo towers found elsewhere in the city. Exuding untamed energy, New York was a city where we'd love to live, even temporarily.

I wondered whether simply breathing the air inspired creativity and literary success as it seemed to do for aspiring writers in books, movies, and real life. Louisa May Alcott's Jo March discovered inspiration and purpose in nineteenth-century New York. A century later Truman Capote's unnamed author/narrator found the inimitable Holly Golightly there. In between and continuing today, the city's hopeful beacon of inspiration has never dimmed.

Unfortunately, like inhabiting London—another dream city—residing in New York was cost-prohibitive. Jim and I weren't young, doe-eyed innocents willing to sacrifice comfort for a Manhattan fix. Middle age and middle-class spoils dull one's daring. Roughing it meant three-star hotels and off-brand clothing. Come to think of it, stories about leaving New York are also quite popular. A legion of budget-minded prestige seekers probably claim New York lineage without ever having lived there. Perhaps after frequent visits, I could tap into the city's inspirational grid and simply pretend we said goodbye to all of that too.

Our stomachs grumbled. We opted for—what else?—Mexican cuisine. Manhattan has no shortage of tacos, burritos, and margaritas. We walked off our heavy dinner with a hardy walk to the Manhattan Bridge. From our perch in the middle of the span, across the East River Gotham glistened like Oz.

Jim sighed. "Wow."

I put my arm around him. "I know. You could live here."

"In a heartbeat." His vigorous head bobs stalled when I held up my hand, rubbing my thumb across my two fingers, the universal sign for "Ka-ching!" He signaled his understanding with a pout.

"But maybe when my book becomes a movie."

A grin returned to his face. "Now you're talking."

After snapping selfies in front of a sample of the amazing graffiti for which NYC is known, we headed back to the hotel. Jet-lagged and content, we went to bed early, our minds mesmerized and our bellies full.

Heat and humidity returned the next day. Sunlight bleached sidewalks and streets as we headed north to Union Square Park for a rendezvous with my older brother.

I was pleased that Scott wanted to join us in New York and accompany us to the awards ceremony. He'd shown only limited interest in my writing, lackluster support that disappointed me. I felt let down, especially since as a musician, he understood creative vulnerability and an artist's craving to be heard. I was also angry. I supported his artistic endeavors for decades. His desire to share in my celebration, therefore, both surprised and pleased me. Perhaps a few days in NYC was the bigger draw, but I didn't care. "It is what it is," Jim said. "Enjoy the moment." I intended to do just that.

We remained hopeful that Scott might visit us in Brussels before we repatriated. He had the means. After we had announced our move, his choir, as a token of their love and support, presented him with airfare and a basket of travel aids including adapters and guidebooks.

Jim and I reached 14th Street early, sticky and parched from our determined pace. After shopping at nearby stores for shoes and books, we headed into the park. The temperature and humidity continued to climb. Water peddlers did a brisk business. We snagged a vacant bench shaded by trees and marveled at the kaleidoscope tableau. We took turns standing to scan for my brother.

"There he is," Jim said, gesturing toward the park's northern entrance.

Scott stood over six foot tall. His shock of white, wispy hair was easily spotted over the crowd. Wearing his customary black short-sleeve shirt and khakis, he held a guidebook in his hand. Despite a relationship that often sparked and sizzled like static electricity, his arrival made me happy. For me, my brother represented home and family, continuity with the past. With our parents deceased and his estrangement from our sister, I was his closest family. Our time together was either great fun or a disaster, the outcome unpredictable—picnic blanket or wrestling mat. As with most families, however, after licking our wounds from the last skirmish we eagerly awaited the next picnic.

Individuals share complete and unredacted histories only with surviving siblings, parents, and a few other close relatives. Spouses don't see the total picture—childhood and early experiences that nuance personalities and shape our characters. Some husbands and wives fill in the blanks, but history pieced together with guesswork and stories filtered through a partner's subjective narrative has many flaws.

As we shared a warm embrace, Scott flashed a smile of genuine affection. "Flight was great," he said replying to our inquiries. "Short and sweet. The sisters even had a car pick me up at LaGuardia."

Scott had secured lodging with the Little Sisters of the Poor at their convent in the Bronx. The price, I surmised, was right. After lunching on burgers and Belgian beer at a nearby restaurant, the three of us spent a delightful afternoon strolling and catching up. Like us, Scott loved New York. He regularly flew in from Chicago for a single day of meandering.

After freshening up at our hotel and changing into dress pants and shirts, we caught the subway north to Columbus Circle. The Providence, a three-level hall and former nightclub, was our destination. Built in the 1920s as the Manhattan Baptist Church, the space had reinvented itself as Mediasound Studios during the 1970s and 1980s. The place oozed with creativity. The Rolling Stones, Bob Dylan, Frank Sinatra, and Barry Manilow recorded there. The three of us posed for photos in front of the building's 57th Street entrance before going inside.

Jim put his arm around me. "I'm so proud of you, sweetie."

In that special moment, I banished self-doubt…for at least one night. The reception and awards ceremony were terrific. Sharing the moment with Jim and my brother made the evening extra special. Recognition by a respected organization in the independent-publishers industry validated me as a writer. Receiving the award in the heart of the publishing world added to the thrill. The honor represented a proud moment in my literary journey.

The next day Jim and I trekked across the Brooklyn Bridge and back again. That evening, Scott joined us for a farewell dinner in Little Italy where I raised my glass in a toast. "To family."

Of course, I felt compelled to blog about our New York adventure.

On Writing, On Travel, On Life

Last week, I enjoyed one of life's rare treats when twin passions, writing and travel, harmonized with my greatest love, my husband and biggest fan, Jim....

The IPPY was a win, a bona-fide medal, complete with bragging rights and marketing possibilities....Still, I wasn't inclined to pack a bag and head across the Atlantic. The trip would cost time and money....Jim, however, insisted we go! One of the many blessings of having him in my life—to kick me in the ass because I can't do it myself....

Writing is hard work. For novelists, the horizon is far. Sometimes the finish line is years in the future; many give up before they cross. Friends know the discipline I bring to the writing table....I don't surrender....

America's preeminent writer of horror stories separates writers into four camps: Bad, Competent, Good, and Great. According to him, badness and greatness are part of one's DNA. Bad writers can't escape their fate and good writers never ascend to greatness, that lofty pedestal where you find Shakespeare, Faulkner, and Hemingway. Wriggle room exists only in the middle. While he doesn't say so, I'm guessing this preeminent writer fancies himself a Good writer, a very Good writer. Four decades of relevance, commercial success, and an entire bookcase at Barnes & Noble support such a claim.

I like to think that I'm a competent writer. If I thought otherwise, I may as well throw down my pen and apply for a job with Cable News. The author's theory offers hope that I can be good, a bit like theological heaven I know, but a carrot nonetheless. But how do I know if I'm making progress? How does any writer?...

Literary competitions offer new authors affirmation, un-biased validation, and new readers. Don't misunderstand me, one contest doesn't a good author anoint, but it's a data point....Only a fool takes one, two, or even three contests as the final word of his or her writing ability. But recognition by objective professionals and peers is a good—*no, great*—feel-ing. It's a chance to take a victory lap, head held high, before returning to the lonely lair armed with pen, the author's lance, to approach, not lightly, the blank page....

IV

Signs of Distress

Any tree or shrub will suffer some degree of stress when uprooted.
The shock of transplanting can be lessened if the task is carried out correctly.

(rhs.org.uk)

Chapter 22

Back in Brussels, we returned to our routines. Jim worked primarily from home now. He had never found his local office overly collegial, and staff reductions and space consolidations rendered it even more uninviting. A remote assistant via a computer replaced the receptionist, a pleasant woman Jim had liked. In addition, he no longer had a dedicated office decorated with personal items including family photos. His options included squatting in someone's office, sitting at a communal bank of docking stations, or working from the comfort and privacy of home. Jim chose the latter. "Wish it weren't so," he lamented, "but I won't be missing anything."

Speakerphone conversations and extemporaneous comments offered up by Jim during coffee breaks gave me deeper insight into his job. Stress took a heavy toll. Despite his brave front, I saw through his stoic resolve. He looked exhausted, worn down. At times, his calm demeanor bubbled over with exasperation. Frustration surged with struggles for resources, mixed messages from senior leadership, and an unsympathetic boss. He dismissed the ordeal as a test, a sink-or-swim exercise to prove his professional grit. In my experience, an astute leader knew when to throw the flailing swimmer a lifeline.

While Jim faced the daily challenges of his job, I found purpose in writing. Early in the year, the head of the BWC had asked me to chair a weekly session. Recalling my tremendous fulfillment and satisfaction facilitating my Chicago group, I gladly accepted. The shoulder tap affirmed me as an insider, at least with my writer peers. I felt honored, accepted, validated, and, in a way, finally anchored.

The IPPY and accolades received in New York also reinvigorated me. I dove into a major revision of my novel *None Shall Sleep*. Each weekday morning after taking Sadie for a short walk, I strolled to my new favorite coffee shop, Bocca Moka on the bustling Chaussée de Charleroi. Arriving as it opened and before I said "Bonjour," the owner and her staff greeted me with my regular coffee, a *lungo grande*. On fair weather days, their lovely garden beckoned. Jim sometimes joined me there with his computer and satchel of work. Staff learned to greet him with his drink of choice, a flat white that he declared the best in Brussels. In the cozy café with bagels flown in from New York, a mural of the Brooklyn Bridge, and genuine hospitality, we felt at home, rooted. Fueled with good, strong coffee, I happily edited away.

I had originally crafted the novel with three first-person narrators, a trio of unique characters referred to as "I." The structure, I concluded, would confuse readers. Rewriting the novel in third person and maintaining the appropriate points of view proved more difficult than I'd imagined. Besides reworking the book's narration and voice, I remolded the main protagonist into a more sympathetic character and changed the ending. This process became a major revision, but a necessary one that, in my opinion, strengthened the story.

I edged closer to publication, confirming the review schedule with my editor. Living in Belgium, I didn't try to peddle the manuscript to literary agents or publishers. The experience with my first book, a teeter-totter of lofty expectations and dashed hopes, had left me exhausted and frustrated. Most of the agents and publishers to whom I sent queries never responded. Those who replied sent terse, uninspiring form letters. My energy was better expended writing and creating a solid final draft. When not editing, I read. Several colleagues from my writer groups in Brussels and Chicago had published new works that I felt obliged to read and review.

In late June, Jim and I celebrated our seventeenth anniversary with dinner at a chic restaurant just off Place Louise, a five-minute walk from the house. The early summer evening was chilly enough for leather jackets. The anniversary carried special significance, our first as a legally married couple. I dined on grilled scallops and white asparagus with shrimp hollandaise; Jim had filet mignon and scalloped potatoes. For dessert, Jim ordered profiteroles with ice cream, and I a strawberry custard tart.

Jim gazed at me, affection in his eyes. "Despite everything, we're pretty lucky."

I nodded. "And wise enough to recognize it. I wouldn't trade any of our time together. The best years of my life."

"Mine too. Love you."

"Love you more." I raised my wineglass and Jim did the same. "Happy anniversary, my handsome husband."

The milestone served as a timely reminder of the strength of our relationship. The shared struggles and adventures of the past eighteen months had brought us even closer together as a couple.

Three days later, great news reached us from America. In what had become a familiar split based on political ideology, the U.S. Supreme Court ruled 5-4, in *Obergefell v. Hodges*, that no state could ban same-sex marriage. The majority found that the fundamental right to marry was guaranteed to same-sex couples throughout the United States by both the Due Process and Equal Protection clauses of the Fourteenth Amendment. Prior to the ruling, at least a dozen states had laws prohibiting such unions. Although the ruling didn't affect us because our Illinois marriage was already recognized at the federal level, we viewed it as a collective triumph for our community. President Obama issued an encouraging statement, "Love just won. Today we can say in no uncertain terms that we've made our union a little more perfect." The

Obama Administration bathed the White House in rainbow-colored light. It was a tremendous anniversary gift. The United States to which we would eventually return was markedly more welcoming than the one we had left nearly two years earlier.

As our lives settled into comfortable routines, Jim's performance review covering his first year in Brussels proved to be an unexpected pivotal point. After his discussion, he phoned me from the office.

"How'd it go?" I asked.

"Well…positive overall…happy about that. But…I expected more acknowledgment of my achievements. Some credit for my leadership." He didn't want to go into details over the phone. "I need to process it," he added before we disconnected. His tone jumbled with an array of emotions. I detected sadness, dejection, but also a mysterious hint of relief.

When Jim arrived home from the office, Sadie, Puhi, and I greeted him at the door.

"Tough day," he replied. "But nothing I can't handle." His mustered smile couldn't conceal the dejection and defeat weighing down his shoulders.

"Sorry, sweetie," I said, giving him a kiss. "I know how hard you've worked. But we both know the game. Your boss was forced to rate on a curve. You're the new kid on the block. The new guy never gets a high rating."

His look informed me that he'd already considered that. "The rating's only part of it. There's more."

I slapped the seat of his trousers. "Go change. We'll talk over a drink."

"Boy can I use one of those." Flashing a clenched-teeth grin, he disappeared downstairs.

Preparing a stiff rum and Coke for him and a vodka on the rocks for me, I suggested we sit on the leather tête-à-tête off to one side of the large formal dining room. The intimate seating area was ideal for serious conversations. Sadie plopped onto the thick Oriental rug at our feet and Puhi jumped into my lap.

Jim took a deep swig from his glass. "Ah," he cooed, pausing to let the alcohol's calming effect kick in. Sensing a simmering volcano of emotions, I didn't rush him. Having kept much of his struggle bottled up, he needed to dole out information on his terms. When he finally spoke, he glanced at me somewhat sheepishly. "Did something I've never done."

Studying his face for clues, I detected embarrassment. "Sounds ominous." My muscles tensed, bracing for his reply.

Dropping his chin, his eyes glanced at me over his beverage. "I…I swore."

"W…what?" Had I heard correctly? My sweet, even-tempered husband used profanity.

His neck straightened. "Used the f-bomb…several as a matter of fact."

"Oh my, that's not like you."

He sighed. "I know. They just came out. I've never done that in my entire career."

"Well, sweetie…can't say she didn't have it coming. Got a few choice words for her myself."

He let out a gentle laugh. "Didn't really swear *at* her, more at the situation…this new role she's created for me." With funding diminished for the project that originally brought Jim to Europe, his boss created a new role for Jim and his team to fill the void.

"Tell me what happened." I grabbed my cocktail off the table and settled in for what promised to be an interesting story. He was primed to share so I didn't do much talking. My sympathetic nods guided him forward.

As Jim recounted their discussion about his boss's expectations for the current year, his tone hardened. He assumed a pained expression. Obviously, this was a toxic memory. To unleash a string of f-bombs, he had to have felt extremely frustrated, maybe even threatened.

"I mentioned obstacles with the new role," Jim explained. "It's something I always discuss when I review my people. You know, how can I as your manager make your job easier, help set you up for success."

"You asked for her help?"

"Not directly, not at first. I took complete ownership. I sought advice, recommendations for solving the problem." After another sip of rum and Coke, Jim elaborated. He told his boss about a European leader, her peer, who refused to engage. "I explained that he's shut me out, cut all communication."

I groaned. "Not very mature."

"What's even worse," Jim added. "My boss already knew. Said he mentioned it to her."

My head shot up. "What? She knew he was refusing to engage with you?" Jim nodded. "And never once warned you or talked about a solution?"

Anger rose in his face. "No, *never*. What's more, he told her that he doesn't see value in the role...or my value for that matter." I hurt for Jim. None of this was the leadership he deserved.

The climax of the performance review centered on an existential question of Jim's job. "So," Jim added, "I had to ask her point-blank if *she* saw value in the role and in me."

My anger surged. "And?"

"She said yes...to both."

"I should hope so. She's stupid if she doesn't recognize your value. As for the role, she created it, for Christ's sake. If she can't speak to its value, who can? And as your boss, it's her duty to be your advocate."

"I asked her to speak to her peer...explain the role...convince him of the role's value...and mine." He scoffed. "Know what she said?"

"I can only imagine."

"Refused. Said to work around him." Jim took a deep breath. "I thought of your frustration driving culture change at United when you were told to work around the CEO."

"Yep, a perfect shit storm," I replied. "You'll fail without the top guy's buy-in."

Jim nodded. "Exactly! That's when I launched my f-bombs. Said, 'No fuckin' way that'll work.' Repeated it a few times. My swearing shocked me more than it did her. Made me realize the role's not for me. I'd never succeed. Told her as much."

Although I was not shocked by Jim's logical conclusion, his raw candor surprised me. I viewed the outburst as a healthy catharsis. "What'd she say?"

"Not much of anything…not then. Maybe she knew it was coming," he said with a shrug. "Anyway, I offered her a deal." My curiosity piqued. We were a package. Any deal included me. "If I don't find another job by year end," Jim continued, "she can count me toward her productivity goal."

Like most corporations, Jim's employer dabbled in doublespeak. Productivity meant layoff, redundancy—a euphemism for thinning the herd, axing someone from the payroll. Management exhorted surviving employees to "work smarter," a justification for expecting the same work and results from fewer people. A year hadn't gone by at Jim's company without layoffs.

Jim continued, "Called it entirely my decision. Said she's willing to work with me… if I decide to stay."

I shook my head. "But she's unwilling to advocate with her peer for you and your new role. Makes no sense. So, what do you think?"

He sighed. "I…I just can't. I'm sorry."

I squeezed his thigh. "Don't apologize. You're right."

We both knew he couldn't go on like that. Wiped out, his confidence shrank with each skirmish. As a passenger on his wild ride, I'd witnessed his white-knuckled grip on the safety bar as the speeding roller coaster whipped around turns, somersaulted, and plunged groundward at breakneck speed. Still, he hung on. No one could have asked more of him. In eighteen tumultuous months, he'd demonstrated courage, tenacity, and grace. He needed a break, a way off the roller coaster. Offering himself up as a sacrificial lamb started the countdown clock ticking. The decision came at great cost. It's hard to abandon a dream.

I grabbed his hand. "I'm proud of you. Takes courage to say what you did."

"Thanks, babe. I know you uprooted your life to come here for me."

"Nonsense. Wouldn't change a single thing. This has been a great adventure."

Jim's tone and demeanor lifted. "Oh, she did say one more thing. Said I had integrity. Unwavering at that."

I raised my glass in a salute. "First sensible words out of her mouth. A high and accurate compliment indeed."

"It sounds funny, but as bad as the day went, I feel okay. A weight off my shoulders." He smiled with the satisfaction that came from taking control of his fate. An end to his ordeal was in sight even if the future path wasn't the one either of us envisioned.

"It'll be great to rid ourselves of your boss," I said. "I feel as if that woman's been living with us for the past year and a half." Despite never having set eyes on Jim's boss during our residence, her daily presence in our lives was palpable and, quite frankly, maddening. Like a conduit, the stress she inflicted on Jim passed through him to me.

She squandered a great talent and, worse, negatively impacted my husband's personality. Throughout his career, Jim consistently rated high in achieving goals. His leadership skills drew top marks. Possessing a core of unshakable values, he nurtured young talent and pushed long-tenured employees to higher performance. He excelled at aligning employees with corporate and departmental strategies. At least his boss recognized Jim's integrity. That noble trait was most evident in his employee engagement. He never asked anything of his people that he wouldn't do. He always made time for his team even though that commitment robbed him of a healthy work-life balance. Coaching, he believed, was a leader's duty and the best way to drive results and meet goals.

From my perspective, Jim embodied *servant leadership,* a management term coined in the early 1970s. A servant leader inverts the traditional management pyramid, sharing power and helping subordinates develop and succeed. Management guru Tom Peters also wrote that leaders best support their teams by removing obstacles. He uses the term Boss-as-CHRO, Chief Hurdle Removal Officer, to describe highly effective managers. Jim could have used a CHRO of his own.

Still digesting the repercussions of the tumultuous review, Jim and I threw an old-fashioned summer barbecue. The diversion did us both good. Our home and spacious garden were ideal for large parties. Over the years, we'd hosted dozens of social events, viewing them as opportunities to gather an interesting mix of people. Sadie shared hosting duties, welcoming visitors with tail wags and nuzzles. Puhi, not to be outdone, sidled up to visitors and plopped into laps. Everyone assumed he was our cat. It began to feel that way to us as well.

In true Brussels fashion, cool and gloomy conditions set in on party day. Dark clouds threatened a downpour but merely delivered a light sprinkle before guests arrived. The cloud cover lightened but didn't disappear. Our guest list reflected our growing social circle of neighbors, writers, Expat Club members, local friends, and a couple of Jim's colleagues. An ideal party mix, the diverse group worked in various professions, hailed from countries across Europe, and included several gay friends—couples and singles.

As we waited for people to arrive, emotions swirled within me: pride, satisfaction, and sadness. Jim and I loved our home. We'd molded it into our own creation. Now as our prospects of remaining in Brussels dimmed, we were on the verge of leaving it behind. We'd have to bid farewell to new friends and our new identities. We weren't the same Midwesterners who had transplanted into Belgian soil eighteen months earlier.

We entertained in our terraced garden. A variety of shrubs, manicured hedges, and a colorful assortment of potted flowers offered a lush, green oasis in the heart of Brussels. The American menu consisted of pulled pork, cheeseburger sliders, and two varieties of sausage. Vegetarian options included macaroni & cheese, quesadillas, guacamole and chips, and a variety of salads. For dessert, chocolate chip cookies and ice cream. The event was great fun. After a rough start, our roots showed signs of thriving in the transplanted soil.

Our Secret Garden

We hadn't abandoned all hope of remaining in Europe. But neither of us had much success canvassing our professional networks for potential jobs for Jim. The lackluster response disappointed us. Close friends provided few leads and scant moral support. The prospect of returning to Chicago became a regular visitor to my thoughts, but I avoided mention of it. I didn't want the incredible adventure to end, especially not when we had started to finally feel grounded in our adopted home. We'd weathered the worst of the transition from old life to new only to find ourselves faced with the likelihood of turning around. It didn't seem fair. But Jim's health and happiness were my top priority.

An unchartered path, repatriation frightened me. The warning from Maria, the writer for *Global Connection* who'd interviewed me the prior spring, rushed back into my head: "Be forewarned. Returning home is a tough transition."

In some ways, moving back to Chicago scared me more than the outbound adventure. Would we slot seamlessly into our former lives? Would we even want that? Would our experience influence us in ways we didn't recognize? Would our life in Brussels—friends, adventures, guest cat—be quickly forgotten…as if it never happened? As July came to a close, uncertainty riddled me with anxiety. Thankfully, December still seemed far away. Anything could happen in five months.

Chapter 23

Jim and I were coming to terms that a return to Chicago was likely. Weekend junkets and holidays didn't mean we were running from our ambiguous future. We simply knew we had little control over what came next. Why not see as much of the world while we could?

Throwing Emerson's caution about travel being a fool's paradise to the wind, we pulled suitcases from the closet yet again. With Copenhagen checked off our list the prior summer, Stockholm was our choice for a long Scandinavian weekend. After a short and uneventful flight from Brussels, we landed at Bromma, Stockholm's older airport located closer to the city's center. Observing our surroundings from the taxi, we were struck by the many rivers, lakes, and bays. Part of a large archipelago, the capital spreads across many islands at the mouth of Lake Mälaren where fresh and salt water mingle. My adrenaline surged with the thrill of adventure. Neither of us tired of sampling new destinations. In Jim, I had more than a wonderful husband; I'd found a Huckleberry friend who shared my wanderlust.

The interplay among geography, history, culture, politics, literature, and art fascinated me. Norrmalmstorg, the square that housed our hotel, was the site of the notorious 1973 bank robbery and six-day hostage drama that introduced the world to "Stockholm syndrome." The term describes a psychological phenomenon in which hostages form emotional bonds with their captors. In this case, after being freed, victims not only defended their captors, they also refused to testify against them in court. Experts used the syndrome to explain the behavior of Patricia Hearst. After her 1974 abduction, the American heiress appeared to embrace the cause of her captors, a group calling themselves the Symbionese Liberation Army. Both events left lasting impressions on my then-adolescent imagination.

Jim and I never passed up an offer of seeing a place through the eyes of locals. Stockholm was no different. A friend put me in touch with her former work colleague, Eva-Lotta, who I'd met years before in Italy. Eva-Lotta emailed us, eagerly offering to show us a few of her favorite attractions. In addition, Andreas, a Swedish acquaintance from the BWC, scheduled a trip home coinciding with our holiday. Jim had met Andreas and his wife Ulrika, a reporter for Swedish television, at the Halloween party we threw the prior year. The couple organized a city walking tour conducted by a friend working toward certification as an official guide.

First stop, city hall. In addition to a stunning waterside setting, the red-brick building, whose single tower and simple roof line blended Venetian and Scandinavian design, also served as the venue for the Nobel Prize awards. Inside, we visited the Blue Hall, site of the awards ceremony and banquet and walked its famous Grand Staircase. Upstairs, the Golden Hall glistened with 18 million tiles. Except for the acclaimed Peace Prize awarded in Oslo, all other Nobel honorees, including laureates in literature, receive awards here. I imbibed the brilliance of such literary giants as Yeats, Shaw, Sinclair Lewis, O'Neill, Hesse, Elliot, Faulkner, Hemingway, Sartre, Neruda, Bellow—idols all.

Additional sites included the cobbled streets and colorful gabled buildings of Old Town, thirteenth-century Stockholm Cathedral with its gothic statue of St. George and the Dragon, and the Royal Palace. Happily veering off the beaten path, Eva-Lotta took us to Rosendals Trädgård, a quaint tearoom set in an organic nursery. There we sampled delicious cakes and strong coffee amidst fragrant roses and fruit trees. After exploring the picturesque waterfront, we boarded a ferry for Södermalm, an island of hipster neighborhoods including idyllic Vitabergsparken, a collective of garden patches and rustic cottages. Above the harbor, the terrace and beer garden of Mosebacke offered sweeping vistas. Here we brought together all of our generous hosts for late-afternoon refreshment and conversation. On this sunny summer Saturday, Jim and I felt like locals, chatting and laughing with native Swedes.

On Sunday, we visited the NK department store. Its rooftop medallion rotating slowly above Stockholm's skyline is a beacon for serious shoppers. After buying some clothes, we ascended to the restaurant floor for coffee and princess cake, the traditional domed dessert layered with sponge cake, pastry cream, and whipped cream covered in green marzipan.

Despite an overactive sweet tooth, Jim shrugged off his sample. "Cake's okay. Chocolate mayonnaise is way better. Still, I could definitely live in Stockholm."

"Would you still say that in January?"

Ending our journey on a sugar high, we found Stockholm to be a place where land, sea, and sky meld together in rich textures, vibrant colors, and harmonic sounds. In addition, the tall, fit, fair-haired Swedes are easy on the eyes. We boarded our flight to Brussels confident of a return visit.

Our next getaway took us to Tel Aviv. A week of business for Jim provided an excuse to arrive a few days early for sightseeing. Jim greeted his first trip to Israel with great excitement. I spoke fondly about my own first visit with United colleagues nearly twenty years earlier. The region teemed with historical and religious significance. Inhabitants of Israel and the Palestinian territories were warm and welcoming.

"Best food in the world," I boasted to Jim. "Meat for you, fish for me."

A rather simplistic review of the cuisine, perhaps, but not an unfounded exaggeration. In the twentieth century a large Jewish diaspora had settled in Israel, bringing their rich culinary traditions. Here, Mediterranean fruits, vegetables, and grains are served up alongside the heavier and flavor-packed comfort food of Eastern Europe. "Oh, and the portions," I added. "Huge. Like in America." As with all my adventures, this one was best shared with Jim.

On our first night, we grabbed an Uber to Jaffa, the ancient port and oldest part of Tel Aviv. An iridescent moon high above the Mediterranean cast a soft glow over the cobblestones and stone walls of the bustling old town. Palm trees swayed in a gentle sea breeze that infused the air with exotic aromas. Jim and I climbed a tall, narrow stone staircase to a quaint restaurant with a menu that suited both our palates—chicken for Jim, fish for me. We sipped a fine local white wine, discussing our future.

"If we do go back to Chicago," I said, "maybe we should live in the city."

Jim looked at me, surprise in his dark eyes. "Huh? Sell the house?"

"Not at all. With the house leased, we could rent a place for a year or two."

"You'd do that?"

"Sure! Fun to do something different. Wouldn't be forever."

Jim loved urban life. Our renters covered the financial obligations of our U.S. house. Their lease ran for another eighteen months. They might even renew. Living in central Brussels hooked me—walking everywhere, not needing a car. Easing into repatriation by moving into a trendy city neighborhood appealed to me.

As Jim processed my suggestion, surprise turned into delight. "Not a bad idea."

"Might even consider New York," I added. A high cost of living made this more fantasy, but the prospect of living in Manhattan even if only temporarily held great appeal. Our recent trip to collect my award had pushed New York's exciting vibe to the forefront of our minds. Besides, when one dream slips from your hand, why not grab another?

With new possibilities of repatriation filling our thoughts, we completed a whirlwind tour of Tel Aviv, Jerusalem, and Bethlehem. The land is a rich and magical amalgam of myth, legend, mystery, faith, and history. Although no longer religious, owing to the Catholic church's harsh and punitive stance on homosexuality, I clung to a deep spirituality. The natural world including the vast cosmos was simply too massive, amazing, and complex for me not to believe in forces beyond human comprehension.

Dusty courtyards, narrow alleys, and ancient structures exuded history. Golgotha, Gethsemane, Damascus Gate, Mount of Olives, and Temple Mount are names of wonder. As on my first visit, the sixth-century Church of the Nativity and fourth-century Church of the Holy Sepulcher filled me with awe. Jim and I donned yarmulkes and passed through tight security to place handwritten prayers and intentions in cracks of the ancient Western/Wailing wall. Unfortunately, as our tour returned us to Tel Aviv before dusk, I was unable to share with Jim my most vivid recollection of my earlier visit—the orange-apricot hue that radiates off Jerusalem's ancient walls at sunset.

A wall of a different type had sprung up since my first visit: a steel and concrete monolith separating Israel from the West Bank. However, the economic barrier observed on my earlier trip remained. Israel and its occupied territories present a stark contrast, the difference between first and third world. Tel Aviv has modern high-rises and multimillion-dollar condos, a thriving business district, and a vibrant commercial scene with luxury hotels, chic boutiques, and fancy restaurants. Bethlehem and other West Bank towns under Israeli military rule are dusty, drab, and depressed. A side-by-side perspective of lands locked in conflict offers visitors an eye-opening experience. A young Palestinian shepherd guiding his flock across the road even halted our van. Here, time stood still, progress measured in decades, not minutes as in Israel.

Our final summer adventure consisted of a full-blown two-week vacation. A friend's milestone birthday sent us to Melbourne where other friends joined us from London and Glasgow. The weekend included a formal dinner and a day of sightseeing and wine tasting in the Yarra Valley including a visit to Coombe Estate Winery, home of Dame Nellie Melba, the late operatic diva.

Jim and I booked a boutique hotel in the city center, the base from which we sampled Melbourne's great food and art scenes including vibrant street graffiti. We reconnected with Jim's former work colleague and her husband, the same couple whose wedding we attended the prior summer, as well as a woman we'd met five years earlier in an outdoor café in Cortona, Italy. We loved nurturing our vast global connections, bolstering social media interactions with face-to-face meetings. These connections made the world a little smaller and a lot more interesting. If more people had passports, perhaps strife, fear, and hate, symptoms of xenophobia and ignorance, would fade away. In Mark Twain's words, "Broad, wholesome, charitable views of men and things cannot be acquired by vegetating in one little corner of the earth all of one's lifetime."

In addition to celebrating our friend's birthday, Jim's rest and relaxation was a top priority. Work stress and a frustrating job search had frazzled his nerves. Although "too many nibbling creatures" served as his excuse to avoid the sea, beach holidays were among Jim's favorite escapes. We chose Hamilton Island, a resort in the Whitsundays, a collection of seventy-four tropical islands 1,200 miles north of Melbourne. Direct flights and access to the Great Barrier Reef sealed the deal.

Our hotel room looked out on palm trees, a sandy beach, and the Coral Sea. Bans on smoking and guests under the age of eighteen made our stay even more enjoyable. Despite rough seas, the Great Barrier Reef amazed us. Jim even donned a wet suit, allowing us to explore the reef together. Sadly, we learned about bleaching. Warming ocean water is causing coral to undergo a physiological change that turns it white.

All Suited Up

Whitehaven Beach, accessed only by boat or helicopter, delighted us. Silky sand, a result of high silica levels that also produced brilliant whiteness, squeaked when walked upon. A vigilant crew member feverishly waved me to shore, saving me from a nasty jellyfish sting and an unpleasant end to our holiday.

After five fabulous nights, we headed back to Brussels, a journey of nearly 12,000 miles. "I'm spoiled," Jim said. "From now on, adults-only resorts for us." Contentment reflected in his sweet smile. Mission accomplished!

Although the autumnal equinox occurs late in September, the month's first days are considered the traditional start of fall. The season of picnics, outdoor parties, and trips to the beach surrender to long pants, shorter days, and thoughts of work and unfinished goals. Whimsy turns serious. For me, the calendar flip from August to September represented more than a change of season. A new month reminded me of the inevitable change ahead. Although I hadn't abandoned all hope that we might find a way to remain in Europe, my mind couldn't silence the relentless ticking of our countdown clock. *Four months left, sixteen weeks, 120 days…*

As flickering rays of summer lingered in my mindset, I crafted two blog posts. The first, "The Things We Did This Summer" summarized our tri-continental adventure with an array of photos. The other, excerpted here but included in the appendix in its entirety, was a wistful piece about the erstwhile harbinger of summer, the iconic and endangered postcard.

Postcards from the Edge…or Maybe Bruges

Have postcards gone the way of handwritten letters, thank-you notes, and the family dinner hour? As a kid, besides birthday cards from a great aunt, uncle, or godparent stuffed with a five-dollar bill, my favorite mailbox find was a postcard. As the jet age dawned, my family didn't know any international globe-trotters. More often, postcards arrived with images of Mackinac Island, Wisconsin Dells, Starved Rock State Park, or some obscure local treasure such as a steel bridge at Steubenville, Ohio. For the rare card that popped into our lives from such exotic locales as Miami Beach, the Grand Canyon, or Hollywood, I skipped into the house from our curbside mailbox squealing with delight. I'd stare at the picture, imagining the magical wonders of such a visit.…

Over the years, postcards became fewer. I miss them. They're long-distance hugs, chances to remind someone that he or she is special in our lives.…Perhaps obsolescence was inevitable. The Internet brings instant gratification. Today, choosing among Facebook, Instagram, and Pinterest, holiday-goers share photos instantly. Messages are personal, timely, and meaningful. No scribbling in long-forgotten cursive, then scrambling for stamp and mailbox to send the mass-produced image, hoping it will arrive home before you do.

I haven't abandoned postcards.…After getting to Brussels,

I strove to keep in touch with family and friends back home. Facebook and email are great but only go so far. I desired a more personal approach, private messages to let people know we hadn't dropped off the planet. I tapped into my passion. Who doesn't love receiving an exotic postcard? I used them to pen birthday wishes and thank-you notes. Colorful images were unique alternatives to staid greeting cards.

In twenty months living in Belgium, I've mailed nearly 100 postcards....I hoped people would view my missives as an attempt to stay in touch, a reminder that Jim and I, though strayed afar, are still part of the flock....

Picture Perfect Bruges

Chapter 24

"Son of a gun." Jim's shout drew me into the living room where I found him staring at the computer screen. "Our tenant," he added with a grimace. "He's invoking the cancellation clause."

"Why?"

"Recalled to London."

Inserted at his employer's insistence, the clause permitted our tenant to break the lease should the company repatriate him. The news added a new wrinkle to our predicament. Rental income helped defray costs of maintaining our property. With the prior winter's water damage, a new hot water heater, and recent news that the sewer line needed replacing, our financial losses were mounting.

I dropped onto the arm of our sofa. "When do they want to leave?"

Jim frowned. "End of the month."

I understood and shared his concern. While we remained in limbo, unsure of our future, we had held onto a sliver of hope that we might manage to stay in Europe. Now, even if we eked out another expat assignment, we'd have to find another tenant after losing several months of rent. The news ended dreams about living temporarily in Chicago or Manhattan. We simply couldn't afford the carrying costs of an empty house.

Soon some more news arrived to temper our concern. A colleague notified Jim of an internal position back in Chicago. Although he had to interview, the long-distance conversation served to assess over-all fit rather than capabilities. Jim simply had to say yes. It wasn't a consolation prize. Jim had actually listed the position, a client-facing role as operational lead for a top customer, on his future career ladder. Contact at such high levels opened up opportunities inside and out-side his company. This step represented victory, not retreat. Still smart-ing over the premature departure from Brussels and hurt by the dearth of job-search support from his network, Jim needed the morale boost.

His current and future bosses were flexible, agreeing to our re-maining in Brussels until year end. Jim would officially assume his new role in January, but the transition would begin from Brussels. Knowing my feelings, Jim likely negotiated this outcome for me. His bosses' flexibility reflected their respect for Jim. Timing meant yet another December move over the busy and stressful holiday season. However, a year-end break minimized issues with taxes and leases. Besides, a new year seemed a perfect metaphor for a fresh start.

With four months remaining in the year, I didn't rush my mental transition from permanent resident to "short-termer." I clung to my routines. Although this might have been called "head-in-the-sand" delusion, such a mindset made it easier for me to cope with our im-pending change. I vowed to hold onto the pretense as long as possible. Sensitive to my emotions, Jim tiptoed around the subject of our return. I may have said all the right things about accepting our repatriation, but my mind churned with disappointment and regret.

"Sent the note today…about our apartment." Jim made this an-nouncement rather sheepishly as we ate dinner in mid-September. His eyes shifted from mine down to his plate and back again.

I bristled. "What note?"

"Our intent to cancel the lease."

My heart sank. Our fairy tale was coming to an end. "Oh!"

"Said we'd be here through December." Jim studied my reaction. "Had to be done, sweetie."

I shrugged. "I know." My gaze drifted down to the plate of chicken and brown rice. What more could I say?

"There's…s…something else."

His silence suggested he expected me to speak. *Something else* couldn't be good news or he would have opened with it. After an uncomfortable pause, I glared at him. "Yes?"

"They want to take pictures."

"Huh?"

"Apartment photos, to get the place onto the market as soon as possible. Told them next Tuesday. That okay with you?"

I took a deep breath. In little more than five minutes, I was reminded not only of our imminent departure from our beautiful apartment but also informed that interlopers would soon traipse through our home. *May as well hand over the keys now.* Sad and frustrated, I merely sighed. "Sure, sure. What do I have to do?"

"Sorry, sweetie. I know this isn't easy." Jim heaved a sigh. "It's not what either of us wants."

I simply nodded. I understood their rush to take photos. Our furniture, art, and overall décor showcased the stately apartment. I recalled an incident from early in our occupancy. Upon entering our front door, a deliveryman had scanned the rooms with wide eyes, asking if it was a museum. Passersby frequently stopped to gaze in through the windows. Once, two women knocked on the glass and asked for a tour. One was an interior designer, the other her client who lived up the street. Gushing with compliments, the designer showed great surprise upon learning that we decorated the place ourselves.

In addition, hard work, perseverance, and love had turned a tired, overgrown garden into a colorful, well-manicured oasis. I lamented the irony. Our love and care for the apartment would facilitate a quick turnover to a new tenant. It pained me to think that whoever rented *our* apartment wouldn't honor its architectural beauty. Images of *my* garden's tragic future popped into my head—untamed shrubs, wild tendrils, dead roses.

As promised, the landlord's daughter came to the house with a photographer. The very next day Jim advised that the first showing was set for the following afternoon.

This is happening all too fast. My frustration turned to anger. "What? Now we're going to have strangers invading our privacy at all times of the day."

"I can tell them no…if that's what you want."

I didn't know what I wanted. I hated this in-between stage—one foot in Brussels, one foot on the plane back to America. I groaned. "No, no. Let 'em come. I'll tidy up."

"You don't have to do that."

With raised eyebrow, I glared. "Then you don't know me." I had too much pride to show our apartment in any condition but pristine. It was still our home, at least for the time being.

Jim smiled. "Nobody knows Todd David better than I do. Right?" He kissed my cheek as we both chuckled. Humor was rare during those trying days.

After two visits, the first prospective renters agreed to take the place. The German couple, EU employees with a young daughter, entered my good graces after heaping praise on our décor.

Jim affected an upbeat tone. "This could work to our advantage."

I glared at him. "I don't see how."

"Think about it. If they rent to the German couple, that'll end the showings. We'll have our life and home back."

He was right. My response had been emotional. I simply didn't like the idea of other people living in our apartment.

Throughout September I kept up the charade of considering us permanent residents by deferring decisions about our move. *I'll think about that next month.* The calendar flipped to October. *Three whole months left.* No sooner had this thought comforted me than Jim rattled my delusion. My ruse started to crumble.

"Any thought to a move date?"

I snapped. "Why the rush?"

"We've got to schedule the movers."

"End of the year. Isn't that what we decided?"

"Kinda like to be home before that."

But this is our home! Don't steal what precious time we have left. "What date were you thinking?"

Jim preferred late November. Resettling into our house before the holidays would give him time to organize before he started his new job at full throttle. "My new boss has been patient, but..."

If thinking logically, I'd have accepted his reasoning. But logic took a back seat to emotion as I clung onto our life. "How about mid-December? Right before Christmas, okay?"

Jim assumed an expression that spouses often do when they understand conditions aren't ideal to argue a point. "Let's see what the moving company says."

"I can tell you right now, whenever we return, I don't want to celebrate Christmas."

Ignoring my non sequitur, Jim merely shrugged. "I'm not in a celebratory mood myself."

Talk of a move date triggered simmering emotions. I began to tell people of our impending transfer. To friends and acquaintances in Brussels, my message was one of sad farewell. Friends and family in the United States reacted to our homecoming news with happiness and delight; I stretched the truth, saying we were thrilled. How could we tell them that all things being equal, we'd prefer to extend our estrangement?

Announcing our departure pained me. It meant no turning back. Quite irrationally, I held out hope of a last-minute reprieve. *Some opportunity will pop up to keep us in Europe.* I viewed Chicago as a step backward. Sure, we had a beautiful home and beloved friends and family. But moving back reeked of retreat, surrender. Our life in Europe was special. I didn't want to unwind that, forget it ever happened. *Our European adventure will fade.* Just as time and neglect would spoil our

Brussels garden, new experiences and old routines would erase our vibrant Belgian memories.

With our departure looming, I contemplated our transition. *Oh, to be invisible, no visitors, no phone calls, no social engagements.* I saw self-imposed isolation, at least for a few months, as welcome decompression. What things from our former life might I change? Perhaps someone new to cut my hair, snipping off a thirty-two-year relationship in the process. My dentist of fifty years and dermatologist of four decades solved my dilemma, announcing their retirements.

"Let's try yoga instead of aerobics," I said to Jim.

"Good idea. What about your writers' group?"

"I don't know." The Barrington Writers Workshop was a great bunch of people. Weekly sessions elevated the quality of my writing. Most of the members made an effort to keep in touch while we were in Europe. Two were among our two-dozen sets of houseguests. Despite my fondness for the group, I viewed it as another step backward. "Let me give it some time."

As I considered our future, waves of nostalgia crashed over me. I'd miss much about Brussels. For starters, the people. I'd become great friends with our neighbor Barbara. We shared weekly coffees and, when Jim was out of town, dinners at a local Thai restaurant. After a rocky start, I befriended a number of people from the BWC. Assuming the role of Tuesday night chair had been an honor. The owner and staff of Bocca Moka warmly greeted Jim and me as regulars. I had my special places: Chatelain market and nearby Bruges, Ghent, and Antwerp. I relished mild winters, dabbling in French, and palate-pleasing cuisines. And what about Puhi, the impish clown of a cat who nuzzled his way into our home and hearts? Leaving him would be heartbreaking. His frequent visits and humorous antics were part of our daily life. I feared that he'd miss us too.

Domestic Bliss

"You won't believe it," Jim said as I returned from my morning writing at Bocca Moka. "Our tenants want to stay through the end of the year." We hadn't yet informed them of our imminent return. As they planned to vacate by September's close, there'd been no need.

I sat on the couch and stared at Jim. "What are you going to tell them?"

"Don't know."

"Ball's in our court." My mind churned with fantastical possibilities. *Couldn't this delay our departure until January? Another Christmas in Brussels!*

Were our tenants, I wondered, also struggling with repatriation? Were they, too, having second thoughts? Our house, I assumed, had been a wonderful home for them.

"Thinking we let them stay through October," Jim added. "We still don't have a firm date from our movers."

No, I thought, studying Jim's determined expression. *That puts us back in Chicago before Christmas.*

Every day brought new information, changed circumstances, and urgent decisions to make. As dynamic churn became our new norm, I retreated into myself. During this period of withdrawal, Jim emailed me, prompting a short but poignant digital exchange. Intimate chats via email were rare. Usually, we saved those for face-to-face discussions.

-----Original Message-----
From: Jim
To: Todd
Sent: Thu, Oct 8, 2015 8:07 am
Subject: Hey Good Look'n
Hi Sweetie,

Sometimes it is easier to write than to speak. I love you so much and am worried about you. You are such a good man; loving, intelligent, kind, selfless...

I tried so hard to keep us here but just couldn't make it happen. I know this move is not what you wanted. You feel like a second-class citizen with no right to be unhappy or complain. People don't place the same meaning on your work—at least not yet. But I do! I love you and believe in you. I know how hard you work and how much you have sacrificed for my dreams. I am eternally indebted to you. Life without you would be miserable.

I know how difficult this is going to be for you and I can already feel you start to slip away, into your own world...without me. I want to hug you but feel like you just want to be left alone.

Please tell me what I can do or say to help you through this difficult process. I am afraid of losing you and I want no part of that life. You are my love, my best friend, my hero and my life. xoxo Love Jim

-----Original Message-----
From: Todd
To: Jim
Sent: Thu, Oct 8, 2015 8:45 am
Dear Sweetie,

Thanks for your note. It means a lot.

I love you too. Please don't mistake my reaction to the imminent turmoil of the move as a reflection of our relationship. That's strong, unbreakable—probably even stronger in many ways because of this experience.

As for the move home, that was inevitable—this year or next. Don't assume the burden for 'failing' to keep us here. I guarantee, I don't view it as a failing in any way. I'm impressed and awed by how you kept it all together and go back with head held very high to a great job you deserve. That's not a failure but a triumph.

I'm probably just filled with conflicted emotions about a number of things. I've made this our home and will be sad to leave, warts and all. And we have a lovely home awaiting us. I'm just trying to figure out my place in the world once we return. I don't want to simply return to my old self as if this experience never happened. Although I don't want that, I'm guessing it's inevitable. Plus, until I achieve more success as a writer, it will be viewed, by most, simply as a quaint little hobby.

Anyway, you're right—my response in times when I have more questions than answers is to retreat into myself. My mind is constantly churning to figure things out. I'm lucky to have you there to wrap your arms around me. That's a great salve.

Just like the move here, we will survive the move home. We'll look upon these two years as a highlight of our life. We will be back, and that experience will be even better than this one. But that can't happen without this move back to Chicago. There's a reason for everything.

You too are my hero, my best friend, and my love. xoxo

-----Original Message-----
From: Jim
To: Todd
Sent: Thu, Oct 8, 2015 9:59 am
Thank you for your response; brought tears to my eyes. I love
you!!!!!!! xoxo

November arrived. Two months slipped by since my countdown clock to repatriation began. I started to think of our departure in terms of weeks, rather than months. The smaller unit of time produced a higher, more comforting number—eight instead of two. October had flown by, filled with trips, visitors, and moving plans. My next blog post's sarcastic title, a jab at the Pollyanna principle, came from my inner conflict. I tried to look at the many positives of returning to Chicago rather than getting stuck lamenting the life we were leaving behind. However, I struggled to keep my disappointment in check. Here is an excerpt. The full post is included in the appendix.

Always Look at the Bright Side of Life, and Other Loads of Crap

The world consists of two kinds of people: those who dwell on life's annoyances and those who sweep them away with a shrug. Maybe each of us is a bit of both. Swearing, however, sure helps us manage through the bad things that happen.

This past month served up healthy doses of bad and good. October reminded us why living in Europe is fantastic. Each weekend served up an exciting treat with a few "tricks" thrown in to keep us grounded and practiced in profanity....

Our list of October weekends, Nice, Amsterdam, Brussels, London, reads like a glossy travel brochure.

Three of the trips threw us curveballs. Most people would roll their eyes and call such glitches "rich people's problems." We get it. These bumps were mere hiccups, petty annoyances that most folks would gladly welcome in exchange for living and playing in Europe. Fortunately, Jim and I are predisposed to letting bad things slip from our memories. Although some issues take a little longer to forget....

As weeks grow into months and months melt into years, experience has taught me that memories of these annoyances will fade. Jim and I will remember that October as a string of lovely weekends reconnecting with old friends. Our ordeals will be inconsequential footnotes, funny anecdotes, and fodder for blog posts and memoirs. We'll recall the people, not the problems. Perhaps that's what it means to always look at the bright side of life.

Aerobics Buddies from Chicago

Friends Peter & Nevi, Hampton Court Park

Chapter 25

When did humanity's obsession with personal possessions begin? Despite small numbers of ascetics who disavow materialism, the majority of our species seems driven to accumulate stuff. Hoarders may be extreme examples, but most of us collect things, stockpiles limited only by space, time, and money. We begin early. Picture the squealing toddler on his or her first birthday placed in the center of a growing mound of toys, trinkets, and stuffed animals. Young brains quickly grasp the concept of personal property. Utterances of "mine, mine, mine" pop early into nascent vocabularies. It's a race to the grave to see who can collect the most toys. Although societal pressures certainly influence us, allowing material possessions to define us is a personal choice. Just how many shoes, automobiles, or houses does one person need? Marketeers and groupthink attach status to almost everything that touches our lives—including brands of cars, fashion, appliances, and even mustard.

Perhaps the pangs of sadness felt as Jim and I prepared to purge much of our stuff were unavoidable. Each piece told a story, a chapter in our life in Brussels. The red toaster and orange blender, replacements for those brought with us after failed experiments with a noisy transformer. The Italian coffee maker hauled on foot from Ixelles when we happened upon the birthplace of Audrey Hepburn. Raclette machines used to host several memorable dinner parties. All these things as well as the memories attached to them, I feared, would soon disappear from our lives.

The purge was necessary. Because of differences in current, electrical gadgets were useless in the United States. We faced the same issue coming over, having to replace such items as a television, iron, vacuum cleaner, and hairdryer. Items to sell ranged from a washer and dryer down to a hand mixer, to a fan. In terms of size and cost, the biggest item was a treadmill. We'd sold a nearly new one at a bargain price when we moved to Belgium. Unlike our outbound experience in the States, we didn't have a vast network of friends to spread the word about items up for sale. Although eBay and Craigslist weren't available in Brussels, a friend told us about two local online auction sites. Jim filled out our online profile and I took photos.

I sat on the couch swiping through images on my phone. "More stuff than I thought. And all in such great condition."

Jim sighed. Time constraints required us to price low. "Great deals for sure."

"Only if things sell," I replied with a shrug. "About the grill, maybe we should simply give it to the neighbors."

"Good idea. Barbara and Patrick have been great." Jim looked up from the computer. "What about Puhi?"

"What about him?"

"Gonna ask Barbara if we can take him?"

I shook my head. "I don't think so."

"But he loves you so much…and you love him."

Jim was right. The clown of a cat had become a regular visitor to our home. I even allowed Puhi a sleepover when Jim was out of town. His frequent drop-ins prompted Jim to buy a litter box and cat condo, which the cat quickly embraced. Even Sadie got used to Puhi. However, I never considered taking him to Chicago. First off, we weren't cat people. But more importantly, he wasn't ours. Despite Barbara's having five other felines, Puhi belonged to her. I couldn't imagine anyone, especially someone who loved animals as much as she did, parting with a prized pet.

"It's up to you," Jim added. "I'm fine with whatever you decide."

"You love him too."

"He's okay." Jim's stifled grin informed me that Puhi had burrowed his way into Jim's heart. Our discussion left me pondering. *What to do about the lovable imp?*

By the first of November, a deluge of repatriation logistics served as daily reminders of our imminent departure. In addition to setting a date with the movers, we had to book our flight to Chicago including arrangements for Sadie. The movers would begin a three-day packing job on Monday, December 7. Exactly one week later, Jim, Sadie, and I would fly home. Before our exit, however, a multitude of tasks remained, including clearing the apartment of our household goods.

Our airline booking offered an unexpected bonus. In speaking with the reservation agent over the phone, Jim learned that a one-way ticket cost substantially more than a round trip. We didn't have to use the return ticket to reap the savings. Based on my years in the industry, the pricing scheme didn't surprise me. Jim, however, voiced his shock to the agent over the phone. "Well, sir," she replied. "I really can't advise you to book round trip, but that's precisely what I'd do." I nodded my concurrence, suggesting for the return flight a random date seven months in the future. Not only had we saved more than $1,000 per ticket, we had reservations to return to Brussels. *Yahoo!* We could leave comforted by knowledge of an imminent return, albeit for a holiday visit.

"Our dog is flying with us," Jim said to the agent. "A pet service will take care of those arrangements. But just for the heck of it, if we were to take a cat, what would that cost?" I chuckled as Jim grinned at me. "Uh-huh...okay...I see. Thank you."

When Jim disconnected, I scoffed. "You're too funny."

He shrugged. "Doesn't hurt to ask, that's all."

"Well, what did she say?"

"Only $100. And he rides in the cabin with us...*if* we decide to take him," he added with a wink.

Our looming departure inspired a heartfelt blog post.

Time to Start Saying Goodbye

This isn't goodbye, *au revoir, vaarwel*—just yet. But our farewell is coming....As good as our life is, change is indeed the only constant....

Full steam ahead! In *four* weeks, movers come to pack up our things for their return voyage across the Atlantic. In *five* weeks, we fly back to Chicago....And as we wait, I measure the time remaining: four more Sundays in our beautiful townhouse that we made into a comfortable, welcoming home. We depart two weeks short of our second anniversary in Belgium.

Other repatriated expats have warned, "Once you tell people you're leaving, they'll start treating you as short-termers. That is, if they don't consider you gone already." I understand that reaction. Why invest emotionally in a short-term relationship? In many ways with its huge percentage of expats, Brussels is a city of interminable goodbyes....

Although we must say goodbye, our excellent adventure has shown us that we're flexible. We can adapt to a new environment, survive, and even flourish outside our comfort zone. There's a certain confidence and strength that comes from knowing that about yourself. Most importantly, we learned that, together, we can make our home anywhere. Home is as much about us as people as it is a physical locale. And how fabulous to learn that the person with whom you've decided to share your life is indeed a perfect fit....

In mid-November, only three weeks remained before movers would pack up our European lives. Many tasks remained, chiefly relating to our apartment. We had to clean and polish the interior and spruce up the garden for the final walk-through. This was no small feat.

Formal inspections are an integral part of the rental process in Belgium. Professional inspectors whose fee is split between tenant and landlord are certified to conduct objective, third-party reviews of the property at the time of initial occupancy and again at the end of the lease. Their detailed notes from the initial inspection serve as foundation for the final review. Blemishes such as nail holes, scratched floors, and damaged walls not noted in the initial review become the tenant's financial responsibility.

Wall paint was a particularly problematic area. A certain amount of normal wear and tear is built into the inspection model. But what did that mean in practical terms? Would we, for example, be liable for shadows left by paintings hung on walls? We were well aware of one task ahead of us. Early in our occupancy, we obtained the landlord's permission to paint the upstairs bathroom and downstairs hall. In addition to filling any nail holes, we had to return the warm red and orange walls back to neutral beige before the inspection.

I viewed the protocol as another archaic Belgian tradition, a process created to protect landlords' interests. We'd get no credit for improvements made to the apartment such as window coverings, stairway carpeting, and landscape plants that cost us thousands of euros. Friends and work colleagues cautioned, "The inspection's an ordeal. A landlord's excuse to nickel and dime you." Others were more fatalistic: "Be prepared to forfeit your entire security deposit." Dire warnings of an unfamiliar process frightened us. Fretting, we suffered nights of fitful sleep. Money was one thing. We prepared ourselves to lose our entire security deposit. The stigma attached to being labeled bad caretakers of our cherished apartment stung as sharp as the loss of a few thousand euros. Only a few weeks remained until the dreaded inspection. And still we had no buyers for the treadmill. We had to get it out of the apartment one way or another.

Before we switched gears to focus exclusively on our grand exit, we held onto a few Brussels traditions. These included one more house-guest, a final day trip to Antwerp, and one last coach tour with the Expat Club to Monschau, Germany, for that quaint town's Christmas market.

Professional concerns competed with departure tasks and social activities. Before we left Brussels, I needed to finalize the cover design and galley edits of my latest book. A combination of glitches including the unexpected need for a review by a second editor as well as missed deadlines by my publisher had pushed the book launch much later in the year than I desired. I now faced a January release date, and then only if I plowed through the remaining tasks. Throughout November, I worked closely with an illustrator. After several iterations, a final cover design emerged. Attention turned to proofing the final text, an exacting process that would drop right on top of the final stages of our move.

Sensational events of Friday, November 13, however, would change the tone and trajectory of our last month in Belgium.

Chapter 26

Keeping to our end-of-workweek routine, Jim and I walked to a neighborhood restaurant whose French name roughly translated as "My Crazy Sister." Intimate Friday dinners, a long-standing ritual, gave us a chance to unwind, catch our breaths, and talk of weekend plans. Martinis were our aperitif of choice although good American versions of the classic cocktail were difficult to find in Europe. Well-intentioned bartenders have served us vodka diluted excessively with vermouth or, worse, Martini Bianco (straight vermouth) on the rocks.

At a small table in a cozy, candlelit room packed with other patrons, Jim dined on roast chicken and I on poached cod. In our two years of dining here, the chalked menu board and specials displayed above the ornate marble fireplace never changed. Nonetheless, we always left the restaurant highly satisfied. With moods mellowed by fine French wine, we spoke of our respective weeks and the moving tasks that remained. Despite it being Friday the 13th, our day and dinner were pleasant and uneventful.

"This time next month," I said with a shrug, "we'll be back in Chicago." Jim nodded, a look of quiet resignation on his face.

After sharing a delicious *tarte Tatin*, Jim asked for *l'addition*—the check, one of the few French words he'd mastered. We paid our bill and offered *mercis* for another *bon repas* to the owners, a polite and efficient French-speaking couple. Parting heavy curtains that protected diners from the elements, we exited onto Chaussée de Charleroi. Bracing against a crisp November chill with wool scarves and leather jackets, we quickened our pace for the short walk home.

Arriving just after ten o'clock, we let Sadie out to roam the garden while we waited on the living room sofa. Surprisingly, Puhi didn't meander inside. Perhaps he'd tried earlier but gave up hope of an evening of television curled up between us on his Scottish blanket.

"*Explosions in Paris.*" Urgency laced Jim's tone.

"What?" I turned to him, his expression serious and surprised. I quickly navigated my phone's screen from Facebook to the BBC. Stories offered sketchy information, reports of loud bangs outside a sports stadium and bursts of gunfire throughout the French capital. I reached for the TV remote. "Sounds like terrorists."

Flipping between CNN and BBC, we monitored news reports for the next few hours. Terrorists had again targeted Paris. But unlike the surgical strike on the offices of *Charlie Hebdo* magazine ten months earlier, these attacks unleashed a fury of violence across the city. Over the course of one hour, suicide bombers and gunmen armed with assault rifles and grenades besieged several restaurants, the Bataclan concert hall, and a stadium where French President François Hollande was among the crowd attending a soccer match between Germany and France. The rampage ended just after midnight. Authorities stormed the Bataclan. Across Paris, 130 people were dead and hundreds more injured, many critically. The widespread slaughter alarmed and saddened but didn't frighten us. With Paris 200 miles to the south, Jim and I felt, perhaps foolishly, insulated and safe.

On Saturday morning I journeyed two stops on the Metro to Gare du Midi to fetch our Italian friend Gia. A visit to the Eurostar website had allayed our concern that the prior night's events had disrupted her journey from London. The Channel Tunnel emerges onto the continent in France and the high-speed train stops at Lille before continuing to Brussels. Fortunately, the delay was minor. Gia noticed only one thing out of the ordinary: additional security personnel on the platform in Lille.

Vivacious and colorful, Gia provided a pleasant diversion from the tragic news reports that filled television and the Internet. Her visit, however, was bittersweet. Another reminder of the ticking countdown clock to our departure. She represented our final houseguest. During our residency, twenty-three sets of overnight guests, forty-two individuals, slept under our roof.

At our apartment, Gia showered a tail-wagging Sadie with love and met Puhi who stopped by on his customary morning rounds. Gia had heard about Puhi and seen him during our biweekly Skype sessions.

"Such a friendly little cat," Gia said, stroking his back. "Are you going to keep him?"

Exchanging looks, Jim motioned for me to respond. "It's undecided."

"Oh," Gia added. "I do hope you decide to take him."

Sharing stories, the three of us spent Saturday touring Brussels on foot. In addition to the Grand Place, stops included the city's medieval cathedral and the Galeries Royales Saint-Hubert. Eye-dazzling chocolate shops that infused the air with rich cocoa and boutiques with chic window displays lured crowds to the handsome shopping arcade. Just outside the arcade's entrance, long lines of eager people waited for *frites*, waffles, and ice cream. The tragic events of Paris hadn't diminished the usual throngs of tourists and shoppers.

Before heading to bed that night, Gia declared our apartment, "Lovely, simply lovely. A veritable palace. Oh, how you both shall miss it."

On Sunday, we drove to Delft to visit an Australian exchange student, the son of mutual friends. Jim and I were eager to visit the historic Dutch city. Known for its iconic blue and white pottery, Delft is also the birthplace of Vermeer, master painter of many famous works including *The Girl with the Pearl Earring*. Brick houses topped by Dutch gables plus canals and squadrons of bicycles were typical of Holland. A gray blustery day with biting winds off the North Sea drew the four of us to the cozy Kobus Kuch café. We fortified ourselves on warm apple cake and hot chocolate, all slathered with rich whipped cream. Having been exchange students ourselves, Jim in Mérida, Mexico, and I in London, we enjoyed hearing our young friend speak with great fondness of his own academic adventure.

Visiting Delft

Noisy seagulls buzzed the square with aeronautical maneuvers as we bade our young friend goodbye with hugs. Watching him peddle away toward his dorm, Gia's smile beamed. "Fabulous weekend. I'm so glad we did this. Nothing beats spending time with friends."

Monday morning we said goodbye to Gia who offered a parting comment, "Keep the cat." Watching her cab turn the corner, Jim and I embraced. Our long string of visitors had come to a quiet end.

With our hosting duties over, we caught up on news. Events in Paris still hadn't rippled across the border. Numbed by chronic violence, perhaps the world shrugged off the latest burst of terror and went about its business. That sense of normalcy, however, was about to change.

Over the next few days, the world's focus turned to Brussels. On Thursday, six days after the attacks, Facebook posts began popping up authored by friends affiliated with the European Union. Authorities, they said, planned to lock down the Belgian capital. I dismissed the reports as social media hype and hysteria. How could a modern European capital shut down? Complex logistics were one consideration. I grappled with the broader philosophical and societal implications. That a modern, first-world metropolis would cease all activity—commercial, political, civic—in the wake of terrorist fears boggled the mind. Civil disruption was precisely the goal of such loathsome cells. If terrorists could shutter Brussels, couldn't they also bring London, Washington, New York, or any city of their choosing to its knees?

That night, Jim's team treated us to a farewell dinner at our favorite spot, the charming Italian restaurant across the street from our apartment. Coincidentally, they were all expats themselves: Dutch, Colombian, Indian. Talk of the rumored lockdown never came up in conversation as we dined from large skillets of fresh pasta dishes, drank robust Italian wine, and spoke of future plans. At the end of the meal, a large plate of cannoli appeared, compliments of the owner-chef, a friendly Italian we came to know from our frequent visits.

The evening's cheery camaraderie heartened me. Jim's team, I observed, admired, respected, and even loved him. They spoke of his nurturing support and skillful coaching. They didn't know as I did the extent to which he had shielded them from the stress and pressures of internal company politics. From Jim's grin and lighthearted mood, I saw that the warm sendoff pleased him as well.

The next day, exactly one week after the Paris attacks, the U.S. Embassy emailed an alert at approximately 6 a.m. to U.S. citizens living in Belgium. A suspicious vehicle, the email read, prompted evacuation of the Renaissance Hotel. Soon thereafter, the embassy reported that authorities had "evacuated/cleared out" the Grand Place as police searched for a suspicious package. Popcorning alerts signaled a city descending into crisis. The irony wasn't lost on me. On the cusp of leaving, Jim and I faced the very situation about which friends and family had expressed grave concern when we first announced our move to Brussels two years earlier.

We didn't panic. Instead, bubbling rumors that turned the world's attention to Brussels compelled me to blog. I hoped to allay fears of friends and family back home.

Alive & Well & Living in Jacques Brel's Brussels

Ever since the atrocities committed in Paris on Friday, November 13, friends and family have reached out to us with concern. Email flurries intensified after Brussels became the focus of investigators. Our thanks to all who checked in with us. We, along with the 1.2 million other residents of Belgium's capital, are alive and well. Streets haven't emptied. This richly diverse city continues to function amidst raids, enhanced security operations, and a steady cacophony of police sirens.

Grand Place Evacuated!

The US Embassy has been dispatching regular warnings, advising American citizens to avoid large public spaces. Although surprised by the extent of the terrorist network operating from Brussels, Jim and I don't feel any less safe than we did before the attacks. Having traveled to hundreds of cities on six continents, we're always cautious. Violence is often random, claiming victims in movie theaters, grade schools, and university lecture halls—places deemed insulated and safe.

What and Where Is Molenbeek?

Brussels Capital Region consists of nineteen semi-autonomous communes. Jim and I live in Saint-Gilles south of the city center. The commune of Molenbeek is northwest of the center. As the world learns about Molenbeek, we who live in Brussels aren't surprised. It's not the first time the commune has been linked to terrorism. In Verviers, authorities apprehended a Molenbeek-connected cell accused of planning attacks on police. The commune also had links to a Jewish supermarket shooting in Paris, the attack on a Thalys train thwarted by Americans, and the 2014 murders of four people at Brussels' Jewish Museum. Many in the press call Molenbeek, a poor neighborhood that most people avoid, the jihadist capital of Europe. Every city has areas deemed seedy and unsafe, our hometown of Chicago no exception. Some people have been lambasted for calling such places "No-go zones." The mayor of Paris sued Fox News for attaching just such a label to parts of Paris after the *Charlie Hebdo* attacks. Arguing over words is senseless. Terrorists, not bombastic newscasters, deserve our focus and wrath. Whatever label you attach to it, Molenbeek isn't all bad. But it's also not a place to wander alone at midnight.

Molenbeek residents even think so. A woman, Muslim by her headscarf, came to our home recently to look at items we're selling as part of our return to Chicago. When asked where she lived, she made a face, held her nose, and said, "Molenbeek." Obviously, she doesn't want to live there either. Although her reasons for remaining aren't my business, I suppose a mix of economic and cultural factors hold her there. Those twin anchors keep most of us rooted in place. The vast majority of Molenbeek's residents are honest, peace-loving people who merely want to live in peace. They too grieve for victims of the Paris attacks.

Why Brussels?

So why does Belgium have more jihadists per capita fighting for ISIS than any other nation? Why is Molenbeek a terrorist hotspot? Many in the press and State Security forces throughout Europe and the world are asking the same questions. An op-ed piece appearing in yesterday's *New York Times* written by Chams Eddine Zaougui, a scholar of Arab studies, offers great background and perspective:

What makes Molenbeek such a hotbed for Islamist radicalism?

The most obvious reason is the deep divisions in Belgian society. The country suffers from a form of linguistic apartheid that divides the Dutch-speaking Flemings and the French-speaking Walloons. Listening to their respective media outlets and politicians, you could be forgiven for thinking that the country of Belgium doesn't exist. The two communities live completely apart. This also leads to administrative dysfunction: Belgium has no less than six governments: a federal government, a Flemish government for the Flanders region, a government of the French community, a government of the German-speaking community, a government of the Walloon region and a government of the Brussels-Capital Region. (*New York Times 11/19/2015*)

I'm no expert, but I agree with much of what Zaougui suggests as reasons for the cluster of terrorist cells in this tiny country. Belgium is a highly fragmented society, a real-life laboratory for sociologists. My views are limited, based on only two years in Brussels. But as a writer, I'm a keen observer. I study people, places, and things. Stories, characters, settings, and motivations are my stock and trade.

Readers of my blog know that I've written much about Brussels. We love living in the hub of Europe and our impressions are mostly favorable. *But*, we found a lack of warmth and welcome from locals. With cold, disdainful sneers encountered on the streets of Brussels, people repel others, creating unnecessary and uncomfortable distance. It's easy to feel alienated here. Most expats we know, even those who've lived here for many years, claim not to have any close Belgian friends. We've been offered many explanations. Discussions on the topic fill the Internet. Belgians prefer family and a tight circle of friends. Many never leave the villages of their births. This last cultural trait is often cited as contributing to massive traffic jams, the worst in Europe. Belgians prefer long, road-clogging commutes to moving away from hometowns.

A great deal of commentary blames the poor assimilation of Muslims into Belgian society for the cluster of jihadist sympathizers. But how can one expect full integration of foreigners in a fragmented society that's wary of each other? The Flemish and French don't like each other—there's even talk of secession.

Communities benefit when passersby look at each other. A sense of connection, however small—humans sharing a place and time. And vigilance—*I see you. You can't get away with anything*. It's the same premise by which neighborhood watches function in the US. By turning away from passersby, society turns a blind eye to those who seek cover to create chaos and mayhem. By all accounts, the terrorists of Molenbeek felt safe plotting their heinous acts in the middle of Brussels, the EU capital and home to NATO.

Belgium is a progressive society. Euthanasia is allowed and the nation was the second to legalize same-sex marriage. But one can draw a fine line between a "live and let live" attitude and the more callous "I don't care what you do, just leave me alone." Both achieve "progressive" results but with very different methodologies and consequences.

I certainly don't have answers for a healthy path forward. That's best left to the Belgians, especially as Jim and I will soon be living 4,000 miles away. But with the world's eyes now scrutinizing them, although Belgians may still turn away from each other, they'll have to look at themselves in the mirror.

<hr />

My message of reason and calm was premature. The day after I submitted that blog post, the situation in Brussels deteriorated rapidly.

Chapter 27

Typical of late November, a cold rain fell on Brussels as residents awakened on Saturday the 21st to news that the government had elevated the city's security threat to Level 4, highest on their scale. Authorities feared a "serious and imminent" Paris-style attack involving firearms and explosives during the manhunt for a Belgian-born man of Moroccan descent suspected of taking part in the Paris attacks. The trail led to Molenbeek.

The declaration closed the city's Metro system, shuttered stores and shopping malls, and canceled sporting events and concerts. Music venues, museums, and galleries closed for the weekend. The U.S. Embassy issued the following statement: "Shelter in place and remain at home. If you must go out, avoid large crowds. U.S. citizens are urged to avoid public places such as major pedestrian walkways and shopping centers. If you were planning to attend an event, we strongly urge you to reconsider. Exercise caution in public transportation systems, sporting events, residential areas, business offices, hotels, clubs, restaurants, places of worship, schools, public areas, shopping malls, and other tourist destinations."

Although concerned, Jim and I had no intention of sequestering ourselves inside our apartment. Only a few weeks remained for accomplishing many moving tasks. Our weekend plans included buying paint to restore a few walls to their original bland shades of white. With stores in Brussels closed for security reasons, off to Leuven we drove for supplies.

We enjoyed visiting the centuries-old university town. The town hall, a fifteen-century Gothic masterpiece, features fairy-tale turrets and an ornate, lacelike facade adorned with hundreds of statues. In addition to a vibrant student population, Leuven is home to Stella Artois beer and the best burrito in all of Belgium…maybe the *only* burrito. On this occasion, probably our last trip to the city, we shunned Mexican fast food and beer for a fine restaurant and a bottle of wine. With each sip of crisp and tart Sauvignon Blanc, the sense of doom fueled by that morning's news reports lifted from our shoulders. Beyond the perimeter of the Level 4 security curtain, Leuven felt relaxed, laid back, safe.

On our drive home after lunch, anxiety slowly returned as we neared Brussels. With news reports on the car radio limited to Flemish and French, I scanned my phone for updates. Headlines spoke to the heightened security risk and strong military presence throughout the city. Later that night, we had dinner plans with another couple, gay American expats like ourselves. We wanted to try a new bar in the Grand Sablon before dining at a favorite nearby restaurant. The upscale area was a ten-minute walk from home.

Mid-afternoon as we sat in our living room, a text arrived from the other couple. "You guys still on?"

"Yep, if you are," I replied. Threats alone weren't sufficient to keep us inside. Perhaps we subscribed to *this won't happen to us* thinking. I ended my text, "I'll call the bar and restaurant when they open to make sure."

Over the next few hours, we monitored news sources. Global media operatives had descended upon Brussels, posting photos of nearly empty streets patrolled by armed military personnel and armored vehicles. As America awakened to news of Brussels' lockdown, we fielded several emails. "Thinking of you both," they said. "Please be careful." The situation slid toward the surreal. One news photo showed four Middle Eastern men sitting on the pavement in handcuffs under police guard in the Grand Sablon, our evening's destination.

"Still comfortable heading out tonight?" Jim asked.

"Let me try the bar and restaurant again."

Replying to my inquiry, the man who answered the telephone at the bar said, "*Fermé*, closed." I received the same response from the restaurant.

The mayor of Brussels asked all restaurants and bars in the city center to close for the night. The decision had been taken out of our hands. We weren't entirely unhappy with that outcome.

The next morning, raising the security shutters that covered our street-facing windows, Jim noted that the sidewalks were emptier than usual even for a cold, damp Sunday. "Good day to paint," he added.

After coffee and breakfast, we divided the painting chores. Jim took the downstairs red hall, and I the upstairs orange powder room. The task required little thought, putting me in a reflective mood. Each brushstroke, as orange became white, erased our imprint on our treasured home. Along with the physical alterations, our emotional connection to the house and our European life were fading away.

Early afternoon, I paused the paint roller and yelled down the stairs. "Hey, sweet pea, how about I go to the market for chicken? Might be our last." Roasted chicken from the Saint-Gilles Sunday market was our favorite. No other chicken we sampled compared to the plump, juicy roasters with golden, salty, crispy skin. We didn't have many Sundays left to enjoy the mouthwatering treat.

Jim wandered upstairs, his T-shirt speckled with white paint. "Sure you want to go out?"

I nodded. "It's only a five-minute walk. I'll grab a chicken, some potatoes, and come right back."

Jim grinned. "Well. I won't say no. But be careful."

Putting on my raincoat and scarf, I grabbed a shopping bag and kissed Jim before heading out into the gray afternoon. I crossed a quiet Rue d'Ecosse and made my way down an abandoned Rue Jourdan. I expected to see blond, round-faced families in their Sunday best who customarily gathered for mass at the Polish mission house. But the street and sidewalks were empty.

Odd, I thought, *especially on market day.*

The laundromat, car wash, and Portuguese bar were quiet. Arriving at the parvis, I stared in disbelief. The vast space was deserted. Cobblestones glistened under a light, steady rain. *Incredible!* The market was an integral part of the commune, its lifeblood so to speak. On a typical Sunday, dozens of vendors and hordes of shoppers filled the square. All that was gone. At the top of the parvis, the simple steeple and clock of the Eglise Saint-Gilles stood as sentinel over the abandoned landscape. The eerie stillness unsettled me; our little world was amiss.

A Nearly Deserted Parvis

Snapping a few photos, I forwarded them to Jim with a text, "Sorry, sweetie, no chicken today." For dinner, we settled for sausage and pepperoni pizza conveniently delivered to our front window by motorbike.

Heading into a new week, Brussels remained on lockdown. Metros weren't running. Businesses told employees to stay home. Having remained inside all Sunday breathing paint fumes, we needed to escape. Strolling the few blocks to our favorite café to work, Jim and I found a policeman standing guard at the front door. Inside, tables filled with unfamiliar faces banging away at computers and speaking into headsets. The café appeared as an oasis of calm and normalcy amidst a city in crisis.

I nudged Jim. "Lockdown's good for business."

Despite my flip comment, we admired the young staff. They worked as usual while most government staffers and EU bureaucrats hunkered down safely at home. Admiration turned to respect after the café's owner relayed an incident from Saturday. A strange man had entered the café and informed staff that a gunman intended to shoot up the place, "just like they did in Paris." Yet despite the threat, staff greeted customers, poured coffees, and prepared bagel sandwiches with eggs, bacon, smoked salmon, and other savories as if it were a regular Monday morning.

That evening, Brussels remained on lockdown. After a day of editing at the cafe, I posted an update on my blog. Here is an excerpt. The full post is included in the appendix.

Winter, Webcam Wonderland

The annual holiday spectacle in the Grand Place draws thousands to the famous square for the Christmas tree, Nativity scene, and light show. This past weekend, Brussels unveiled this year's tree, a real beauty. But no ogling spectators came.

Instead, dire warnings of an imminent terrorist attack put Brussels on lockdown. A week after the attacks in Paris while the rest of Belgium remains at Threat Level 3, authorities elevated Brussels to Level 4....

Images coming out of Brussels are surreal, scenes from a Dystopian future. Military carriers rolled into the city. Soldiers toting machine guns patrolled the streets alongside the city's police force. Metro entrances blocked with police tape. Cinemas and stores closed. Brussels, a world capital of 1.2 million people, on lockdown. The US Embassy sent emails advising citizens to stay indoors. The US Department of Defense issued a 72-hour embargo on its employees and contractors for travel to Brussels. DOD personnel already in Brussels were told to stay inside....

We're still not sure what tomorrow will bring. All we can do is trust that authorities are doing what's necessary to keep us safe. Kudos to soldiers and police for putting themselves in potential peril to keep the city secure....

Hunkered down in our Brussels home, I scanned local news for updates. I happened upon the Brussels City website where I found webcam links, real-time windows into our besieged city. There's a webcam at Place de Brouckere, one of the city's busiest squares, another in the Grand Place with a view of the Christmas tree and Starbucks.

It's sadly ironic that the Christmas tree, a symbol of peace, joy, and hope, stands alone. Viewing the tree from the safety of a webcam feels a bit unseemly, like a Peeping Tom or Orwell's Big Brother. It's not very satisfying to window-shop on life. I'd rather stand below the mighty balsam's branches, gaze upon the dazzling lights and sparkling ornaments. I'd prefer to feel the nip of crisp air on my face, hear the wonderment in children's voices, and inhale the comforting scent of pine....

Christmas trees, like life itself, are best experienced up close and in person, their beauty and majesty firing each of our senses.

⸻ ◦〇◦ ⸻

On Monday November 23, the country's Prime Minister announced that security measures would last at least another week. Brussels remained on lockdown. As the manhunt for the Paris terrorist suspect continued, sensationalist headlines told of police raids and roundups of suspects.

The immediacy of the crisis was inescapable. The constant wail of sirens blared outside our favorite café. Blue and white police cars escorted green transport vans hauling suspects between the prison in Saint-Gilles and criminal court at the Palais de Justice. Most of these arrests amounted to nothing. Detainees were generally released after questioning, updates relegated to minor footnotes in news reports. Police helicopters buzzed the sky above our garden more than usual. Soldiers wearing camouflage uniforms and toting automatic weapons patrolled neighborhood streets alongside augmented patrols of regular police in dark blue uniforms. Armored vehicles strategically parked throughout the city served as backdrops for tourist photos and selfies. We lived in a city primed for battle.

The global media wasn't kind to Belgian intelligence. News outlets questioned the efficacy of intelligence gathering and data coordination. Reports cast a critical spotlight on police effectiveness. A law banning police raids between 9 p.m. and 5 a.m. drew sharp rebukes. To many, it appeared that authorities were spinning their wheels. Officials responsible for the city's safety and security faced a dilemma. With the Paris terror suspect still at large, no significant arrests made, and no cache of weapons found, the declared threat to Brussels remained unresolved. An indefinite lockdown of the country's capital and commercial hub was unsustainable, economically untenable.

One politician suggested a laughable solution. Create Threat Level 5—accept the current situation as the new normal, a baseline. A higher and as yet untriggered threat level would give authorities cover to restart the city. Reason prevailed and the ill-conceived scheme was shelved.

Despite some criticism, on Wednesday the 25th schools restarted and the Metro chugged back into operation. Despite a lingering terrorist threat and strong, visible military presence, Brussels stirred back to life. Tensions, however, remained high.

Chapter 28

"I've made up my mind. I'm throwing you and Jim a traditional American Thanksgiving."

Weeks before the holiday and prior to the Paris attacks and Brussels' lockdown, our neighbor Barbara made that declaration as the two of us dined at our favorite Thai restaurant. Jim's absence on a business trip allowed me to satisfy my craving for the exotic cuisine. Barbara, always a willing accomplice, had a cheerful demeanor and stockpile of fantastic stories that made for a fun and entertaining dining experience.

I set my wineglass onto the table. "Are you sure? That's a lot of work."

She wagged her finger. "You simply can't refuse. Not with you leaving." Speaking in Slovenian-accented English, she affected a pout, her customary expression when talking about our impending repatriation. "Poor, poor, us."

I snickered. "Okay, okay. We'd really love that."

Her blue eyes sparkled as she clapped her hands. "Good, good, good. It will be great fun. We'll need turkey of course. Yes, a turkey for sure." Her round, fair-skinned face, framed by wisps of blonde hair, assumed a determined expression.

Her undertaking struck me as endearing and humorous. Barbara, a proud, proselytizing vegetarian who abstained from meat out of compassion for animals, proposed to roast a turkey for her American neighbors.

Her impish grin returned. "But you'll have to fill me in on all the other traditions. For example, the flags."

"Flags?"

She nodded above the bowl of aromatic green curry placed before her. "Yes. American flags and fireworks."

I laughed. "No flags or fireworks. Different holiday. This one's all about food. Families and friends gather in thanks to share the harvest."

"Friends, huh…" With narrowed eyes and pursed lips, her expression became that of an eager student. "Then I'll invite friends."

"You don't have to. That's more work."

"No, if Thanksgiving calls for friends, then friends we shall have. Auguste, Carlos…" Her mind churned with other names. "Oh, and besides turkey and stuffing, what other food do we need?"

"Mashed and sweet potatoes, cranberry sauce, Brussels sprouts, green bean casserole, and gravy…lots and lots of gravy. And for dessert, pies. Pumpkin, maybe pecan…but this being Brussels, any sweet will do."

As the menu items increased, Barbara's eyes widened, her shoulders sagged. "Oh," she said almost as a gasp of defeat.

I waved my hand over the table. "But don't you worry about any of that. Leave the sides to me. Besides, finding a turkey in Brussels will be challenge enough."

Lifting her wineglass, she batted her eyes. "*Au contraire*, the biggest challenge will be learning how to stuff and roast the bird."

In America and for Americans across the globe, November 26 was Thanksgiving. In Belgium, that Thursday marked another day under Threat Level 4. For Jim and me, it meant a regular workday. Barbara's dinner party, however, promised a special treat, an oasis of civility and camaraderie in a city shrouded by threat and suspicion. More importantly, we regarded her enthusiastic desire to celebrate our American holiday as a precious gesture that honored not only our national customs but also our friendship.

As promised, I spent a great deal of time in our kitchen preparing half a dozen side dishes including rich, creamy gravy, Jim's favorite. Our apartment filled with familiar aromas, triggering fond remembrances of Thanksgivings past. Vibrant images flickered through my head: my siblings, cousins, aunts, uncles, parents, and grandparents, many now deceased, gathered around my mom's meticulously set table. Thanksgiving was one of only a handful of occasions when Mom used the dining room, her cherished tablecloth and fine china. These memories enveloped me with comforting feelings of family, security, and home.

I considered the prior year's Thanksgiving our first in Brussels. We had dined alone while Sadie recovered from surgery. And now, this night. Regardless of how Barbara's turkey debut turned out, the gathering at her home represented the closest surrogate for family that Jim and I had in Brussels. Anticipation and excitement swept over me just as they had done when, as a child, I peeked out the front window anxiously awaiting our cherished guests.

I penned a blog post that served as a holiday greeting to folks back home as well as an update on events in Brussels. The world remained riveted by the crisis that continued to grip our adopted city. Here is an excerpt. The full post is included in the appendix.

Thanksgiving & Terror Threat Level 4

With so much wrong in our world and our own city under a cloud of terror, are we foolish, naïve, or, worse, hypocritical to celebrate Thanksgiving? Pope Francis has gone so far as to call this Christmas, with the world pimpled by war, a *charade*.... When the Pope sounds jaded and cynical, what hope is there for the rest of us? Yet the world keeps spinning forward; and we manage to hang on. We're survivors....

With an abundance of craziness closing in on us, and cable news feeding us infinite loops of ugly chaos, it's easy to lose sight of the world's beauty and humanity's decency. For just as beauty exists beside ugliness, so too does goodness coexist with evil....

We shouldn't forget the *cornucopia* of goodness, beauty, and love that also exists in our world. Today, Jim and I will pause to celebrate our Thanksgiving tradition and give thanks to the bounty of good fortune in our lives. In addition to our wonderful families and friends, we're thankful for the past two years in Belgium. In years to come, we'll remember our time here, not for these final weeks living under threat of attack, but for the country's amazing wonders. Thank you, Brussels, Belgium, for enriching our lives with culture and for providing us a beautiful home into which we welcomed so many dear friends, old and new.

Happy Thanksgiving from the Arkenbergs!

———

As darkness descended on Brussels, Jim and I bade farewell to Sadie with promises of turkey leftovers. Into our arms we loaded two potato dishes, two vegetable dishes, cranberry sauce, gravy, and two bottles of wine, from our home at number 4, next door to number 6. The irony was hilarious. Jim and I, proud carnivores, prepared non-meat dishes while our vegetarian neighbor roasted the turkey.

"Happy Thanksgiving," we said as Barbara opened her front door.

"Oh my," she replied glancing at our full load. "That's a lot of food."

We both chuckled. "There's more," Jim replied. "I'll put this down and run home for the rest."

"Ungodly amounts of food are part of the tradition," I said as Barbara welcomed us into the foyer with three kisses to the cheeks. "By the way," I added. "How's the turkey?" Lifting my nose, I detected only the faintest hint of roasted meat.

Barbara looked a bit frightened, a deer-in-the-headlights glare. "I'm worried it's not cooking. Can you check it for me? Oh, some good news," she added leading me into the kitchen. "The bird came pre-stuffed."

Good news indeed.

The small kitchen looked like a disaster zone. Dishes, utensils, and cutting boards filled the sink and every inch of counter space. Did I want to know what exploded in the half-opened microwave? Barbara opened the oven. The slightly browned turkey was barely warm to the touch. "Poor, poor me," she muttered.

By my estimates, we were two hours away from dinner. It wasn't my first experience with the creeping delay of undercooked turkey. My mom's oven once broke in the middle of roasting. Her microwave saved the day. In addition, on several holidays, Jim and I arrived at my brother's home for a late-afternoon meal only to find ourselves waiting hours to dine on properly cooked meat.

I put my arm around Barbara. Her sad pout melted my heart. "Don't worry, a delayed bird's also part of the tradition."

She looked up into my eyes, despair surrendering to joy. "Really?"

"Most emphatically yes. The appetizers and champagne I spotted on your table will humor us until the bird's done. I'll keep my eye on it."

Her blithe spirit returned. "Thank heavens you're here."

Despite the delay, the evening was magical. Barbara and Patrik's home radiated with cozy warmth that included a wood-burning fireplace and comfortable, cat-proofed furniture. The large, round wooden dining table glistened with silver and sparkled with crystal and fine china set for seven. Our Slovenian hosts were also sharing the feast with Carlos, a Spaniard; Auguste, a Belgian; and Mortem, a Norwegian. Puhi and a few of Barbara's other cats made appearances.

While waiting for the turkey to cook, we settled onto the couch and chairs in the living room before a generous fire.

"Tell us about this Thanksgiving tradition," Carlos said during the champagne toast.

"When did it start?" Auguste added.

"I've heard bits and pieces," Mortem interjected, "but not from an actual American."

As I told the story of the pilgrims and Indians and the first Thanksgiving, I recognized parallels between our American tradition and that evening's communal feast. All of us gathered that evening were pilgrims of sorts—expats, wayfarers, risk-takers—uprooted people pulled together by chance.

Barbara's First Thanksgiving Turkey

Barbara's stuffed turkey was juicy and flavorful. She beamed with pride as we praised her efforts. My side dishes were gobbled up as seconds and even thirds were requested. As expected, the gravy was a hit. Instead of pie, in true Belgian fashion, a creamy chocolate mousse torte was served along with coffee and digestives. The cheerful little party embraced the spirit of the holiday, forgetting the security threat that lurked outside the door. Swept up by the camaraderie, Jim and I set aside the sadness of our imminent departure. In the soft glow of firelight and candles, and touched by the warmth of friendship, our American and Belgian roots grafted together seamlessly. The perfect evening meandered toward a pleasant and satisfying end.

"Thank you for sharing your lovely tradition with us," Auguste said.

"Not at all what I expected," added Patrik.

"Even better than the stories," said Mortem.

Carlos nodded. "Simple, yet so pleasant."

We hugged our way around the table. Embraces were sincere and affectionate. "*Au revoir et bonne chance,* goodbye and good luck" were common refrains. We saved our strongest hugs and fondest words for Barbara who, retrieving a small bag of leftovers for Sadie, showed us to the door.

"Best Thanksgiving ever," Jim said.

"*Merci, merci, ma bonne amie,*" I said. "Everything was fabulous. We'll cherish this evening always."

She affected a pout. "And soon you leave. Poor, poor me."

V

Uprooted Again

The definition of a successful transplant is a tree that survives.
(deeproot.com)

Chapter 29

In the days after Thanksgiving, little more than two weeks remained until our departure. Au revoir, goodbye, and "If you're ever in Chicago…" dominated our vocabulary. In addition to close friends and colleagues, our cleaning lady, hair stylist, house and dog sitter, dog groomer, and staff of our favorite café received our spoken farewells. Our dentist and her husband, befriended on an Expat Club adventure, warranted a goodbye dinner at our home.

As for our doctor, we had parted ways months earlier. Without even an X-ray, he diagnosed my aching hip a result of insufficient padding around my pelvis. *Huh?* I later learned the hip required total replacement. The doctor had given me another reason to question his judgment. During my consultation he casually dropped a pamphlet into my hands. "Hope you and Jim can make it," he said with an encouraging nod. "One of your countrymen. Smart fellow loaded with facts. You won't believe the things your government's hiding from you." My interest piqued. As I began to read the brochure, my blood pressure spiked. Despite knowing that I'd worked for United Airlines, a company that lost two airplanes, nineteen employees and dozens of passengers in the terrorist attack, our physician had just invited me to a lecture by a renowned conspiracy theorist who claimed that September 11 was a hoax. Dumbstruck, I walked out of his office. *Not the best way to instill confidence in a patient—quack!*

Besides farewells to people, Jim and I also wanted to experience a few of our favorite places and activities one last time. Antwerp topped the list for an enjoyable Saturday excursion. First stop, Bakkerij Dellafaille for cappuccino and *strikje,* the flaky bow-tie pastry we had discovered early in our residence. Fortified with sugar and caffeine, we took an extended farewell stroll through the city's charming streets, squares, and neighborhoods. "I could live here," Jim's customary endorsement of a place, applied equally to me. Antwerp is a gem.

Before heading back to Brussels and at my urging, Jim used a portion of his eco check allowance, funds provided by his employer for environment-friendly purchases and activities, to buy a bicycle. He'd eyed the Dutch-made bike on prior visits but needed my push. "Go ahead," I said. "Spend the money on yourself. You deserve it." Wheeling his shiny purchase to our car, Jim grinned like a little boy. "Now, whenever you ride it," I added, "you'll always think of our Belgian adventure." His trilling of the bike's bell signaled his concurrence.

The next day we boarded a chartered coach for our final adventure with the Expat Club. The organization had entertained and educated us with day trips to Cologne, Champagne, Trier, the Mosel River valley, and Holland's famed tulip gardens. Our last tour took us to Monschau, Germany, for a Christmas market. We stepped from the bus into crisp, spruce-infused air that carried the hushed roar of rushing water. Nestled in the Rur River valley, the medieval village was picture postcard perfect: half-timbered buildings, gabled houses, slate-roofed shops, and a fast-flowing river. A centuries-old castle perched on a hill above the town completed the fairy-tale tableau.

Grinning Like a Boy

Monschau proved an ideal diversion from our repatriation blues. By their nature, Christmas markets are cheery places. Bright tents full of colorful, glittery wares tempted our eyes. Our noses twitched with the savory aromas of grilled sausages, onions, and fried potatoes that mingled with sweet scents of roasted chestnuts, candied almonds, mulled wine, and spiced ciders. Children's playful squeals punctuated the happy banter of adult revelers fueled by beer and glühwein. As the sky turned from sapphire-blue to indigo and then to black, a chill descended over the valley. Jim and I grabbed bratwursts and locally brewed beers before the long ride home. When a light mist began to fall, we took refuge at a high-top table under a tent on a terrace above the river. On the opposite bank, lead-pained windows of rustic cottages glowed with warm light that reflected upon the river's surface. Such idyllic scenes were common in the Europe we loved.

After swigging his beer, Jim rested his glass on the table. "I'm gonna miss all of this."

Putting my arm around him, I replied, "Me too."

As December opened, we had one final week of near normalcy in our apartment before packers dismantled our expat life bit by bit. Strangers dropped by to collect items bought through our Internet sale. They'd been kind enough to wait to take possession of household necessities such as our vacuum cleaner, coffee maker, washer, and dryer. Lack of interest in our treadmill, however, continued. The machine wasn't some small, inconsequential object we could simply leave behind hoping no one noticed. We had to get rid of it. As a last resort, Jim phoned the sports store where we bought it and offered it free of charge. The giveaway represented a loss of three thousand euros. Minor consolation came in the form of three very fit, handsome guys in snug jeans who dismantled the machine and hauled it away—eye candy for a hefty sum.

Farewell lunches, coffees, and drinks continued to fill our calendar. Michel, our neighbor at number 2, a congenial purveyor of sandwiches and neighborhood news, invited us into his shop for complimentary coffee, candy bars, and casual banter. In addition, I strolled into the city center for a final Tuesday night with the BWC. My fellow writers toasted me with Belgian beer and presented me with parting gifts of notebooks and pens. Teary-eyed, I expressed my gratitude. "You made Brussels feel like home."

As for Jim, the need to return his company car and computer gave him the chance to bid farewell to his office. That morning he left the house with an air of contentment about him. When he walked in our front door later that evening, his attitude assumed a mix of anger, amusement, and befuddlement.

"What's up?" I asked after we exchanged a welcome kiss.

Dropping his bag onto the desk, Jim heaved a sigh. There wasn't time for a drink. I sensed his need to vent. "First off, no one's ever heard of an exit interview. Guessing they agreed to one only to humor me."

Jim desired closure with his boss. Their relationship, as the saying goes, was complicated. From my perspective, it bordered on toxic. Jim had hoped to use the exit interview to have a constructive dialogue about the experience and thank his boss for bringing him to Brussels. He wanted to leave on a positive note.

Based on his account, he led the discussion. "Told my boss what I'd learned. Admitted my weaknesses. Acknowledged our difficulties. Thanked her too. And I meant it, you know I do." I nodded as we both moved to the couch. "Then I asked what she learned from me..." He rolled his eyes. "Apparently, she's learned *nothing* from me or our experience...*nothing*."

"Good grief."

"Oh, wait," he added. "She did learn one thing. Said she found my paraphrasing technique annoying. 'Yet another reason,' she said, 'why you'll never succeed in Europe.'"

My jaw dropped. Pricey consultants hired by United Airlines to teach executives how to better communicate called paraphrasing a valuable tool used by highly effective leaders to get teams onto the same page. To me, it seemed tailor-made for Jim's far-flung team and complex project that crossed multiple disciplines, languages, and borders. Her dig about his not making it in Europe seemed gratuitous and cruel, salt for the wound. He had every reason to be proud of his accomplishments with European teams, those who worked for his current employer as well as his prior one, Daimler Financial.

"Wait, wait," Jim added. "That's not even the best part."

How can it get any worse, I thought, clenching my jaw.

"I mentioned some soul-searching," Jim added. "Told her that I'd asked myself would I take the assignment again, knowing what I do."

"And?"

"I said, 'Yes, of course I'd do it all over again. It's been an amazing experience for which I thank you.'"

His suggestive smirk prodded me. "There's more, right?"

His smirk became a sarcastic sneer. "Uh-huh, the *best* part. After sitting stone silent for a few awkward moments, she finally speaks, 'Hmm, asked myself the very same question, Jim. Would I do it again? Bring you to Brussels?'"

"This ought to be good."

"Again, she pauses. Finally, her face contorts. I swear to you, she looked as if she was passing a kidney stone." Jim mimicked her contortion. "Then, she looks me in the eye and says, 'Yes, I'd do it again.'" He shook his head as he relived the agonizing moment. "I mean really! She couldn't have looked more miserable."

The situation demanded drinks, which I fetched from our bar. Not knowing whether to laugh or cry, I simply raised my glass. "Cheers, sweetie. You survived. Did great work too. That's all that matters. And now she's out of our lives."

Veterinary certification remained. Pets traveling internationally required an examination within ten days of departure. The vet had to stamp a pet's EU passport, certifying that all vaccinations were current and the animal healthy to travel. Sadie's house-calling vet cleared our princess to fly.

And Puhi?

Jim warmed to the idea of bringing him to Chicago despite warning me that the gregarious cat was probably a "good-time Charlie," a precocious imp who toyed with the affections of many. I'd already given Puhi a piece of my heart.

Fearing a painful rejection, I hemmed and hawed about asking Barbara's permission to take Puhi. What if she said no? For as much as she encouraged his visits and commented on our affection for him, Puhi belonged to her. She, no doubt, loved him too. However, with our departure date quickly approaching, I worked up the courage to ask her. Doubtful of the answer, I didn't even tell Jim.

"I want to ask you something," I said one afternoon to Barbara over coffee. My stomach knotted. "It's okay if you say no—"

"Of course, you're taking Puhi." She didn't even let me finish my sentence. "He's already made up his mind he's going."

Gaping at her, I felt my tension ease. "Are you sure?"

"Absolutely! Cats pick their owners. He picked you."

After I hugged her, she replied with a giggle. "Puhi's going to be a Yankee. Not the only Slovenian immigrant to America either. Puhi and Melania Trump." Barbara considered Puhi Bruxellois by birth but Slovenian by adoption. We both laughed heartily.

Barbara accompanied me to the veterinary clinic. "Poor, poor Puhi," she said. "He's going to need every vaccination."

We asked the vet to replace Barbara's name with ours on the cat's passport and chip registration. After he did so, I exclaimed. "It's official, Puhi's an Arkenberg."

Due to many questions fielded from friends about Puhi, and in recognition of his formal adoption, I created a blog post. Here is an excerpt. The full post is included in the appendix.

Guest Cat No More

Puhi made inroads into our garden...and into our hearts. The little fellow was persistent. He wanted in. Puhi quickly had me in the palm of his little paw. To gain entry, however, he learned that he'd have to work on Jim and Sadie....Absent a few swats and nibbles of Sadie's feathery tail, Puhi behaved reasonably well. The ole girl grew to tolerate him—first hurdle cleared.

Jim wasn't going to be a pushover. My kind husband humored me and my new feline buddy but made it clear he wasn't a cat lover. Besides, he had allergies! Jim explained his passive acceptance of Puhi into my life, "These are the things we do for love."

Family is an all-or-nothing proposition. What was Puhi to do? Answer—shower Jim with affection and counter his objections to a cat...by acting like Sadie. "He's just like a dog," Jim declared, arriving home from work as Puhi waited at the front door beside Sadie. *Well played, Puhi, well played....*

And Jim's allergy? By some miracle, he's not allergic to Puhi. *Oh, the things we do for love!....*

When the Arkenbergs board the plane for Chicago, we will be four. Puhi wouldn't have it any other way. We just can't tell Sadie that although she must ride in the cargo hold, Puhi gets to accompany us in the cabin.

We'd be remiss if we didn't acknowledge the understanding and generosity of our neighbor....As Puhi's owner, Barbara recognized his decision to adopt the Arkenbergs and accepted his emigration with all of her heart. We know she'll miss the little clown. But sometimes love means you have to let a piece of your heart take flight.

⸻ ❖ ⸻

We knew that our final week in Brussels would be emotional. Movers planned to pack boxes on Monday and wrap up our furniture on Tuesday. On Wednesday, they'd load the cargo container that would transport our belongings to Chicago. We set aside Thursday and Friday for cleaning and the formal turnover of keys.

Packers arrived on schedule. Cupboards and closets emptied. I stood aside and watched. As boxes piled up around us, sadness swept over me.

"Sweetie," Jim said sensing my mood shift. "Don't you want to move to the hotel tonight?" He'd booked a room at a nearby hotel for us until our departure in a week's time.

I flashed my *are you kidding me* face. "We've already discussed that. The longer I sleep in our bed, the happier I'll be."

"Even if it's only for one extra night?"

I nodded. "Even if it's only one more night." I guess I wanted to hold onto our old life as long as possible. My feelings were the same two years earlier when we moved from Chicago. At that time, I slept on an air mattress after our furniture shipped, delaying my departure to the very last moment.

Jim, Sadie, and I found refuge in the living room, the last space we asked movers to clear. When they reached it the following day, we'd relocate to the hotel. Sadie would lose access to her garden. Puhi posed a problem. He was accustomed to hopping over the wall and wandering into the house at will. Because the movers needed to keep our doors and windows open to the street, we feared the curious imp might wander off. Barbara agreed to keep him indoors until the movers left for the day. The free-spirited feline who bristled at a collar and scratched at any closed door wasn't happy.

On Monday evening, we texted the *all clear* to Barbara. Sure enough, Puhi soon wandered over. Once inside, he studied the boxes. But after touring the apartment, he jumped onto the couch and curled into a ball. With Sadie at our feet, the four of us enjoyed one final evening of domestic harmony in our cozy Brussels home.

Wednesday evening signaled the point of no return. Movers cleared out everything, packed the cargo container, and hauled it away. I returned to the empty apartment to collect Jim after a farewell drink with a friend. After a stop at Barbara's for cocktails, we'd grab dinner. We were making the final rounds to our favorite neighborhood restaurants.

Sadie Surveys our Empty Home

Saying Goodbye to our Home

When I walked in, Jim looked distressed. "What's wrong?"

"It was horrible." He explained that he texted Barbara and opened the back door to await his visitor. Soon, Puhi scrambled over the garden wall. "He strolled through the door, looked around at the empty space, and started howling. I've never heard such a pitiful cry. I'm sure he thinks we're leaving him. He's utterly distraught."

"Where is he now?"

Jim shrugged. "Don't know. Guessing back at Barbara's, sulking. Poor little guy."

Puhi, finding his adopted home cleared out, probably figured that his cozy evenings curled up between us on the sofa were over. His friends were abandoning him. In one agonizing moment, he expressed the feelings that Jim and I had weeks to work through. Puhi could have used a valium and Jim an extra-stiff drink.

In those tumultuous last days as the movers inched closer to displace us, I huddled in the living room behind tall French doors. The BWC's co-chairman asked me to write a farewell piece for the group's website. With sentiments befitting valediction for our entire adventure, I also shared the piece on my blog, my last post from Brussels. Here is an excerpt. The full blog post is included in the appendix.

A Fond Farewell to the Brussels Writers' Circle
Coming Full Circle—BWC says Farewell to Chairman Todd Arkenberg

"One does not discover new lands without consenting to lose sight of the shore for a very long time."
—Andre Gide

A favorite quote speaks to the necessity of risk—courage to leave behind the safety of the familiar—in order to grow. As authors, we soar highest when we push beyond the familiar. Readers crave fresh perspectives, unique story lines, unfamiliar settings. Experimentation is a great teacher. But as rewarding as discovery is in our writing, losing sight of the shore in our personal lives can unsettle.

As I prepared to leave the USA two years ago, apprehension tempered my excitement. What would life be like in Brussels? What about my writing?...

Surfing the Internet from the security of my Chicago home, I found the Brussels Writers' Circle....A safe haven awaited me on that distant, unknown shore.

Within a fortnight of my arrival...I made my way to La Maison des Crêpes....All of the writers had journeyed to Brussels from some other shore. Many had even crossed another frontier, language. BWC members for whom English is not their native tongue amazed me....

Among the circle, I found the same dedication, resource-fulness, imagination, and support that endeared me to the colleagues left behind in Chicago. Similar passions, I guess, drive those who yearn to write. We have an innate need to tell stories, stir emotions, share truths. Maybe even more important than providing a place to hone my craft, the BWC offered friendship to Jim and me. That social outlet allowed us to adapt much quicker to expat life. Settled physically and mentally, I could focus on writing....

We face resettlement with apprehension and excitement. We've come full circle. But we return richer because of our experience. I'm a better writer because of the Brussels Writers' Circle. Thank you.

———— ((◍)) ————

With our apartment cleared, only days remained before we said goodbye to Brussels and our expat life.

Chapter 30

Barbara invited us into her home every evening of our last week for a bit of whiskey and sympathy. "Poor, poor me," she said. "I want to spend as much time with you two as possible. Not to mention show my gratitude. Rue d'Ecosse simply won't be the same."

She and Patrik gushed over our parting gifts that included a gas grill, garden supplies, perishables, spices, and several bottles of liquor. Barbara beamed with pride displaying the fully loaded liquor cart.

Jim and I viewed the visits as a chance to console Puhi. His woeful lament at the sight of our empty apartment suggested he felt abandoned. Our dark, lifeless house and closed door, no doubt, added to his sadness and confusion. Sipping cocktails before Barbara's crackling fire, we attempted to shower Puhi with affection. But in true feline fashion, he gave us a cold shoulder. Adopting an air of aloofness, he squirmed out of our arms and scurried into the darkness of the overgrown garden. He was giving us a taste of our own medicine. Comforting ourselves, we explained his behavior as a defense mechanism, a way of coping with our perceived abandonment. He'd experienced rejection before, finding refuge with Barbara after being booted outdoors by his former owner's new girlfriend.

With echoes of Puhi's cries in his head, Jim felt especially pained. "If only we could make him understand it's only temporary. Maybe we could tell him we're just redecorating."

Finding the idea both endearing and absurd, I wasn't entirely sure

Jim didn't mean it. He'd grown very attached to the cat even if his words, sometimes, masked his true affections.

Besides patching up our friendship with Puhi, two apartment-related tasks remained before we turned in the keys—a full day preening the house with a cleaning crew, and the final dreaded inspection.

With echoes back to our very first week in Brussels, early Friday morning we grabbed coffee and croissants from a local bakery before arriving at our soon-to-be-former apartment. Entering the emptied space felt odd. Our emotional detachment had begun. The cleaners had done a thorough job. Wood floors shone and windows and mirrors sparkled. Still, we awaited the landlord's agent and the inspector with the same anxiety that greeted a dentist's drill. Regardless of the apartment's condition, we knew they'd ding us. Our ally, a personable woman from the same firm that assisted us in our move into Brussels, confirmed our suspicions. "The inspector," she said with a shrug, "needs to find something to show objectivity. Merely a question of how much." Jim and I exchanged pained looks.

When the buzzer rang, our stomachs fluttered with nerves. I opened the door to find not only the inspector, a slender older man, but also the landlord's agent, Madame Goosen, the femme fatale with flowing blonde hair, bangles, and fur vest. Were those dollar signs I spied in her intense eyes?

Jim recognized the inspector. The same man had documented the apartment's condition before we moved in. Walking from room to room with clipboard in hand, the inspector scrutinized walls, floors, ceilings, and doors. We trailed behind hoping for clues. His face, however, remained inscrutable as he rendered silent judgment on our tenancy. With each note jotted on his worksheet, our tension rose. Occasionally, Madame Goosen pointed at something and spoke to the inspector in French. We were completely at their mercy.

Madame Goosen ran her finger along the glass of the door separating kitchen and dining room. "Hmm."

The inspector bent his head toward the glass. "Hmm."

"Hmm what?" I asked. "What are you looking at?"

"Here," the inspector replied, "scratches." Where the glass met the door frame, I observed a series of vertical scratches. "Did you affix a decal or something similar to the glass?"

"No!" I protested. "We didn't touch the glass."

Madame Goosen flashed a sneer of disbelief. "Maybe a cleaning product."

Jim studied the door. "Must have been there when we moved in."

Madame Goosen rolled her eyes. "It wasn't noted."

The inspector sighed. "If it wasn't noted it's your responsibility."

I recoiled. "You must be joking."

"Afraid not," he replied stone-faced.

"Wait!" An idea came to me. I had snapped many photos of the apartment on our house-hunting mission. Perhaps an image showed scratches prior to our occupancy. I flipped through my phone but the screen was too small. Laptop enlargements weren't clear either. *Damn!*

I turned at the sound of Jim's voice. The inquisition had moved to a corner of the kitchen.

"You must be joking," Jim said, in words that became our recurring refrain. "How is that not normal wear and tear?"

Shaking his head in unison with Madame Goosen, the inspector faulted us for shadowy smudges on the wall above the radiator. "Should have wiped the wall down on a regular basis." The agent nodded in concurrence.

Doomed, I thought. *We're doomed.*

By the time the pair left, Jim and I were exhausted. The exercise left us feeling dirty, as if we were derelict tenants. No one loved that apartment more than we did.

"Cheer up, guys," said our ally, reviewing the inspection summary. "All things considered, you fared pretty well. I've seen entire security deposits wiped out."

Despite her encouragement, we didn't feel victorious. Not only were we faulted for scratched glass and radiator dust, we had to pay seventy euros each for two burnt-out light bulbs and fifty euros for a crusty oven pan. The inspector also charged us for a light that never worked but, like the glass, wasn't noted on the intake inspection. Our penalty came to about five hundred euros. A far cry less than our security deposit perhaps, but a lubeless screw nonetheless. Our penalty due the landlord approximated the amount of money he owed us for two dehumidifiers he bought. Coincidence...*or not!*

Jim and I had one last weekend in Brussels to rest and recover before our flight home. Living in a hotel, we played tourist. We spent Saturday afternoon touring the city's Christmas market and buying gift boxes of chocolate.

On Sunday we enjoyed a farewell brunch at the home of Philippe and Laurent who ran a bed-and-breakfast, the Dame de Carreau. The congenial couple, rare locals who befriended and invited us into their home, gave us as a parting gift, a bottle of Belgian champagne. Perhaps their dominant gay genes suppressed the *Belge Face* chromosome. The fact that Jim's American coworker, a cousin of one of the guys, had brokered our initial introduction didn't hurt either.

Well before dawn on the morning of our departure, the pet transport service collected Sadie. After Jim lifted her into the van, our little princess stared at us from her crate. "See you in Chicago," I said. Our hearts melted as we blew kisses until the door closed.

With Sadie on her way to the airport, I grabbed the empty cat carrier and hustled down the still-deserted streets toward Barbara's home. My adrenaline surged; my stomach knotted. What would I find there? Would she have second thoughts? What if Puhi, still angry, resisted me? What if he hadn't returned home the prior night? Our flight wouldn't wait.

I hurried past the shuttered windows of our former apartment but had no time for winsome nostalgia. Next door, I pressed the bell. Barbara buzzed me in immediately, as if she'd been waiting. During the prior evening's cocktail session, she'd prepared me for a short goodbye. "No long goodbye," she had said. "I don't want to cry."

Opening her door, Barbara greeted me with three kisses. "Poor, poor Puhi," she said. "Doesn't know what he's in for."

As she left me in the foyer to retrieve the little fellow from somewhere inside the dark apartment, I wondered how she felt. Had she awakened sad? Did she shed tears for her beloved imp? Maybe she was happy for his new adventure. Whatever her feelings, she was either too much the free spirt or a damn good actress like her mother, a famous Slovenian theater and television personality, to let on.

"Here he is."

My heart lifted at the sound of Barbara's voice and the sight of the little tiger cat in her arms.

After kissing Puhi's head, she placed him in the carrier. "Au revoir, little Puhi. Safe travels."

My eyes welled with tears. "Thank you, Barbara."

"Promise me." Her expression and tone turned serious. "If he doesn't fit in or like his new home, you'll call me." I nodded. "I know, I know," she added, offering a faint smile. "He'll love it, but if he doesn't…I'll fly to Chicago to pick him up."

I kissed her cheek. "I promise." Although I didn't say it, I shared her concern that Puhi might not adapt to his new life. I hoped that wouldn't be the case, but Barbara had warned me that cats are very territorial. They have difficulty transitioning to new environments.

She opened her front door. "Okay, you better go. No long goodbyes."

"Au revoir, dear friend. See you in June."

Her head bobbed up and down. "Yes, yes, June. I'd forgotten your return ticket. June's right around the corner. So, this isn't goodbye." She blew me a kiss and I was out the door.

Puhi cried in the taxi to the airport. One stressful task remained. At security, the empty pet carrier had to be X-rayed. Having no prior experience with cats and only one hour under our belts as Puhi's owners, we feared the worst. What if he bolted from our arms as he'd done every night the prior week? We'd never see him again.

As we approached security, Jim reached for the carrier. "I'll take him."

"Fine by me." I had enough jitters.

Once extracted from his carrier, Puhi appeared more nervous than we did. He pressed himself against Jim's sweater. He took in the strange airport world, his green eyes widening to the size of saucers.

Puhi eagerly returned to his carrier. As we headed to our gate, Jim whispered to him, "Next time you're out, Lovebug, you'll be home."

With security behind us, my focus turned to the journey ahead. I simply wanted to get home, to reunite our family—Sadie, Puhi, Jim, and me—in our house to start rebuilding our life in Illinois. The sadness and stress of leaving had faded away...or so I thought.

After the loudspeaker announced our flight, I stood with my carry-on. "That's us."

Jim rose to my side. "Let's remember to ask the flight attendant to confirm Sadie's onboard."

Stepping up to the agent, I scanned my boarding pass. The machine triggered a red light, a problem with my assigned seat. My already churning stomach fell. I anxiously looked to the gate agent. She smiled. "We've got new seats for you two." She handed me two boarding passes. "Business class."

I must have flinched. I was flabbergasted. How or why we were upgraded, I didn't know. As we walked down the jet bridge, tears streaked down my cheeks. That kind and unexpected gesture uncorked the stress of the preceding weeks that I'd kept bottled up. As we settled into our bulkhead seats, I tried in vain to contain my tears.

Jim squeezed my hand. "I love you, babe."

"Love you too."

The purser allowed us to keep Puhi's carrier at our feet. There was ample room. In addition to confirming Sadie's safe boarding, we learned that our benefactor was another flight attendant, a dear, sweet friend. She'd asked the crew to upgrade us if they had space. Halfway through the nine-hour flight, Jim reclined his seat and placed Puhi's carrier on his chest. We departed Brussels in style. However, we agreed not to tell Sadie that her upstart brother Puhi got upgraded to business class.

We arrived home via taxi. Although it was mid-December, no snow covered the ground. Grass retained hints of green. As we pulled up the long driveway, the house greeted us with familiar warmth and simple beauty. Excitement stirred within me. I'd not set eyes on our house in two years. Entering felt comfortable, almost as if we never left. Although we had to pull Puhi from his carrier, our concerns about his reaction quickly faded. After an initial sniff-about, the feline expatriate strutted around as if he always belonged there.

A few days earlier, Jim's mom had accepted delivery of rental furniture. The Spartan décor would suffice until our belongings completed their long journey across sea and land. Jim's mom also stocked the refrigerator and pantry and left us homemade cookies. In our reclaimed nest, only Sadie was missing.

A couple of hours later, the doorbell rang. "It's Sadie." Jim bolted for the door, opening it to an older woman who held our girl on a leash. "She's a gentle lamb," the woman said handing the leash to Jim.

With her leash unfastened and before we could make a fuss, Sadie scurried through the hall and kitchen. She made her way to the mudroom for water, the exact spot where the bowl formerly stood.

"She remembers," I said.

Jim replied with enthusiasm, "Did you see that smile? Our princess is smiling."

We were all home. Three Arkenbergs who traveled to Brussels two years earlier had come home safely accompanied by the newest family member, a tiger cat named Puhi.

Jim and I spent a quiet Christmas alone, no tree, no decorations, no lavish holiday feast to plan and prepare. Family understood our need for breathing room, a chance to adjust to repatriation. After catching a new *Star Wars* movie at a crowded cinema, we dined at a packed Chinese restaurant. We never knew that so many people enjoyed an unorthodox Christmas.

A month after our return, my third book, *None Shall Sleep,* launched.

The National Indie Excellence Awards honored the novel as a finalist in their literary competition. That same year, the Brussels Writers' Circle published an anthology, *Circle of Words*, that included my short story, "Hollywood Calls." The collaborative project was a comforting sign that my departure hadn't severed all ties with my Brussels writer friends.

And despite the upheaval of our move, I dove back into my writing, publishing my first memoir, *Two Towers*, in 2017 and *A Belgian Assortment*, a collection of short stories, in 2018—the first of many Brussels-inspired writing projects. Harvesting tales from our fertile adventure, my Belgian short stories grafted fiction onto fact. Chatelain market, Bruges, Ypres' battlefields and breweries, and a Brussels locked down under threats of terror are a few of the seeds I sowed into my stories. The appendix includes a more detailed discussion of these "story seeds."

Eventually, I found my way back to the Barrington Writers Workshop where I received warm and genuine welcomes. A few weeks after our return, I wrote one final blog post.

Cuddling in Chicago

Our Expat Adventure Comes to an End

Hard to believe four weeks have passed since Jim and I boarded a plane in Brussels for our flight to Chicago. Returning to our house and lives after a two-year absence has been a chore. We've suffered separation pangs and slogged through Christmas and New Year's. Our furniture and possessions are still en route from Belgium, but we feel somewhat settled. With a bit of distance, emotional and physical, and a chunk of resettlement tasks behind us, I can blog about our farewell.

If given a choice, we'd hop a plane back despite the "imminent" and "probable" terror threat. Maybe that's natural. It's hard to break out of a familiar orbit, especially one that delivered great adventure. We made a great life for ourselves in Belgium. Even though we left behind family, friends, and our beloved house, Brussels became home. Or rather, *we made* Brussels our home. There is a difference. Left to passive indifference, a deep connection with our adopted city probably wouldn't have happened.

Brussels isn't Paris, London, or even Chicago. The city's sophistication is imported. NATO headquarters and the European Commission, Council, and Parliament populate the place with legions of interesting foreigners. Service and infrastructure are mediocre. Frankly, Brussels always looks in need of a good power washing. Yet despite its many blemishes, we embraced Brussels and befriended many great people who call the city home.

I welcomed our posting. "Years from now when we look back on our lives," I told Jim, "we'll remember Brussels. We'll call it a highlight of our lives." We don't have to wait that long. Acknowledging our good fortune, we already recognize Belgium as a prized adventure. Would we do it again? We both respond with an enthusiastic *YES!*

Although we'll carry pieces of Brussels with us until our dying days, in time memories and faces will fade. In place of vivid and detailed recollections, we'll be left with gentle musings and comforting reflections of a most excellent adventure.

———— ⊙ ————

Three months after our return, news outlets reported that police raids in Molenbeek resulted in the capture and arrest of the man wanted in connection with the Paris attacks of November 13. Eluding authorities for four months, the Belgian-born French citizen of Moroccan descent had triggered the Brussels lockdown. Four days after this report, on March 22, we awakened to the horrific news that terrorists attacked Brussels. Suicide bombers detonated nail bombs in check-in terminals at Zaventem Airport. An hour later, another attacker detonated a bomb on a Metro train at a station near the European Commission. Thirty-two people died and hundreds more were injured, dozens critically.

News of the attacks made Jim and me ill. We retained great affection for Brussels, a place we once called home. Our minds raced to our many friends. Any one of them had valid reasons to be at the airport or on the Metro near the EU. Guilt stirred within me for not being in Brussels to show camaraderie with our city and friends. Jim spoke of similar feelings. Although nobody we knew was hurt, as happens in places that suffer random acts of terror, the trauma scarred the survivors. We suffered gut punches when Facebook asked us to check ourselves, "Marked Safe in Brussels." Confused, I soon realized that we'd never changed our "current city" from Brussels back to Chicago.

Three months later, Jim and I used the return coupon of our round-trip ticket to travel back. Combined with an add-on trip to Dubrovnik, the return visit to Brussels served as a perfect eighteenth-anniversary gift to ourselves. Unfortunately, we misconnected in Newark. The reroute through London got us into Brussels too late for a planned rendezvous with writer friends at Chatelain market. Although greatly disappointed, we got cheered up at dinners on subsequent evenings at two favorite restaurants with Jim's former team and a dozen friends. We spent time at our favorite café and reconnected with our kind-hearted former neighbor Barbara, who wanted to know all about Puhi's expat adventure.

We stayed at the same hotel where we'd spent our final week in Brussels the prior December. When we checked in, staff members asked, "How's your dog?" Pleased by their recollection, we replied, "Sadie's good. She loves her house and yard."

Our former residence lured us. Peering into the window, however, gave further proof to Thomas Wolfe's iconic phrase, "You can't go home again." In place of our lovely furnishings that complemented the apartment's stately grandeur, the current occupants' furniture was drab. Our lovely living room had transformed into an adolescent's messy bedroom. "No mistaking it for a museum now," I said to Jim, my tone laced with sarcasm.

Despite customary drizzle and chill, Brussels felt warm, familiar. Jim pulled me into an embrace. "Feels just like home, doesn't it?"

"Guessing it always will."

That summer, Jim received a prestigious leadership award for his work in Brussels that launched the company's European Pride group. With no fanfare or explanation, the boxed award simply arrived at his home office. He also learned that his Brussels business unit very successfully implemented the strategy he had developed. A former employee also shared news that the team adopted many of Jim's American leadership tools and techniques.

As for Sadie, our precious golden retriever loved repatriation. She enjoyed rediscovering her large yard. No longer able to dash along the long fence line, the lovable senior chose instead to spend long summer days lounging on the soft, green grass she had missed in Brussels. Her smile showed contentment. Sadly, nine months after our return, our dear girl suffered a seizure. The gentle giant and intrepid traveler passed away in our arms at the age of twelve.

Puhi, the impish clown of a cat, adapted easily to America. Pampered and showered with love, he adjusted to life as an indoor cat. Of the many souvenirs Jim and I acquired in Brussels, Puhi is our favorite, a daily reminder of our expat adventure. Memories of his antics transport me back to our house and garden. Closing my eyes, I picture our introduction. From his perch on our garden wall, the little tiger cat studied Sadie and me. An unexpected tumble brought him into our lives. Over several weeks on a kitchen chair carried outside after dinner, Puhi and I became friends. I grin recalling his initial sprints into the house and the cautious détente with Sadie. I see him delighting guests at our Halloween party, curling up under our magnificent Christmas tree, and snuggling on Jim's legs to watch television. Puhi taught us that the best keepsake didn't have to be expensive or showy. Sometimes, a simple pleasure in the guise of a precocious housecat surpasses the most exciting of adventures. He's a reminder that things don't always go as planned. Surprise and delight can enter your life through an open door, even if that door is cracked just enough to let in a small cat.

Expats No More

All love stories come to an end. For everything in life is temporary. But as experienced lovers know, tender memories linger long after a great romance ends. And so it goes with our Belgian love story.

Appendix

Selected Full Blog Posts, 2014–2015

Mussels in Brussels–*Moules-frites*
November 6, 2014

If you think of mussels merely as shellfish in a bucket, a gastronomic tour of Belgium will convince you otherwise. I arrived in Brussels unimpressed with the bivalve mollusk. In the States, I avoided the dish, wrinkling my nose at what looked like a pile of dark blue shells sitting in a puddle of lukewarm water. Why would I eat that? Looks like more work than it's worth. I couldn't possibly fill up on the tiny, rubberlike morsels. And there's the gritty grains of sand.

Then we moved to Brussels. I thought I'd give mussels a shot. Why not? The food known as *moules-frites* is, after all, the national dish of Belgium. I'm a brave adventurer when it comes to sampling cuisine. How many people would eat squirming baby eel served with a fried egg over hashed potatoes as I did in Barcelona?

Was I in for a surprise! The mussels, *moules*, are prepared in steam pots shaped like buckets. The secret and flavor are in the broth—marinara, white wine, pernod, beer, etc. One restaurant that's become a favorite, Le Chou de Bruxelles, has thirty preparations. My particular favorite is called *Moules du Chef*, a mix of leeks, celery, and onions added to cream, white wine, and garlic with a hint of ginger. We've taken many visitors to this restaurant for buckets of *moules*, and cones of home-cut *frites* served to a soundtrack of Jacques Brel.

The experience? A bucket arrives at your table, lid in place. Invisible vapors carry irresistible scents of herbs, wine, and garlic. And *voilà*, with a flourish, your server removes the cover. A cloud of steam rises to your nose. Closing your eyes, a punch of flavor knocks your senses. Placed beside the pot, the lid becomes a receptacle for discarded shells.

You dig in. Slowly at first, pulling plump pink morsels from the shell. It's love at first bite. The pace quickens, interrupted only by an occasional *pomme frite* (never French fries in Belgium). Belgian *pommes frites* are exquisite, a golden yellow crispness that adds texture and flavor to your dining adventure.

You take a deep breath. Lid fills with empty shells yet the bucket seems as full as when you started. And still the juices that fan delectable aromas are out of reach. In search of broth, your spoon plunges down between *moules* yet to be tasted. But the spoon comes up empty. A *frite* is your best option. Spearing deep into the broth, the crispy tip of the *pomme frite* absorbs the refined goodness, whetting your appetite for more. Your pace quickens. You fall into a satisfying rhythm, a percussion of fork against shell, shell against lid and other shells. Sips of Chablis, Sauvignon Blanc, or Pinot Noir fill your mouth with a different pop of flavor. You emit a spontaneous sigh.

And you continue. The pile of used shells slowly grows. At last you reach the broth. The flavorful liquid, soaked up by fresh bread, is your reward for persistence. Other treasures are yet be discovered. Steamed vegetables and, best of all, a renegade *moule* dislodged from its shell. It bathes in the broth, luxuriating in the savory juices. Heaven. After trawling for other *moules* and a final slurp of the spoon, you're finished. You can't believe you ate that enormous bucket, emptied the cone of *pommes frites*, and devoured a sizable chunk of bread. Yet, the mound of dark shells serves as proof of your deed.

You swear off *moules-frites*...at least until the next opportunity presents itself. Besides, dessert awaits...*creme brûlée, dame blanche, gateau au poire, profiteroles*, etc.

You now understand how 1.6 million tons of *moules* can be consumed every year. But none is as delectable as those served up in Belgium.

⚬

There's No Place Like Home, or Is There?
November 17, 2014

Where is home? As expats are wont to do, we traveled back from whence we came—Chicago, or more specifically the Village of Arlington Heights. Ten short months ago, Chicago was "home," Brussels a pretty flirtation.

We didn't sell our house. How could we? It meant home. My parents built the original structure in 1967 and raised three kids there. Buying the house after their deaths, Jim and I made it our own, a custom-built home on a foundation laid by my parents. With the length of our European adventure unknown, we rented out the house and turned our attentions toward Brussels. Slowly and almost unnoticeably, Brussels claimed a piece of our hearts.

Our first trip back since moving, Jim and I had an aggressive agenda. We only had four days and nights to squeeze in everything. We had to check on our house and renters, hoping both would weather the coming winter's polar vortex better than the last. There were licenses to renew. We had favorite restaurants and foods—cheeseburgers, Italian beef, Mexican cuisine. And a long list of supplies unavailable in our adopted home.

Dry cleaning was a luxury in Brussels—five times the cost in the U.S. I took up ironing to avoid paying $6 to launder and press a single shirt. A friend introduced us to Dryel, a do-it-yourself dry-cleaning product. We saved thousands of euros, using some of the savings to buy even more clothes for me to launder at home.

Peanut butter and grape jelly, staples in most American pantries, are hard to find. Belgian peanut butter is dry and grainy while grape jelly is nonexistent. Even Sadie had her wish list. A special brand of dog treats and canned pumpkin, the latter a nutritional diet supplement. Hard to find processed pumpkin costs nearly $6 per can in Brussels.

There are also nice-to-haves: favorite toothpaste, hand soap, breakfast cereal, deodorant, hand cream, kosher salt, pancake mix and syrup, etc. We had to buy an extra suitcase to cart everything back.

Most importantly, there were visits with friends and family, our beloved roots. These included the Barrington Writers Workshop, talented writer friends who pushed me to become a better author. While Facebook, FaceTime and Skype have kept us in touch across an ocean, these people are precious. In Brussels, friends are limited to a rare few. It will take years to recreate the extensive social network we've cultivated in Chicago.

Can you go home again? Of course! But where is "home"? Ten months of grand adventures and simple moments have transformed Brussels from a shallow flirtation into a promising new partner. At the end of our visit, we looked forward to going *home*. We meant Brussels. Home may be where you hang your hat, but more importantly, home is where you share a life with the person you hold most dear.

Lest we forget Chicago's claim on us, we only have to enjoy a breakfast of pancakes with faux maple syrup, lunch of peanut butter and grape jelly, dinner of perfectly seasoned chili, while recalling faces of family and friends.

Perhaps the best definition of all—*Home is in your heart!*

———————— ((()) ————————

Nuts & Nutcrackers, Christmas in Belgium
December 18, 2014

Jim and I are about to celebrate our first Brussels Christmas. Our tree, *un sapin de Noel*, is lit, table decorated, and candles glow. Christmas music plays throughout our home—Nat King Cole, Bing Crosby, Rosemary Clooney, Ella Fitzgerald, and a smattering of French carols, *les chants de Noel*. This is our first Christmas alone, away from home, friends, and family.

We're not the only Americans ever to find themselves in Belgium, alone and far from family at Christmas. Not by a long shot. This week marks a significant anniversary for our nation. Seventy years ago, in the waning days of 1944 with a cold and snowy winter upon them, American forces came under German attack in what we call the Battle of the Bulge. British Prime Minister Winston Churchill said, "This is undoubtedly the greatest American battle of the war, and will, I believe be regarded as an ever-famous American victory."

On December 16, German troops launched a surprise offensive in the Ardennes, in eastern Belgium. Since D-Day in June of '44, Allied forces had been pushing the Germans east. With the Red Army advancing on his eastern front, Hitler planned a drive toward the port of Antwerp, a counteroffensive aimed to split English and American forces. The Germans counted on the element of surprise. Their plan required poor weather to neutralize the Allies' superior air power. The Germans hoped for a rapid push toward the Meuse River, halfway to Antwerp. With an artillery assault on thinly spread American forces, the Germans scored early victories.

By the 20th, the Germans seemed poised to take Bastogne, a strategic town at the crossroads of seven paved roads essential for a swift advance. On the 22nd, German General Luttwitz sent a note demanding surrender to US General Anthony McAuliffe, acting Commander of the 101st Airborne Division. Rejection, warned Luttwitz, would mean total annihilation. As the story goes, when presented with the ultimatum, McAuliffe mumbled, "Aw Nuts!" Pressed for an official response, the Americans couldn't come up with anything better. They sent the following:

To the German Commander,
NUTS!
The American Commander

Initially confused by the American slang, Luttwitz soon learned the term was American for "Go to Hell.' For the next several days over Christmas, outnumbered five to one, the Americans held firm. Finally, on December 26, Patton's Third Army broke through the encirclement. American fighters would become known as the Battered Bastards of Bastogne. Clearing skies on the 26th restored allied air support. By mid-January, American forces pushed the Germans back but not without significant casualties on both sides.

I was honored to visit Bastogne and the battle memorial in 1993 with my parents. My dad was a World War II veteran. Living in Belgium, I returned this July with Jim and a visiting friend from Chicago. The star-shaped memorial is somber. This is sacred American ground akin to Normandy's beaches, Pearl Harbor's Arizona Memorial, and New York's Ground Zero. A visit induces goose bumps, tears, pride.

To commemorate the battle's seventieth anniversary, Belgium's King and Queen traveled to the area. Stars and Stripes filled Bastogne's windows along with the black, yellow, and red vertical stripes of the Belgian flag. Simple signs of "Thank You" in English expressed the sentiment. In what's become an annual tradition commemorating McAuliffe's blunt reply, the King and Queen led the crowd in throwing *nuts*.

So, this Christmas, pause to thank the brave men who hunkered down in Bastogne seventy years ago without a tree, holiday table, or loved one to embrace. Think also of the brave military men and women who will be away *this* Christmas. Hug your loved ones extra tight. Give thanks you are together. 'Tis the Season…to once again wish, hope, and pray for an end to all war. 'Tis indeed the season to dream…

Comfort Food, Alpine Style
January 14, 2015

Raclette, Tartiflette, Fondue. If you're like most Americans, you've probably only heard of one of these dishes. *Quelle dommage!* Perhaps this post will whet your appetite to explore what you've been missing.

Parisian friends invited Jim and me to join them for a short holiday between Christmas and New Year's. They suggested Annecy, a charming town in the foothills of the French Alps on the shores of a pristine lake of the same name. The region is Haute Savoie, once a part of the Kingdom of Sardinia before France acquired it in 1860. Geneva, Switzerland and its eponymous lake are thirty kilometers to the north. Having never visited that corner of France, we jumped at the chance.

Europeans travel everywhere with their pets. Therefore, we loaded Sadie into the car for the seven-hour drive from Brussels. A sudden snowstorm, however, slowed our journey. After more than fourteen hours in the car with the worst traffic we've ever experienced, we arrived at our destination. The silver lining: a fresh dusting of snow turned Annecy into a winter wonderland, a magical, medieval fairy-tale city.

We lunched at a Michelin-starred restaurant, Le Belvedere, a gastronomic delight—artistic, palate-pleasing French cuisine at its best. But what about the comfort food the title promised? Although less glamorous, a Savoyard indulgence proved equally satisfying after a stroll along Lac d'Annecy on a crisp, clear day. In a restaurant decorated in Alpine motif, we found raclette, *tartiflette*, and fondue.

In its purest form, fondue is a pot of melted cheese into which diners, using long forks, dip bread cubes and possibly potatoes. Cheese is key. In Haute Savoie, that usually means a blend of Beaufort, Comte, and Gruyère to which white wine is added. Beware the diner who drops bread into the communal font. Double dipping is sneered upon.

Tartiflette, a dish with a name derived from a word meaning "potato," is a casserole made with Reblochon cheese. To the cheese, lardons, onions, and potatoes are added along with white wine before being baked to a golden-brown crust.

A variation replaces lardons with smoked salmon. As with fondue, crisp green salad is an ideal accompaniment.

Raclette is a cheese as well as the name of the dish. The French verb *racler* means "to scrape." Diners scrape melted cheese onto steaming hot potatoes. Traditional accompaniments include cornichons, pickled onions, and dried meats. While originally heated on a fire, today raclette is offered using an electric gadget found at most kitchen supply stores or Internet sites. Introduced to the dish by European friends living in Chicago, Jim and I have hosted several raclette parties. We replace traditional accompaniments with a variety of sides such as caramelized onions, pineapple, prosciutto, Italian sausage, and sautéed chicken. Let your taste buds design your menu.

So, next time you crave comfort food, think beyond chili, pot roast, and mashed potatoes. Travel to the Alps even if only in your own imagination and kitchen. Savor the creamy richness of raclette, *tartiflette,* and fondue. Serve crisp white wine although beer is just as good. Put on some soft French music and cuddle with your sweetie beside a fire. I guarantee you'll derive great joy from Alpine comfort food. Bon Appetit!

Afternoon Tea & Friends
February 13, 2015

"I believe it is customary in good society to take some slight refreshment at five o'clock." —Oscar Wilde, *The Importance of Being Earnest*

We set up the date weeks ago. The purpose, a condolence call. Dear friend Gia, an Italian woman living in London, lost her aged mother in November. Jim and I were in the States at the time and couldn't attend the funeral. But our friendship is precious and the occasion too important not to acknowledge. We proposed afternoon tea, the most sensible and civilized of all English traditions. Gia was keen on the idea. But where to go? Five years before on one of our London visits, the three of us opted for a low-key, informal tea.

That simply wouldn't do on this occasion. Condolences demanded top tier—the Savoy, Ritz, Dorchester, Claridge's, Brown's. London is, if you'll pardon the expression, awash in afternoon teas. In the two centuries since the tradition's birth, afternoon tea is more popular than ever.

We chose the Savoy. "Comfier chairs," said Gia, "and oh, the food," she added with a sigh. "Nonstop!" But savvy Londoners and visitors alike must know about the Savoy's plush chairs. Despite the £50 ($76.50) per person cost plus a 12.5% "discretionary" service charge, the first available Saturday was three months in the future. Apparently, those with idle hours in the middle of the day don't mind that a box of Twinings—enough Earl Grey for a fortnight—could be theirs at Sainsbury's for less than £4. Tushes must be cushioned and palates pleased, at any price.

Afternoon tea, however, isn't about cost, venue, or even the eponymous brew from which it takes its name. An afternoon away from angry work tussles and monotonous routines is special—rejuvenation without massage, refreshment without alcohol, relaxation without sleep. Teetotalers aren't the only fans squeezing into uncomfortable chairs at low tables— champagne is also offered.

The Savoy, Claridge's, and Dorchester were fully booked. I suggested Brown's Hotel. Located in Mayfair, mere blocks from the Ritz and Berkeley Square, Brown's was recently voted the most quintessential of English teas.

Gia and I had tea at Brown's nearly 24 years earlier with mutual friend David. It was a mini-reunion. The three of us met years earlier at London Business School. Never mind that David got deathly ill after that earlier tea and spent the night running to the toilet, blame placed on smoked salmon sandwiches. Tea, after all, is about tradition. We'd raise our cups to our friend and his delicate constitution.

We arrived promptly at 4:30. An email warned that the table was ours for precisely ninety minutes. Perhaps it's the polite English way to limit intake of tea and nibbles–*Old Country Buffet take note*. We crouched onto low seats and a sofa, tiny chairs and tables reminiscent of a child's party—tradition.

One chooses tea from a long list of blends: black, green, herbal, and fusion. We made it simple, all opting for Darjeeling. Two shiny silver pots quickly arrived steeping with aromatic leaves—*never, never, never bags*. A third pot provided a reservoir of hot water to replenish the magic elixir.

Does one add milk to the cup before or after tea is poured?

The feast begins. Genteel grazing with tiny plates, forks, and napkins. A caddy containing two plates of savories topped by a third of colorful tea cakes, a subtle reminder to leave room for dessert.

Sandwiches are crustless, dainty, and...traditional: smoked salmon, cucumber, ham & cheese, egg mayonnaise, and chicken. Our delightful server offered to replenish the sandwiches as often as we liked. (NOTE: When taking afternoon tea, one should consider skipping lunch and dinner.) The next course draws universal squeals of delight—warm scones with strawberry jam and clotted cream—a sticky mess of delectable goo.

How could something so deliciously innocent be embroiled in controversy? It's not the scones themselves, but the cream and jam, or more precisely, the order in which one applies the ambrosia that causes strife. Cornwall and Devon, two English counties that both claim originating cream teas, are at the center of the spat. Cream first and jam second or vice versa? A bitter battle akin to the great ketchup/mustard debate surrounding Chicago hot dogs. Is there no room for compromise, a proposal worthy of Solomon? How about the swirl technique? Mix together both toppings on a plate, dolloping them simultaneously onto the scone. At such a thought, good Lords, Ladies, and Downton devotees might toss their crumpets with cries of "Colonial rubbish!"

Suppress the urge to lick your plate, knife, and all surfaces coated with clotted cream. It's time for sweets or, as hungry Hobbits call it, *second dessert*. Time to dig into those petite tea cakes staring you in the face—creamy mousses and delicate flavors that evoke an English garden—rose, violet, strawberry. *But wait!*

The server offers a hefty slice of red-velvet cake or Victoria Sponge. Who could resist? Okay, after having your cake and eating it too, you finally dig into those dainty tea cakes. *(Reason prevails—you decide to cancel your dinner reservation.)*

That's a traditional English tea—*never, never, never high tea.* But just as Lewis Carroll's mad tea party wasn't about tea, our afternoon wasn't really about cucumber sandwiches, scones and clotted cream, sweet cakes, or even tea. Much of life plays out below the surface in subtext, shorthand, and rich, unspoken passages. Our lovely Saturday at Brown's Hotel did the same. Conversation glided over a thirty-year landscape—shared experiences, personal joys, triumphs, tragedy, and loss. Discussion piloted toward the horizon—hopes, worries, dreams…friendships nurtured over time by admiration, respect, concern, and yes…tea!

Battlefields & Breweries of Flanders
February 26, 2015

Jim and I recently joined a small group of expats for a tour, aptly called Trenches & Trappistes. The itinerary featured two things for which Belgium is known—battlefields and beer. The country is awash in war history and sudsy splendor. An odd mix, perhaps, or maybe a perfect pairing.

Our day took us to the flat Flemish countryside, the area of Belgium abutting France and the North Sea. We joined our tour in Ypres (Ieper), ill-fated site of three World War I battles. Befuddled by French and Flemish pronunciations, English-speaking troops simply called the town "'Wipers."

Ypres' current charm belies the fact that at war's end, the medieval town stood in ruins. Artillery reduced its thirteenth-century Cloth Hall to rubble. Between 1933 and 1967, painstaking efforts restored the historic structure. It's now home to In Flanders Fields Museum, which offers a great introduction to WWI. The town's Menin Gate honors more than fifty thousand Commonwealth Troops killed in the war and whose final resting places are unknown. Each night at 8 p.m., as it has for nearly 90 years, Last Post sounds for fallen warriors.

This tiny country, the size of the Maryland, has endured more than its fair share of battles. A year doesn't seem to pass without an anniversary of a major conflict. 2014 marked the centenary of the start of WWI. Much of the fighting occurred on "neutral" Belgian soil. The same year marked the seventieth anniversary of the Battle of the Bulge, fought in the Ardennes. June 2015 marks 200 years since Napoleon met his Waterloo at the eponymous town, today a suburb fifteen miles south of Brussels. One can dig deeper into history for more Belgian tragedy. 2015 marks the 320th anniversary of the bombardment of Brussels by Louis XIV in his war with the Hapsburgs.

In his *Commentaries on the Gallic War*, Julius Caesar wrote, "The Belgae are the bravest of them all." Sadly, that bravery has been tested for centuries. In August 1914, Belgian fighters, outnumbered 34 divisions to 6, held off German invaders far longer than anyone expected. Belgians paid a hefty price for enraging the Germans. *Fusillé par les Allemands* (Shot by the Germans) is inscribed on many civilian tombstones.

As we left Ypres, we stopped first at Essex Farm Cemetery located on the west bank of the Ypres-Yser canal. Exactly one hundred years before our visit, the site was a forward dressing station on the western front. The second battle of Ypres in the spring of 1915 is considered the war's first gas attack. Germans released chlorine gas on Canadian troops. On this spot in May of that year, Canadian Dr. John McCrae penned his poem, *In Flanders Fields,* as a tribute to a dead comrade. McCrae's poem inspired the use of the poppy, still seen today, to honor war veterans.

In Flanders Fields
(John McCrae, 1872–1918)
In Flanders fields the poppies blow
Between the crosses, row on row,
That mark our place, and in the sky,
The larks, still bravely singing, fly,
Scarce heard amid the guns below.

We are the dead; short days ago
We lived, felt dawn, saw sunset glow,
Loved and were loved, and now we lie
In Flanders fields.

Take up our quarrel with the foe!
To you from failing hands we throw
The torch; be yours to hold it high!
If ye break faith with us who die
We shall not sleep, though poppies grow
In Flanders fields.

Later, we stopped at Vladslo Cemetery, final resting place of more than 25,000 German soldiers. A sculpture, *The Grieving Parents* by German artist Käthe Kollwitz casts a somber shadow over the grave of her youngest son, Peter, killed in battle. Young people sent off to fight in foreign fields is history's tragically repeated thread. Regardless of one's sympathies, graves of ordinary soldiers are a sad reminder of war's human toll.

English author Thomas Hardy wrote *Drummer Hodge* for a casualty of a different war, a British soldier killed in South Africa during the Boer War. Hardy's images and sentiment of youthful idealism wasted by war, and soldiers never to return home resonate in any foreign field.

Drummer Hodge
(Thomas Hardy 1840–1928)

They throw in Drummer Hodge, to rest
Uncoffined—just as found:
His landmark is a kopje-crest
That breaks the veldt around:
And foreign constellations west
Each night above his mound.

Young Hodge the drummer never knew—
Fresh from his Wessex home—

The meaning of the broad Karoo,
The Bush, the dusty loam,
And why uprose to nightly view
Strange stars amid the gloom.

Yet portion of that unknown plain
Will Hodge for ever be;
His homely Northern breast and brain
Grow up some Southern tree,
And strange-eyed constellations reign
His stars eternally.

A trench surviving from WWI serves as tribute to brave soldiers caught up in the insufferable war of attrition. This memorial bears the ominous name Trench of Death.

Our tour guide also promised beer. After steeping in the tolls of war, not one of us refused a sample of Belgium's best. I won't attempt to review the beers. Blogs too numerous to cite fill the Internet. Chief among these is Ratebeer.com whose reviews turned many Belgian beers into brewery equivalents of rock stars. We had time for three visits. With some alcohol contents drifting above 12%, that's probably all our systems could bear.

At Westvleteren Trappist Brewery peaceful devotion coexists with beer lust. For certification, *Trappist* beers must be brewed on monastery property. Monks must be involved in the process. 6-8-12 isn't the prayer schedule, but the alcohol content of their brews. Over lunch, we sampled beer in their café before catching a prayer service officiated by white-robed monks. Monasteries began brewing beer at the time of the Crusades, permission granted by the Catholic Church for fundraising purposes—the precursor to B-I-N-G-O.

Production is limited. Rumor is that the monks are busy brewing to pay off a recent addition. The day we visited, they were selling the 8% brew in brown, unmarked bottles—très chic! To deal with high demand, when the monks announce a production, they initiate a hotline. Orders are fulfilled on a first come, first served basis. License plate numbers are tracked to prevent cheats from absconding with someone else's stash. These were the most cheerful monks I'd ever seen. Coincidence? I think not.

Two brothers founded Dolle Brouwers Oerbier Dolle in 1980. Along with Chouffe Beer founded two years later, in 1982, Dolle Brouwers get credit with sparking the Belgian beer renaissance. One brother stopped to chat and take a picture with us in the brewery's cozy tasting room.

A transformed schoolhouse is the home of Struise Brouwers. They have thirty brews on tap in their tasting room for as little as 1 euro a taste. Their flagship brand is Pannepot. If only every school had a tasting room...

By the end of our mellow afternoon, we were hopped up on hops. Not even a missed train for our two-hour journey back to Brussels deflated our buzz.

Over the centuries, Romans, French, Burgundians, Spanish, English, Austrians, Germans, and others overran the land that comprises modern-day Belgium. With such an embattled history, who wouldn't drown sorrows with beer?

————)(◉)(————

It's a Bulb's Life: Nature's Lessons for Life
April 22, 2015

A tulip is a tulip is a tulip
Oh to be in Holland now that April's there...
A tulip by any other name would smell as sweet
(Adapted from Stein, Browning, and Shakespeare
with apologies)

Inspiration, sweat, patience—almost everything I've attempted in life comes down to those three ingredients. A combination of head, heart, and simple body mechanics.

Inspiration is the seed, or for that matter, bulb of an idea or desire. Sweat is the effort— physical, mental, spiritual— that turns thought into action. Patience is the will, whether powered by passion, duty, faith, or sheer discipline, that keeps us marching forward.

This past Sunday, Jim and I visited Holland's famed Keukenhof where master planners and a small brigade of gardeners plant seven million bulbs annually. Each spring for eight short weeks, the gardens inspire and delight one million visitors. After their splendorous moment in the sun, bulbs are dug up and destroyed. The fleeting spring spectacle should remind us to seize upon our own brief moments in the sun—*carpe diem*.

On our first visit six years ago, I'd just begun my journey to become a writer. On this second visit, whiter at the temples and, hopefully, a bit wiser, parallels between Keukenhof and my experience as a budding author came into focus.

Although we associate the tulip with Holland, the flowering bulb didn't start there. The genus *Tulipa* had a lofty beginning. Most sources place its origin in the Himalayas. The flower was not yet known as *tulip*. That name would come later.

Just as inspiration undergoes transformation to become an idea, the bulb began a long and arduous journey. In the 11th century, the Seljuk Empire that included present day Turkey brought the flower west. Their successors, the Ottomans, noted the striking resemblance of bulbs to turbans worn by nobility, *tulipan* in Persian. The flower had a name. But the tulip's journey didn't end there. The Dutch, master traders, imported the tulip to the Low Countries in the 16th century. The little bulb born in the Himalayas, adopted and named in Turkey, had a new home in Holland. Its popularity and commercial value soared. Today, that well-traveled flower inspires gardeners worldwide and has grown into a multi-billion-dollar business.

But what does that have to do with writing?

A gardener looks beyond drab, lifeless bulbs to see a bed of vibrant and stately blooms. So too must a writer look beyond the mere kernel of an idea to envision the poetry of his or her completed work. Both efforts start with inspiration.

As a gardener may scan catalogues or visit flower shows for ideas, inspiration for literary projects springs from many sources. The idea for my second book came to me on Mykonos as we learned of Jackie O's exploits on the Greek island. My dear friend Gia's passion for opera nurtured global friendships and inspired my upcoming third novel. Scenes, characters, themes, and phrases pop into my head—raw fields of ideas without shape or form.

Writing and gardening both require patience, perseverance, and time. A tulip *seed* requires four years to transform into a *bulb*. And bulbs need up to twenty years before the tulip variety is ready for commercial distribution. Every home gardener knows that planting bulbs requires *faith* that the little bulb will take root. And *patienc*e that vibrant flowers will blossom after a long winter.

Like a gardener scanning the frosty barren landscape, I've

stared at blank pages waiting for vibrant ideas to take root. Writing shares long planning horizons. Moving a story from idea to published book takes years even when writing every day. I published my first novel after four major drafts and countless minor rewrites five years after the idea was born. Likewise, the time from inspiration to publication with my second novel was more than five years. Like gardening, writing isn't for those who tire easily or who crave immediate gratification.

And like the gardener who spies the first tulip of spring, a writer experiences joy and delight when he tears open a corrugated box and stares for the first time at his glossy-covered book. The humble bulb emerges as a majestic tulip.

I continue to hone my craft, aspiring to become a better writer. But good writing can't be rushed. And unless you're satisfied with a silk flower, a tulip of unique grace and elegance requires care, patience, and time.

Floral fireworks can spark your creative center by touching your heart, nurturing a sagging spirit, and restoring faith in nature's beauty and bounty. Creating anything of value (gardens, stories, etc.) requires inspiration, sweat, and patience. Forgive my borrowing from Mr. Wordsworth and allow me to let my mind wander for inspiration, back to the hour of splendor in the grass, of glory in the *tulip*...

━━━━ ((●)) ━━━━

Champagne: A Name Bubbling with Joy
April 30, 2015

Champagne, one of those rare words that triggers an explosion of sensory neurons. The name conjures up images of celebrations, coronations, christenings, and myriad other happy occasions. Champagne is most often paired with smiles, laughter, and joy. Movies brim with references to champagne. No other prop has a cachet that immediately conveys class, refinement, sophistication, wealth, and a zest for life. Think Cary Grant, Audrey Hepburn, Julia Roberts, Leonardo DiCaprio. Many consider champagne all glamour and giggles. However, there's a dark side. The sparkling wine is under immense pressure (pun intended) to pop consistently with delight. Most of us would shatter under such lofty and unrealistic expectations. Besides a chic reputation, how much do we know about the drink we call Bubbly?

Recently, Jim and I had the pleasure of traveling 170 miles from Brussels to Champagne, a region in northeastern France. The trip was bittersweet. We toasted a safe farewell to friends who, after eight months in Belgium, are returning home to New Jersey. With its large international community, Brussels is full of farewells, lives in constant motion like bubbles in a flute of champagne.

We sampled the region's *eponymous* (always fun to use a *New York Times* word) nectar and learned along the way. I managed to retain some of that knowledge despite losing countless brain cells in the process. The sacrifices one makes in pursuit of knowledge. (For a primer on champagne, I've included some basic facts at the end of the blog. You can impress others over caviar, canapés, foie gras, and, of course, champagne.)

Let's begin with a familiar refrain. Once upon a time the inhabitants of Champagne envied their southern neighbor, Burgundy, a region known for remarkable wines. The Champenois, as natives are known, tried to replicate the rich, full-bodied Burgundies. However, a cool and rainy climate and chalky soil dashed their dreams. Though inferior for producing red still wines, the region was ideal for growing the grapes that give champagne its trademark fizz and flavor. The lesson? Greatness comes not by imitation, but by embracing your uniqueness.

We started our tour in the town called the capital of Champagne, Épernay. Situated on the left bank of the Marne River eighty miles northeast of Paris, Épernay is home to the Avenue of Champagne. The street boasts many of the best-known producers, known as "Houses." These include Moët & Chandon, Pol Roger, Mercier, Perrier Jouet.

We visited the House of Castellane founded in 1895 by a wealthy, aristocratic family from Provence. Our tour of the production facilities included the caves in which champagne is aged. Our guide taught us the basics. The sparkling wine known as champagne begins its life much like any still wine. Grapes separated by variety—Chardonnay, Pinot Noir, Pinot Meunier—undergo a first fermentation in stainless steel vats. Topless vats allow carbon dioxide, a byproduct of sugar-eating yeast, to escape. The result is a still wine. To produce champagne's signature effervescence, the still wine undergoes a second fermentation. In this phase, wines are mixed to produce a desired blend. A Brut Traditional, for example, may contain equal parts of all three grapes. Second fermentation occurs in bottles. Early riddlers, workers responsible for rotating bottles, often suffered injury from flying glass. 19th century tourists to the caves had to wear protective gear to protect against shards of flying glass. The solution? Heavier, more durable bottles. First Lady Bess Truman learned the hard way that champagne bottles are built to last. In 1945, at a ceremony christening a military ambulance plane, a stubborn bottle refused to break.

Our second stop was Hautvillers, pronounced something akin to "O-vee-lay." The town is home to the Benedictine Abbey where champagne icon Dom Perignon lived, worked, and died. Slick advertising made champagne the drink of kings *and* commoners. Smart marketeers—kings are few while commoners are a dime a dozen. Hautvillers provided great views of the region's vineyards.

Then onto Reims. Champagne's largest city began as a Roman settlement, Durocortorum. Mars Gate, dating to the third century, still stands. But first things first, pronouncing the city's name. It's not "reems" or "rhymes," but "rans" that rhymes with "Hans" or "wants" with a rolled "r" and a nasal "n." The pronunciation's origin is anyone's guess. The city's Notre-Dame de Reims is a 13th century cathedral in which 25 French kings were coronated. Champagne, very likely, flowed.

Reims is also home to top names in Champagne production: Taittenger, G. H. Mumm, Veuve Clicquot, Pommery, among others. The Pommery tour is not to be missed. By chance, we visited during an exhibition. Modern art adorned the caves. Champagne, we also learned, should be enjoyed soon after purchase. A bottle stored properly may last five years, but in a home refrigerator, less than six months. Jim and I learned this the hard way when a friend popped open a bottle of Dom Perignon that he'd kept for fifteen years. The fine wine tasted like cat piss. *C'est dommage!*

This final excursion with our friends couldn't have been more delightful. We saluted them with champagne wishes and caviar dreams. Life, like champagne, is meant to be consumed, not stored away till it's too old to enjoy. Seize the day. Share a bottle of bubbly with those you love. You never know how long someone will be in your life. No one wants to drink cat piss, no matter how fancy the label.

A Toast to Champagne

Creating champagne is a complex process, worthy of a bit of study. Here are a few basic facts best learned over a flute of champagne:

1) Only sparkling wines produced in Champagne from grapes grown in Champagne have the right to be called champagne. Hope it won't come as a shock to some of you that André Cold Duck, therefore, really isn't champagne. Most big-name producers do not grow their own grapes, they buy them.

2) Champagne is NOT a grape variety. All champagne is produced from some combination of three grape varieties. Two as a matter of fact do not have white skins at all. *Blanc de blancs*, literally "white from whites," refers to a champagne made exclusively from Chardonnay grapes. The skins of the pinot varieties have colored pigments; the juicy flesh is white.

3) There's method to the madness. Méthode Champenoise is the name of the process that turns still wine into champagne. While sparkling wines the world over use the same method of double fermentation, only that wine produced in Champagne has the right to call the process Méthode Champenoise. All others including Spain's Cava and the sparkling wines of California must call the process something else. Most use the term *méthode traditionnelle,* often found on the bottle. A basic principle of this method is that the second fermentation takes place within the bottle.

4) Vintage is a rare year indeed. Most champagne is produced from grapes blended from several growing seasons. But in years when grapes are deemed to be exceptional, individual producers declare a "vintage year." There is no "regional announcement" or "vintage decree." Producers use grapes from that single season to create a vintage Champagne. You can recognize vintage champagne, as bottles display a year.

According to our guide, champagne is intended for near immediate consumption. Vintage champagne beyond ten years old is undrinkable.

5) Sweetness decoder. Champagne has an array of sweetness. The list below illustrates the different amounts of sugar found in each type of champagne. For example, Extra Brut has LESS, not more, sugar than Brut. Demi-sec has MORE, not less, sugar than Sec.

- Extra Brut (less than 6 grams of residual sugar per liter)
- Brut (less than 12 grams)
- Extra Dry (between 12 and 17 grams)
- Sec (between 17 and 32 grams)
- Demi-sec (between 32 and 50 grams)
- Doux (50 grams)

6) Dom Perignon (1638–1715), the Benedictine monk who lends his name to the pricey cuvée of Moët & Chandon did *not* invent champagne. While Perignon spent his life as a cellarer in the Abbey of Hautvillers, the myths surrounding his influence were fabricated more than one hundred years after his death to bolster the Abbey's prestige. The quote attributed to Perignon's first quaff of sparkling champagne, "Come quickly, I am drinking the stars!" seems to be the advertising creation of 19th century 'Madmen'.

7) Veuve, as in Cliquot and Pommery, is a French word, meaning "widow." Both of these savvy businesswomen led their respective houses to greatness after their husbands died.

8) Impress your friends with champagne trivia. In the second fermentation process, small plastic concave cups are placed in the neck of the bottle. As the bottles are turned, or "riddled," these caps collect the fermentation sediment.

When the secondary fermentation is complete, the necks of the bottles are chilled to a temperature of -25 Celsius (-13 Fahrenheit). When the temporary bottle cap is removed, the pressure inside the bottle disgorges the plastic cap. These plastic caps are known as *bidules,* the French equivalent of "thingamajig" or "widget." The little wire cage that secures the cork has a name, Muselet, derived from the French verb *museler,* meaning "to muzzle."

Finding Arkenberg
May 18, 2015

What's in a name? Surely an identity: a way for the laundry to track your shirts, the pizza parlor to match your order, an inventory system for people—Bueller, Bueller...A surname identifies your tribe and is usually a source of pride. Sometimes, families change their name, the British Royals among the most notable to do so. At the outbreak of WWI, they quietly replaced German-sounding Hannover with the very British Windsor. Royals, however, like Cher, Charo, and Bono are so important they don't need a last name. Hollywood manufactured glamorous names: Kappelhoff became Day, Sherer became Hudson, Morrison became Wayne. Literature gives us pen names: Twain from Clemens, Eliot from Evans, Orwell from Blair. Prisons take your name and give you a number, the ultimate humiliation.

A spouse who shares not only your life but also your name is the ultimate validation. On our fifth anniversary, my spouse legally changed his name. Now, we're both Arkenbergs, as is our pooch, Sadie.

With the world's population mushrooming to more than seven billion, human beings feel less connected. A popular theory suggests that six mere degrees separate us from one another. If the six-degrees theory links every human from Chicago to Shanghai to Chennai—what about individuals who share a last name? Certainly, the degree of separation among our own tribe must be considerably less. But how many of us know our roots? How many of us care?

Everyone who shares my surname, I hypothesize, is related in some fashion whether by blood, marriage or adoption. I'm pretty fortunate that my name is Arkenberg. If it were Smith, Jones, Anderson, Patel or Lee the search for relatives may not be as easy.

About six years ago, I started to get more serious about family genealogy. Between writing sessions, Internet searches provided therapy like Sudoku or crossword puzzles. Piecing together family history was challenging and fun. The Internet made the search painless. A cousin who's researched our family tree for decades in the pre-Google era needed the patience of a saint and tenacity of a Rottweiler.

With a little digging (actually a lot of digging), one search led to another and so on. Any dabbler in genealogy understands the addiction. Without leaving the comfort of my kitchen and coffee cup, I traced back five generations to my Great, Great, Great Grandfather and Grandmother. Bernard and Mary Arkenberg were born in or near Damme, Germany in the late 1700s. Their son, my Great, Great Grandfather, Ferdinand Heinrich Arkenberg, was born in Damme in 1822 or 1823. The family migrated to Ohio with several other residents in 1831. One of these other families, that of Johann Surmann and his wife, Catherine, had a daughter, Elizabeth, who married Ferdinand. Their oldest child, Joseph Ferdinand, is my Great Grandfather.

I was curious to see these roots firsthand. Several years before my family hunt began, I located a place called Arkenberg on the Weser River between Bremen and Hannover near Liebenau, Germany. Other than today's trendy baby names of Madison, Brooklyn, Memphis, *et alia*, who has an authentic, GPS-recognized town with their surname? (Washington doesn't count. Why? My blog, my rules!)

After fulfilling a pilgrim's need to visit our namesake town (actually more hamlet with one street and lots of farmland), all genealogical signposts pointed to Damme, forty-eight miles to the west. The road between Arkenberg and Damme took us over the rolling landscape of Lower Saxony. Here was the landscape that Arkenbergs have traversed for centuries whether on foot or horseback, or in donkey cart, Volkswagen, or Audi.

Today, Damme is a well-manicured little town of 16,500 residents, the economic center of an affluent area of 40,000 inhabitants. Grimme, headquartered in Damme, is a leading global manufacturer of potato harvesters and other planting equipment. The company employs 4,500 in its factory. Area farms, according to one local, raise more pigs and chickens than anywhere else in Europe. With restaurant menus filled with *Schwein* this and *Schwein* that in addition to *Hahnchen*, I didn't doubt the boast.

But what of Arkenbergs who never left? Would mention of our name be met with rolled eyes and sneers or positive tales and grins? We had our answer when the owner of the hotel at which we booked, Hotel Tepe, pulled up our reservation. Her eyes widened. "You're an Arkenberg." A broad smile swept across her face. "They're Arkenbergs," she repeated louder to her mother and co-owner of the 4-Star property. "The Arkenbergs are all such nice people. One of my girlfriends married an Arkenberg." Although Jim, Sadie, and I didn't get the keys to the city of Damme, we weren't run out of town either.

Where to begin exploring Damme? Saint Viktor's Church is often mentioned in genealogy searches connected to Arkenberg marriages and christenings. The current church dates to 1904, but the stone tower of a centuries-old structure still stands. How many of my ancestors stood on that very spot? I expected a jolt of electricity to rush through my body, channeled by ancestral spirits. That didn't happen.

In addition to Damme, we drove through other towns mentioned in Arkenberg genealogy including Osterfeine, Ruschendorf, and Vechta. Turns out, the Arkenbergs who remained did very well for themselves. Theodore Arkenberg owns and operates a large factory in Damme. Another Arkenberg family has one of the finest homes in Osterfeine, a neat little town five kilometers from Damme. There, we experienced the same reaction we got at our hotel. A friendly woman tidying up the lovely Friedhof (cemetery) beamed a smile when we identified ourselves. "We've got five Arkenberg homes in town," she said. "All really nice people." We found the Arkenberg burial plot although I don't know how we're related to that branch of the family.

Perhaps the Arkenbergs who sailed from Bremen to Baltimore two hundred years ago to make new lives in America did a big favor to those left behind, giving them room to grow and prosper.

Am I satisfied with my search? Although Jim, Sadie, and I didn't meet any German Arkenbergs, we got to spend time in the land of my forefathers seeing, breathing, and listening to the world from which I came. Yes, that was worth it. In addition, I spent time with the most important branch in my family tree—Jim & Sadie.

Will I continue my search? My cousin has traced the family tree back to the fourteenth century. And while I'm tempted to peek at his work, it feels to me like flipping to the page with the crossword puzzle solutions. Curiosity tempts, but getting help with the answer isn't very satisfying. Besides, I have hordes of Irish and Polish relatives yet to discover. Road trip!!!!

<hr>

Postcards from the Edge...or Maybe Bruges
September 4, 2015

Have postcards gone the way of handwritten letters, thank-you notes, and the family dinner hour? As a kid, besides birthday cards from a great aunt, uncle, or godparent stuffed with a five-dollar bill, my favorite mailbox find was a postcard. As the jet age dawned, my family didn't know any international globe-trotters. More often, postcards arrived with images of Mackinac Island, Wisconsin Dells, Starved Rock State Park, or some obscure local treasure such as a steel bridge at Steubenville, Ohio. For the rare card that popped into our lives from such exotic locales as Miami Beach, the Grand Canyon, or Hollywood, I skipped into the house from our curbside mailbox squealing with delight. I'd stare at the picture, imagining the magical wonders of such a visit.

As years passed and my circle of friends expanded, my postcard trove increased. Greetings came from every corner of the world. Messages were similar. *Having a grand time, wish you were here.* But cover images and stamps were truly exotic—Piccadilly Circus, the Eiffel Tower, Rio's Copacabana Beach, an Australian kangaroo, a Nepalese temple, the Great

Pyramid at Giza. Who wouldn't want to welcome bits of our amazing world into his or her home—the next best thing to being there?

Over the years, postcards became fewer. I miss them. They're long-distance hugs, chances to remind someone that he or she is special in our lives. A few years back, Jim and I were in Rome. I'd scribbled out greetings on cards featuring images of the Colosseum, Spanish Steps, Trevi Fountain, and Vatican City. Wandering down to the front desk, I asked for postcard stamps. Behind the desk, a blonde Millennial flashed a deer-in-the-headlights look. "Postcard?" Her expression, a mix of bewildered judgment, made me feel as if I asked for the nearest telegram office. This wasn't a language barrier as much as a generational divide. Young people, I surmised, no longer appreciated the romance of postcards.

Perhaps obsolescence was inevitable. The Internet brings instant gratification. Today, choosing among Facebook, Instagram, and Pinterest, holiday-goers share photos instantly. Messages that are personal, timely, and meaningful. No scribbling in long-forgotten cursive, then scrambling for stamp and mailbox to send the mass-produced image, hoping it will arrive home before you do.

I haven't abandoned postcards. Although the number we receive in a year can be counted on one hand, I relish them. Rarity increases the delight. When Jim and I moved to Belgium, we had a massive estate sale. Hundreds of people trudged through our suburban home on a damp December weekend snatching up a lifetime of possessions. Among these was a prized box of postcards accumulated over the decades, those received and others bought as souvenirs. I freely put them up for sale. Time to let go, give the postcards a second chance to bring someone joy and delight.

After getting to Brussels, I strove to keep in touch with family and friends back home. Facebook and email are great but only go so far. I desired a more personal approach, private messages to let people know we hadn't dropped off the planet. I tapped into my passion. Who doesn't love receiving an exotic postcard? I used them to pen birthday wishes and thank-you notes. Colorful images were unique alternatives to staid greeting cards.

In twenty months living in Belgium, I've mailed nearly 100 postcards. Only about a quarter of recipients acknowledged the gesture. In their defense, a postcard doesn't ask for a reply. However, the scarcity of acknowledgment surprises me. Perhaps people don't consider postcards prize finds anymore. Are they considered *junk mail?*

I admit to being a tad obsessive when it comes to acknowledging correspondence. I thank people for thank-you notes. I send a quick email of thanks to senders of postcards. Unusual, I admit. However, it's my tactic to keep the flow of postcards coming. Besides, I hoped people would view my missives as an attempt to stay in touch, a reminder that Jim and I, though strayed afar, are still part of the flock.

I started sending my brother postcards the moment we arrived in Belgium. Off went a postcard with a sweet, brotherly message from Bruges, one of his favorite places. I never heard a peep. Off went a second—still no reply. With visits to Bruges on every houseguest's list, opportunity allowed me to dash off postcards to my brother again and again—six greetings from Bruges in all. Still no response. My brother is a kind man with good intentions. He merely stumbles on the execution. For example, last year he didn't send Jim a birthday card. "No," my brother replied when I inquired. "I certainly did *not* forget Jim's card. It's sitting right here on my kitchen counter."

And so, apparently, the card still sits on that kitchen counter in Chicago, a daily reminder that he did *not* forget Jim's birthday.

Should I stop sending postcards? I'd save time and money and avoid the disappointment of non-repliers. Why keep sending them? Sometimes there's a payoff—a note that my postcard made someone's day, put a smile on their face. Just last week, cousins sent me notes and pictures. Postcards sent to my 87-year-old aunt and 86-year-old uncle brought smiles to their faces. My cards gave them something interesting to pass around at the family breakfast. "As if you and Jim were there," one cousin wrote. Reactions like that motivate me to keep sending postcards.

By the way, in early October Jim and I are expecting more houseguests. Of course, they want to go to Bruges. Guess what I'll grab off a kiosk to mail to my brother?

———————•(◉)•———————

Always Look at the Bright Side of Life, and Other Loads of Crap
November 2, 2015

The world consists of two kinds of people: those who dwell on life's annoyances and those who sweep them away with a shrug. Maybe each of us is a bit of both. Swearing, however, sure helps us manage through the bad things that happen.

This past month served up healthy doses of bad and good. October reminded us why living in Europe is fantastic. Each weekend served up an exciting treat with a few "tricks" thrown in to keep us grounded and practiced in profanity. Because Jim and I have October birthdays, the month is usually busy.

Europe has an abundance of exciting places. For Jim's special day at the beginning of the month, we flew to Nice for a long weekend. For my birthday at the end of the month, we visited London. In between, we took the train to Amsterdam, spending the month's second weekend with eight friends from Chicago. Over the month's third weekend, we entertained dear friends from Glasgow, showing them Brussels and Ypres. Our list of October weekends, Nice, Amsterdam, Brussels, London, reads like a glossy travel brochure.

Three of the trips threw us curveballs. Most people would roll their eyes and call such glitches "rich people's problems." We get it. These bumps were mere hiccups, petty annoyances that most folks would gladly welcome in exchange for living and playing in Europe. Fortunately, Jim and I are predisposed to letting bad things slip from our memories. Although some issues take a little longer to forget.

Take Nice. Friends who arrived days before us snapped photos of themselves in Speedos on sunny Côte d'Azur beaches splashing in pristine blue water. Jim and I packed swimsuits in glorious anticipation of escaping the chilly gloom of Brussels. However, storm clouds formed the moment we landed. Jim and I will forever refer to the Riviera as the Côte de Gris—the Gray Coast! We remember Nice as chilly and wet. The sun came out only as we climbed into a taxi for the trip to the airport. Our friends who remained in Nice for a couple of extra days sent us more photos, back in their Speedos, frolicking in the sea.

Problems of a different kind impacted our trip to Amsterdam. A strike by French-speaking rail workers halted all train traffic out of Brussels. Living in Belgium, we're used to national strikes that occur as often as national holidays! Coincidentally, strikes never actually occur on a national holiday. Most take place on a Monday or Friday. Do you suppose that's done to give folks a three-day weekend? While I respect the rights of people to protest, Belgian protests usually take the form of disruptive work stoppages. Striking workers show little or no respect for those they disservice, effectively raising a collective middle finger at management and customers simultaneously.

Despite the rail strike, we didn't give up trying to join dear friends from Chicago. We had a nonrefundable hotel booking. Zigzagging across Brussels, we scrambled for an alternative. Instead of a fast train to Amsterdam we climbed aboard a cramped, sluggish bus. Instead of a ninety-minute voyage and mid-morning arrival into Amsterdam, we endured a four-hour bus ride and evening arrival. We were exhausted. As usually happens, however, once reunited with our friends and soaking in the ambience of the charming city of canals, frustrations with our journey faded. We didn't even need a trip to Amsterdam's fabled "coffee" houses to help us mellow.

The month's most challenging incident awaited us in London. What could possibly go wrong? Never ask yourself that question; the answer is, plenty of shit can *always* happen. And, boy did it. Our lovely afternoon tea at the Savoy was barely digested before catastrophe struck. I noticed the problem as Jim and I transitioned from a friend's flat in central London to the suburban home of other friends.

After thirty-eight years without incident, my passport was missing—lost, or stolen. I didn't panic. Why let the loss impact our lovely weekend? I calmly called stores, restaurants, and train station Lost and Founds, retracing our steps. Other than station personal (perhaps correlated with a penchant for striking), people were kind and sympathetic. My search, however, didn't turn up my passport.

The US Embassy was unreachable by telephone (by design). Their website scheduling tool could only guarantee an appointment two weeks into the future. Jim and I had tickets to leave London the next afternoon. Would I be stuck, an undocumented refugee inside Great Britain? From a table in the tearoom of Hampton Court Palace, Jim dashed off a late-afternoon email, twenty minutes before 5 o'clock on Monday.

Fortunately, the Embassy monitored emails. They gave me an early appointment for the next morning. I maintained a sliver of hope that I could make my train home. Unable to sleep, I rose hours before dawn. Our kind hosts had to get up early to ferry us to the train station. Not only did we have to get to central London, I also had to find a photo kiosk and make my way to the Embassy before 8 a.m.

Imagine my delight when, an hour later, I walked out of the US Embassy with a shiny new blue passport. A fantastic birthday present, a terrible weight lifted from my shoulders. The weather in London matched my sunny mood. Three weeks earlier we shivered under umbrellas in Nice. Now, we enjoyed lunch outside on a sun-drenched terrace in Leicester Square. My problems were behind me...or so I thought.

Jim and I arrived at the Eurostar terminal at Saint Pancras. All we had to do was pass through security, flash our passports, and be on our way home. Seemed easy. My first hint of trouble came at the pre-screener. As he looked at my new passport, he shook his head disapprovingly. "Have anything else? Residency card or work permit, perhaps?" My heart sank as I stammered, "W...why?" He nodded over to stone-faced immigration officers encased in a glass booth. "They don't like these passports." Crestfallen and scared, I pulled out my Belgian resident card and trudged to the glass booth. *Will I be forever marooned at Saint Pancras?*

Forcing a smile, I pushed my passport and resident card through the slot. The burly, sneering man took the passport. Holding it as he might a stale fish, he flipped the pages forward, then backward, repeating the scan half a dozen times. The inspector sharing the booth stopped. After an exchange of mumbles, he too grimaced. My heart sank to the floor. I heard about the UK not letting people into their country, but never refusing to let them leave. Tom Hanks made a movie about being stuck in limbo at the Paris airport.

The humorless man grunted. "Belgium doesn't like this kind of passport. Probably won't accept it."

"But it's a US passport, issued by the Embassy this morning. I'm a US citizen," I said, wanting to add, *But, it's my birthday! Let me pass.* After a little more haggling he picked up the phone. *Oh no…am I about to be hauled away?*

After a ten-second conversation, the personification of Cerberus, Guardian of the Underworld, hung up the phone, closed my passport, and slid it through the slot. "Have a nice trip."

I felt as if I'd been thrown into a washing machine for an extended spin cycle. Yet, I survived the ordeal and passed into Belgium without incident. The birthday trip to London will be remembered more for great friends and weather and less for the passport fiasco. As weeks grow into months and months melt into years, experience has taught me that memories of these annoyances will fade. Jim and I will remember that October as a string of lovely weekends reconnecting with old friends. Our ordeals will be inconsequential footnotes, funny anecdotes, and fodder for blog posts and memoirs. We'll recall the people, not the problems. Perhaps that's what it means to always look at the bright side of life.

Winter, Webcam Wonderland
November 23, 2015

The annual holiday spectacle in the Grand Place draws thousands to the ancient square for the Christmas tree, Nativity scene, and light show. This past weekend, Brussels unveiled this year's tree, a real beauty. But throngs of ogling spectators didn't come. Instead, dire warnings of an imminent terrorist attack put Brussels on lockdown. A week after the attacks in Paris while the rest of Belgium remains at Threat Level 3, authorities elevated Brussels to Level 4, fearing "A Serious and Imminent Threat."

A Surreal Scene!

Images coming out of Brussels are surreal, scenes from a Dystopian future. Military carriers rolled into the city. Soldiers toting machine guns patrolled the streets alongside the city's police force. Metro entrances blocked with police tape. Cinemas and stores closed. Brussels, a world capital of 1.2 million people, on lockdown. The US Embassy sent emails advising citizens to stay indoors. The US Department of Defense issued a 72-hour embargo on its employees and contractors for travel to Brussels. DOD personnel already in Brussels were told to stay inside. The mayor of Brussels asked bars and restaurants in the city center to close at 6 p.m. Our reservations were canceled. People who count on customers to earn a living were hit hard.

On Sunday, the same story. Our local market at the Parvis Saint-Gilles, usually packed with vendors and customers, was canceled. This hub of economic and social activity is a cornerstone of Brussels' life. Other popular markets at Flagey and Gare du Midi, which draws tens of thousands of people, were also canceled. At a news conference on Sunday afternoon, the Prime Minister announced that Brussels would be shut down again on Monday. Three days of unprecedented lockdown. Twitter filled with reports and photos under the hashtags, #BrusselsAlert and #Brusselslockdown. Twitter feeds became our pipeline for information.

Loose Tweets Compromise Streets!

On Sunday night, authorities asked residents to refrain from using Twitter to telegraph police activity to terrorists. In a show of humor, a pillar of civilized society, residents flooded Twitter with pictures of cats as guardians of the capital. Brussels' feline population pounced into action. If you want a smile in these troubling times, check out #Brusselscats. Our own Puhi may look like he's lying down on the job, but he's not. The impish cat is enforcing the Twitter blackout by blocking access to our computer keyboard.

We awoke this morning to news that overnight raids in Brussels and the depressed southern city of Charleroi netted arrests of sixteen people. Later accounts reported that no guns or explosives were found. A prime subject of the manhunt, a man wanted for the Paris attacks, remains at large. Even if he's caught, then what? Authorities have repeatedly stated that the threat extends beyond this fugitive.

Is This Our Future?

A civilized world held hostage, forced indoors by terrorist threat. If this siege can happen in Brussels, a world capital that headquarters NATO and the European Union, could terrorists not shut down other cities? Such an action has ramifications for commerce, education, transportation...every aspect of our modern world. On a nearly empty street this afternoon, I overheard one young woman, sidelined from her job by the lockdown, complain to a friend, "I'd like to tell the Prime Minister to pay my rent. I have to work." That's the practical reality of the situation.

As of Monday afternoon, we're still not sure what tomorrow will bring. All we can do is trust that authorities are doing what's necessary to keep us safe. Kudos to soldiers and police for putting themselves in potential danger to keep the city secure.

Can a Webcam Be a Surrogate for Life?

Hunkered down in our Brussels home, I scanned local news for updates. I happened upon the Brussels City website. There I found webcam links, a real-time window into our besieged city. One webcam is at the Place de Brouckère, one of the city's busiest squares. Another is situated in the Grand Place with view of the Christmas tree and Starbucks.

It's sadly ironic that the Christmas tree, a symbol of peace, joy, and hope, stands practically alone. Staring at the tree from the safety of a webcam feels a bit unseemly, like a Peeping Tom or Orwell's Big Brother. It's not very satisfying to window-shop on life. I'd rather stand below the mighty balsam's branches, gaze upon the dazzling lights and sparkling ornaments. I'd prefer to feel the nip of crisp air on my face, hear the wonderment in children's voices, and inhale the comforting scent of pine.

I shudder to think of a future viewed solely through webcams. I'd miss the magic and wonder. I'm hoping that we'll soon be able to visit the Christmas tree. Like Charlie Brown's sad little sapling, our Grand Place Christmas tree must feel forlorn—all dressed up with no visitors to awe. Christmas trees, like life itself, are best experienced up close and in person, their beauty and majesty firing each of our senses.

Thanksgiving & Terror Threat Level 4
November 26, 2015

For those in the USA, it's Thanksgiving. For the rest of the world, it's simply the fourth Thursday in November. And for those of us in Brussels, it's the sixth day of life under Terror Threat Level 4. Despite the heightened security level, normalcy is gradually returning to the Belgian capital. Schools and most stores are open. About half of the Metro is operating. Yet armed soldiers still patrol the streets and armored military vehicles remain visible throughout the city. Perhaps, this is simply the new normal.

On this sunny Thanksgiving Day in Brussels, Jim and I are grateful for the many people, concerned for our safety, who have reached out to us this past week. The many calls, emails, and FB posts have been heartwarming. We're also thankful for the new friends we've made here in Brussels including our Slovenian neighbors, Barbara and Patrik. We'll be heading to their home this evening to share a Thanksgiving feast, European style. Yes, even amidst terror threats, we make time for tradition and celebration. Our neighbor has even snared a turkey, a rare bird in Belgium!

Christmas a Charade?

But with so much wrong in our world, and with our own city under a cloud of terror, are we foolish, naïve, or, worse, hypocritical to celebrate Thanksgiving? Pope Francis has gone so far as to call this Christmas, with the world pimpled by war, a *charade*. Isn't that a bit like Aunt Jemima waging war on pancakes or Donald Trump dissing...well, Donald Trump? When the Pope sounds jaded and cynical, what hope is there for the rest of us?

Yet the world keeps spinning forward; and we manage to hang on. We're survivors. Today, by coincidence, also marks the fourteenth anniversary of my mother's passing. But I choose to remember her not in death but in life—vibrant & vivacious. Resiliency is one of humanity's most noble traits.

With an abundance of craziness closing in on us, and cable news feeding us infinite loops of ugly chaos, it's easy to lose sight of the world's beauty and humanity's decency. For just as beauty exists beside ugliness, so too does goodness coexist with evil. I'm reminded of Blake's poem, "The Tiger." How many of us had to memorize in high school, "Tiger tiger burning bright..."? In the penultimate stanza, the narrator ponders the juxtaposition of innocence and savagery in our world.

> When the stars threw down their spears,
> And water'd heaven with their tears,
> Did He smile His work to see?
> Did He who made the lamb make thee?
> —William Blake, "The Tiger," 1794

We ask ourselves, how can the same species that spawns terrorists and insidious evil also grace us with breathtaking beauty? Take Belgium. The country of 11 million people has faced scrutiny and criticism in recent days for the many terrorist cells that seem to operate unimpeded in Molenbeek, one of Brussels' nineteen communes. But we shouldn't allow terrorists to tarnish, or, worse, hijack Belgium's rich legacy. The tiny nation has also given the world great beauty. So instead of Belgian terrorists and their evil deeds filling your screens, this Thanksgiving Day consider positive images of Belgium: picturesque, historic cities; stunning cathedrals; brilliant Flemish painters Rubens and van Dyck.

That's not to say we should ignore terror threats or turn our eyes from evil. Rather, we shouldn't forget the *cornucopia* of goodness, beauty, and love that also exists in our world. Today, Jim and I will pause to celebrate our Thanksgiving tradition and give thanks to the bounty of good fortune in our lives. In addition to our wonderful families and friends, we're thankful for the past two years in Belgium. In years to come, we'll remember our time here, not for these final weeks living under threat of attack, but for the country's amazing wonders. Thank you, Brussels, Belgium, for enriching our lives with culture and for providing us a beautiful home into which we welcomed so many dear friends, old and new.

Happy Thanksgiving from the Arkenbergs!

<hr />

Guest Cat No More
December 4, 2015

Jim and I will soon leave Brussels. Our farewell is bittersweet. Sure, we're looking forward to seeing our American friends and family. But we'll miss our adopted home, now familiar routines, and the people and places we've come to love.

And what about Puhi? I've blogged about a clown of a cat that dropped into our lives quite literally. Our neighbor's tiger cat began watching us shortly after we moved in. His favorite surveillance perch was the top of the wall that separates the two gardens. At some point during that first summer, he lost his footing and fell into our garden. Was his fall accidental or a sly move to make a dramatic entrance into our lives? We'll never know for sure.

From the moment Puhi plummeted to Sadie's paws and my feet, our household hasn't been the same. Jim and I never considered ourselves cat people. I don't think I'm too far out on a limb to suppose that Sadie, our lovable golden retriever, wasn't a cat lover either. Perhaps cat owners could have guessed what was in store for the Arkenbergs, but we didn't foresee what awaited us.

Puhi made inroads into our garden...and into our hearts. The little fellow was persistent. He wanted in. Puhi quickly had me in the palm of his little paw. To gain entry, however, he learned that he'd have to work on Jim and Sadie. The golden girl is our princess. Aside from a few swats and nibbles of Sadie's feathery tail, Puhi behaved reasonably well. The ole girl grew to tolerate him—first hurdle cleared.

Jim wasn't going to be a pushover. My kind husband humored me and my new feline buddy but made it clear he wasn't a cat lover. Besides, he had allergies! Jim explained his passive acceptance of Puhi into my life, "These are the things we do for love."

Family is an all-or-nothing proposition. What was Puhi to do? Answer—shower Jim with affection and counter his objections to a cat...by acting like Sadie. "He's just like a dog," Jim declared, arriving home from work as Puhi waited at the front door beside Sadie. *Well played, Puhi, well played.*

After several months of his campaign, Puhi is in. No longer mere guest cat, Puhi is now family. Litter box, scratching post, toys, food and water bowls, and treats. No one is more surprised to find themselves attached to the little guy than the rest of the Arkenbergs. And Jim's allergy? By some miracle, he's not allergic to Puhi. *Oh, the things we do for love!*

Many people have been following the exploits of the Arkenbergs in Europe via Facebook and my blog. As they come to learn about our imminent departure they all ask, "What will happen to Puhi? He'll be devastated when you leave."

The story has a happy ending. When the Arkenbergs board the plane for Chicago, we will be four. Puhi wouldn't have it any other way. We just can't tell Sadie that although she must ride in the cargo hold, Puhi gets to accompany us in the cabin.

We'd be remiss if we didn't acknowledge the understanding and generosity of our neighbor. Barbara has a heart of gold. She's saved the lives of countless cats and dogs through her foster efforts and animal advocacy. As Puhi's owner, she recognized his decision to adopt the Arkenbergs and accepted his emigration with all of her heart. We know she'll miss the little clown. But sometimes love means you have to let a piece of your heart take flight.

<hr />

A Fond Farewell to the Brussels Writers' Circle
December 8, 2015

Coming Full Circle—BWC says Farewell to Chairman Todd Arkenberg

> "One does not discover new lands without consenting to lose sight of the shore for a very long time."
> —Andre Gide

A favorite quote speaks to the necessity of risk—courage to leave behind the safety of the familiar—in order to grow. As authors, we soar highest when we push beyond the familiar. Readers crave fresh perspectives, unique story lines, unfamiliar settings. Experimentation is a great teacher. But as rewarding as discovery is in our writing, losing sight of the shore in our personal lives can unsettle.

As I prepared to leave the USA two years ago, apprehension tempered my excitement. What would life be like in Brussels?

What about my writing? A new continent and city would certainly provide fresh material. But writing is lonely, an occupation pursued in silent refuge. In Chicago, I found a cure for isolation. I joined the city's two oldest groups for writers. Bonds formed with fellow authors gave me personal and professional fulfillment. Camaraderie was only one benefit. Members inspired and motivated, helping me become a better writer.

Surfing the Internet from the security of my Chicago home, I found the Brussels Writers' Circle. The website was informative and welcoming. With a favorable first impression, I dashed off an email of introduction. Upon receipt of the Chairman's reply, I felt comforted. A safe haven awaited me on that distant, unknown shore.

Within a fortnight of my arrival, during the dark, drizzly evenings of early January, I made my way to La Maison des Crêpes on Tuesdays and Le Falstaff on Thursdays. The first *tour de table* of introductions allayed my fears. All of the writers had journeyed to Brussels from some other shore. Many had even crossed another frontier, language. BWC members for whom English is not their native tongue amazed me.

Weeks turned into months. BWC didn't disappoint. Among the circle, I found the same dedication, resourcefulness, imagination, and support that endeared me to the colleagues left behind in Chicago. Similar passions, I guess, drive those who yearn to write. We have an innate need to tell stories, stir emotions, share truths. Maybe even more important than providing a place to hone my craft, the BWC offered friendship to Jim and me. That social outlet allowed us to adapt much quicker to expat life. Settled physically and mentally, I could focus on writing.

I've been very productive. While living in Brussels, I published two novels and nearly completed the initial draft of my next project, a memoir. Throughout this time, BWC members offered encouragement.

Perhaps that explains why so many BWC writers are published authors. Sessions provide a safe forum. I felt comfortable experimenting with nonfiction and poetry. Honest critique based on trust and respect explains the circle's success. The opportunity to co-chair weekly meetings pleased me.

Jim and I both hoped to stay longer in Brussels, but a life open to adventure knows few certainties. A new job for Jim takes us back to Chicago. As for me, I may take a playwriting course to turn two ideas into dramas.

Things are starting to disappear from our home as our departure date nears. A barbecue grill, vacuum cleaner, blender, even Jim's car. Of course, this is mere *stuff*. We'll miss many things about Brussels. But most of all, we'll miss the people, especially, our many good friends of the Brussels Writers' Circle.

We face resettlement with apprehension and excitement. We've come full circle. But we return richer because of our experience. I'm a better writer because of the Brussels Writers' Circle. Thank you.

Story Seeds: A Belgian Assortment

In October 2018, nearly three years after Jim and I returned from Brussels, I published, *A Belgian Assortment: Brussels Short Stories*. Work on the collection began shortly after we resettled in Chicago while the vibrant images of our expat experience were still fresh in my mind. Although fiction, each tale is based in fact, growing from a setting, conversation, person, or incident that left an impression on me. I call such inspirational catalysts, "story seeds."

In chapter 8 of this memoir, for example, I describe my wide-eyed excitement stumbling upon the market that springs up every Wednesday in a parking lot in Chatelain. "The bountiful market assumed a carnival atmosphere…a sensory feast." In my story, *Chatelain Market*, a wounded shop clerk journeys to the market to escape loneliness and finds herself indulging in romantic fantasies. My chance conversation with a public-school teacher over wine at Chatelain, offered yet another seed. The young woman's experience as a Flemish transplant in French-speaking Brussels and the difficulties she faced teaching middle-school boys of Turkish and Moroccan descent gives my story, *Aftershock*, texture and authenticity.

Our experience during the terrorist-triggered lockdown described in the memoir's last chapters, seeded *Lockdown*. In the story, a Lebanese immigrant tries to comfort his brother who struggles with a secret, his own personal lockdown. The humorous, *In Bruges…Again*, got its title from the fact that nearly every one of our houseguests wanted to visit the picturesque medieval city *ad nauseam*. The setting of *Christmas Carousel*, a story of young and complicated love, was inspired by Brussels' sprawling Christmas market, described in chapter 16: "Jim and I especially enjoyed watching the whimsical carousel on which grinning children squealed atop giant squid, flying ostriches, bobbing seahorses, and other exotic creatures. The spectacular contraption looked as if it were ripped from the pages of a fairy tale."

Each story in my collection sprouted in similar fashion from fertile reality. What's next? Puhi's memoir, *My Single and Extraordinary Life*, a story seeded by our serendipitous encounter with our neighbor's impish scamp of a cat.

Acknowledgments

I extend my deepest gratitude to:

My husband Jim. The dream of living in Europe became a reality only through his hard work and perseverance. He has my unyielding love, pride, and admiration.

Friends and family who journeyed to Brussels. The best adventures are shared. Their visits made transitioning into our European life easier. Special thanks to those who carried staples from home such as Sadie's canned pumpkin and American peanut butter.

Jim's parents Barbara and Michael whose Skype sessions regularly brought Chicago into our Brussels living room.

The fine writers of the Brussels Writers' Circle. Besides encouragement, support, and insightful feedback that helped better my work, their friendship and camaraderie entertained and nurtured Jim and me throughout our stay. Risking omission, I especially thank Nick, Anne-May, Dimitri, Klavs, Sarah, Patrick, Lida, Mimi, Océan, Richard, and David.

Other dear friends and colleagues who befriended us in Brussels especially those from Edgar Hütte's Expat Group, Pat Bob, Cecilia, and

Tom plus Jim's direct reports, and Karina and her team at Bocca Moka. Their kindness and companionship sweetened our adventure.

Our good neighbor Barbara. Her friendship was a welcome oasis in a neighborhood of strangers. Among other things, we shared laughs, gripes, Thai dinners, cocktails, and her collection of cats that breached our garden wall. Above all, heartfelt thanks for allowing Puhi to become a Yankee.

Supportive friends Barbara, Gia, Jerry, Janice, Libby, MaryEllen, David, Charlie, Lorna, and Jeff. Reading early drafts and sharing feedback helped shape and polish the final draft.

Talented authors at the Barrington Writers Workshop. They saw me off to Brussels with hugs, tears, and good cheer and welcomed me back into their fold with the same genuine warmth. Even in my absence, they made me feel part of the BWW family.

My editor and friend Meera Dash. Her keen eye and relentless pen make me look good.

Susan Jackson O'Leary for creating yet another fabulous cover design.

Sadie, our cherished golden retriever, and Puhi, our lovable Brussels cat. Their love, tender affection, and loyalty brought smiles to our faces and happiness to our hearts.

CPSIA information can be obtained
at www.ICGtesting.com
Printed in the USA
LVHW070213100720
660306LV00022B/2087